I met a little cottage Girl:
She was eight years old, she said;
Her hair was thick with many a curl
That clustered round her head.

She had a rustic, woodland air,
And she was wildly clad:
Her eyes were fair, and very fair;
—Her beauty made me glad.

"We are Seven",— William Wordsworth

The Eye of the Beholder

How to See the World Like a Romantic Poet

Louis Markos

THE EYE OF THE BEHOLDER:
HOW TO SEE THE WORLD LIKE A ROMANTIC POET

Copyright © 2011 Louis Markos
Hamden, CT

All rights reserved. Except in the case of quotations embodied in critical articles or reviews, no part of this book may be reproduced or transmitted in any form or by any means, electronic or mechanical, including photocopying, recording, or by any information storage or retrieval system, without written permission of the publisher. For information, contact Winged Lion Press www.WingedLionPress.com

Winged Lion Press Press titles may be purchased for business or promotional use or special sales.

10-9-8-7-6-5-4-3-2-1

WINGED LION PRESS

ISBN 13   978-1-936294-01-5

With joy and thanksgiving for
20 years of Christian marriage,
I dedicate this book, with love,
to my wife, Donna

August 12, 1989 - August 12, 2009

TABLE OF CONTENTS

Preface

PART ONE: INNOCENCE AND EXPERIENCE

Chapter I	The Externalization of the Internal	1
Chapter II	The Songs of Innocence	13
Chapter III	The Songs of Experience	30
Chapter IV	Gnostic Myth-Making	46

PART TWO: NATURE AND SUPERNATURE

Chapter V	Lyrical Ballads	64
Chapter VI	Wise Passiveness	80
Chapter VII	The Willing Suspension of Disbelief	96
Chapter VII	The Dark Side of Inspiration	114

PART THREE: CRISIS AND RESOLUTION

Chapter IX	Abundant Recompense	132
Chapter X	Solipsism with a Vengeance	153
Chapter XI	Trumpet of a Prophecy	167
Chapter XII	Process in Stasis	184
Epilogue	The Darkness Within	201
Appendix A	Timeline	206
Appendix B	Bibliographical Essay	209
Index		217

PREFACE

If you were to ask a random group of American college students how many of them had written at least one poem in their life, you would likely see about a third of their hands go up. But if you were to follow your first question with a second—"how many of you have ever written a poem that was not in the first person?"—you would see most of those hands go back down. I do not exaggerate when I say that in the minds of most Americans—students or otherwise—poetry in particular and the arts in general are considered to be mostly, if not exclusively, a form of self-expression. Such has been the common wisdom for the past two centuries. Could you go back in time, however, to any period before the Romantic Age and poll a group of poets and critics as to what poetry and the arts were, you would be hard pressed to find a single person who would answer that poetry is a form of self-expression. They might have told you that the role of poetry was to imitate nature or to glorify God or to celebrate heroism or to explore theological, philosophical, and scientific beliefs or to teach and please or to woo women or to dramatize human character, choice and motivation—but not to express in rhyme their depression and angst or to work through personal crises or to project their inner mood onto the external world.

True, one can find exceptions to the rule. In the lyrics of Sappho and Catullus, the sonnets of Shakespeare and Donne, and the love poems of Dante and Petrarch, one hears the authentic, often anguished voice of the poet. Still, none of these writers would have reduced poetry to self-expression. The idea that one's diary or journal should serve as the primary raw material for serious poetry would have seemed foreign to nearly all poets who lived before the French Revolution. The role of the poet was not to air in public his personal struggles nor spin "original" ideas out of his head nor remake the world in accordance with his own unique, radically individual genius; rather, it was to use his creative gifts and craftsman-like talents to give a more perfect and lasting shape to pre-existing material: a shape that squared with beauty, that resonated with truth, and that aspired to goodness.

All of that changed during the Romantic Age. Born out of the French Revolution and its radical faith that a nation could be shaped and altered by the dreams and visions of its people, British Romantic Poetry was founded on a similar belief that the objects and realities of our world—whether they be natural or human—are not fixed in stone but can be molded and transformed by the visionary eye of the poet. This key romantic notion—that things are as they are perceived, that the external world is, in part, a projection of the internal mood of the poet—found its first full flowering in two collections of poetry that form a sort of arch or doorway to the rich and vibrant world of British Romantic Poetry: William Blake's *Songs of Innocence and Experience* and Wordsworth and Coleridge's *Lyrical Ballads*. Were I writing an exhaustive study of the subject, I would begin by considering the work of such eighteenth-century pre-Romantic poets as James Thomson, Edward Young, Thomas Gray, Thomas Chatterton, Thomas Gray, William Cowper, and (especially) Robert Burns. For the purposes of this book, however, I will narrow my focus to these two age-defining collections.

Accordingly, I will devote most of Part I to a close study of Blake's *Songs*, a work whose deceptively simple, nursery-rhyme-like stanzas mask a depth of mature thought and insight. I shall show how, in these timeless poems, the same images and events take on a different coloring, form, and reality when viewed through the eyes of innocence and experience. After explaining how Blake uses the terms "innocence" and "experience" to define not external realities but internal perceptions, I will contrast the pastoral vision of the former with the angst-ridden, overly-self-conscious vision of the latter. I will conclude Part I with a look at Blake's brilliant but esoteric mini-epic, *The Marriage of Heaven and Hell*, a work that offers us Romanticism in its most radical form. Here, and throughout the book, I will attempt to show that though Romanticism brings with it the promise of freshness, growth, and freedom, it also carries with it a dark side.

Although my analysis of the Romantics and their poems will be traditional in focus and content, I should mention here that in my handling of Blake I will be going off somewhat on my own. In my own personal reading of Blake, one that is not meant to reflect the views of traditional scholars or of the publisher of this book, I chart a movement in which Blake slowly but inexorably morphs from a position that is fairly close to orthodox (incarnational) Christianity to one that is essentially Gnostic. Part II will take up *Lyrical Ballads*, another work whose simple stanzas are more complex than they might at first seem. I shall show how Romantic poets can present both common, mundane objects with a freshness and a wonder that lends them an air of the mystical, and strange, supernatural objects with an emotional intensity and psychological truth that makes them seem real and natural. I will conclude Part II by exploring both the joys and dangers of inspiration and "specialness" by a close look at three of Romanticism's weirdest and most haunting lyrics.

In the third and final part, I shall broaden the scope of the book to encompass a key Romantic movement—or turn—that undergirds many of the greatest works of the Romantic Age and that makes them read like private journals set to verse. The movement is an internal one from despair to hope, crisis to resolution; the turn an emotional and psychological one from feelings of dejection and isolation to a renewed and restored sense of oneness with nature and the self. Although this crisis/resolution motif is sometimes played out solely within a present moment, in the more complex lyrics, it includes a brief but terrifying rupture between the poet's past and present selves, a sense of alienation between what the poet once was and now is. It was the Romantics who were the first to tap fully the power of memory (or recollection), the first great explorers of the dark, hidden areas of our psyche. Indeed, a century before Freud and Piaget, the Romantics had already explored and mapped the unconscious mind and defined, in some of the most beautiful verses ever written, the stages of childhood through which each of us must progress.

The first half of Part III will focus on the central crisis/resolution poems of Wordsworth and Coleridge. These two poets, along with Blake, make up the first great generation of Romantic poets: those who grew up during the French Revolution and who saw their hopes for political freedom both raised and dashed by the success and failure of that great event. It is the work of these three poets that shall be my chief concern in this book. I will, however, in the second half of Part III, devote two final chapters to the poetry of Shelley and Keats. Together with Byron, these two poets make up the second great generation of Romantic poets: those too young to be disillusioned themselves but who inherited the internalized angst that the Revolution produced in their Romantic predecessors. I shall trace in the poetry of Shelley and Keats a kind of internal dissonance between the Romantic desire for pure, unmediated inspiration and joy and its dark opposite—the tendency toward over-self-consciousness. In nearly all of their greatest poetry, Shelley and Keats long to escape from their heavy, burdensome existences into a perfect, aesthetic world of process in stasis: an intense state of suspension in which there is, simultaneously and paradoxically, both static perfection and dynamic growth. Unable to find this perfection in the world around them, they seek it in the higher worlds of nature, art, and love. In songbirds whose melody is pure and un-self-conscious, in ancient statues and urns that seem to dwell in an eternal state of beauty, in the perfect embrace of lovers who seem able to freeze time by the passion of their love, Shelley and Keats encounter a vision of life as it should be lived: simple, direct, emphatic.

Unlike many of the books written on Romanticism, which devote many pages to the poets and few pages to their poetry, I shall keep my focus firmly on the poems themselves. Indeed, in order to facilitate that focus, I shall overlook such epic-length Romantic poems as Wordsworth's *Prelude*, Byron's *Don Juan*, Shelley's *Prometheus Unbound*, and Keats's *Lamia* and confine myself almost exclusively to short lyrical poetry. Aside from the lengthy *Rime of the Ancient Mariner* and two prose pieces that are central to the thesis of this book (Blake's *Marriage of Heaven and Hell* and Wordsworth's "Preface to *Lyrical Ballads*"), all the works covered in this book will be brief and in verse. As I hope to draw the reader as closely and intimately as possible into the life of these poems, I shall be using very few footnotes. Instead, I will provide a bibliographical essay that will both indicate some of the secondary sources that have influenced my own view of the Romantics and provide the lay reader with accessible biographies of each poet and critical studies of their work.

PART ONE

INNOCENCE AND EXPERIENCE

I
The Externalization of the Internal

On July 14, 1789, the people of Paris rose up en masse and seized control of a notorious state prison known as the Bastille. The French Revolution had begun.

On the other side of the English Channel, nineteen-year-old British poet William Wordsworth had just completed his second year at Cambridge. A decade later, Wordsworth would begin work on a poetic autobiography (*The Prelude*) that would eventually swell to epic proportions. In Book XI of *The Prelude*, he would capture, in two immortal lines, what it was like to be a college student in the shadow of the storming of the Bastille:

> Bliss was it in that dawn to be alive,
> But to be young was very Heaven! (108-109)

The Age of Aquarius had dawned over France, and it would only be a matter of time before liberty, equality, and fraternity spread their warming rays over all Europe. To those entrenched in the old power structures of Europe, this might not have seemed like good news, but to the young it seemed to promise nothing less than a return to Eden.

Had the Revolution occurred in Wordsworth's Britain it would have been a shocking event. But that it should have happened in France was almost inconceivable. True, France had given birth to the Enlightenment, but France was also one of the most hierarchical nations in Europe. Her monarchy and her privileged classes—aristocracy and clergy—wielded almost absolute power over the peasants and rising middle class, crushing them with heavy taxes and entangling them in a social and economic system that was still strongly feudal in theory and practice.

On the one hand, the French Revolution might be viewed as Act II in a drama of freedom whose first act was played out in the American colonies. On the other hand, the declaration that was signed 13 years and 10 days before the storming of the Bastille was far less revolutionary in its scope and its effects. Thomas Paine was right; it was only "common sense" that the colonies would secede from England. After gaining our independence, we conducted ourselves very much as we had done before, with little change in our social, economic, political, educational, familial, or religious lives. The American Revolution shares less in common with the French than it does with the successful twentieth century struggle for Home Rule in southern Ireland.

In contrast, the French Revolution is better compared to the twentieth century revolutions that so greatly altered the still semi-feudal nations of Russia and China. Though all three of these revolutions eventually went sour, they all promised to effect radical social, economic, political, and religious changes that would usher in a new and lasting era of freedom and equality. The old was to be swept away and a new order established.

In France the unthinkable had occurred. The people had risen up *within* a nation built upon inequality and entrenched class privilege and demanded to be free. In the famous—or, perhaps, infamous—opening sentence of his *Social Contract* (1762), Jean Jacques Rousseau had boldly proclaimed that man was born free but was everywhere in chains. 1789 held out the hope that that insidious process could be reversed, that man could throw off his chains and return to his original state of freedom and innocence.

To a certain extent city-dwelling westerners—from fifth century BC Athenians to Renaissance Florentines to twenty first century New Yorkers—have always cast an eye of longing upon the primitive inhabitants of Tahiti or Tibet or the Kalahari. When compared to their own hectic, jaded, inhibited lives, the lives of these noble savages seemed simple, peaceful, and natural. However, while most pre-eighteenth century writers had treated the myth of the noble savage as a species of nostalgia or wishful thinking, Rousseau turned it into a rallying cry for political action against the corruption of modern civilization. We could be "noble" again, Rousseau promised, if the social-political-religious slate could be wiped clean. The French Revolution seemed to offer up this possibility not as an idyllic dream of Arcadia or El Dorado or Utopia, but as an historical reality.

Indeed, it held out an even greater possibility: that our internal dreams, hopes, and desires could reshape the external world around us—that we could, quite literally, will ourselves to be free. There would be no need to climb an ice-capped mountain or sail on a black ship over the wine dark sea to find our way to Shangri-La or the fabled land of the Hyperboreans. Here and now, we could transform our *own* world into a utopia of peace and plenty.

In its early stages, the French Revolution had been relatively bloodless, and it seemed to many in Europe that just such a utopia was forming before their very eyes in the charmed city of Paris. In the glow of that hope-filled expectation, British poet William Blake (1757-1827) published a series of deceptively simple poems that celebrate a world in which man and nature are reunited and all division is healed. He titled his collection *Songs of Innocence* (1789), and he peopled it with rich pastoral imagery that fuses into one the Judeo-Christian longing for the Garden of Eden with the Greco-Roman yearning for the lost Golden Age.

Alas, the new dawn promised by the French Revolution and embodied in Blake's pastoral effusions was never to reach its zenith. The Revolution grew increasingly violent and intolerant, culminating in 1793 with the executions of Louis XVI and Marie Antoinette. The shedding of royal blood begat, in its turn, the spilling of rivers of aristocratic blood, and the would-be Age of Aquarius morphed into the Reign of Terror. Under the tyrannical rule of Robespierre, thousands of aristocrats and out-of-favor revolutionaries lost their heads to the guillotine, a year-long orgy of guilt, fear, and cruelty that only ended when Robespierre himself was beheaded. There was to be no return to Eden, only the forging of a new and heavier chain of oppression. Out of the crucible of the revolution would arise not utopia but Napoleon.

During the height of the Terror, Blake republished his *Songs* in conjunction with a new set of poems, *Songs of Experience* (1794). This time, Blake conjured for his readers a dark, brooding world of angst, dread, and isolation, one in which joy and hope have turned against themselves and sickened into despair. He titled his combined collection *Songs of Innocence and Experience* and then, that his readers—at least those with eyes to see and ears to hear—might grasp the full meaning and import of his work, he added to it a subtitle: "Shewing [showing] the Two Contrary States of the Human Soul."

Those who would rightly understand Blake's great work and its centrality to the themes and perspectives of the Romantic Age must pay close attention to the wording of the subtitle. For if we overlook it, we are apt to conclude that by "innocence" and "experience" Blake means two different socio-political states: the first of peace and equality; the second of injustice and exploitation. But such was not his intent. By innocence and experience, Blake did not intend to refer to external realities but to internal perceptions.

For Blake, the central question is not whether the world itself is one of innocence or experience; what really matters is how we perceive that world—through eyes of innocence or eyes of experience. On one level, Blake's decision to privilege the way things are perceived over the way they are may be seen as a legacy of the French Revolution. Perhaps if true freedom could not be realized in the social or political realm, it could be cultivated within. Certainly, as the French Revolution—not to mention the later Russian and Chinese Revolutions—demonstrated, if a people who are still enslaved in their minds throw off an oppressor, they will inevitably end up enslaving themselves to a new and harsher taskmaster.

However, Blake's privileging of internal perception over external reality also reflects a general change in the philosophical atmosphere of eighteenth century Europe, one that shifted the focus from the world around us to the world within us.

From Ontology to Epistemology

Traditionally, philosophy, theology, and aesthetics concerned itself with the essence of things, whether those things were natural or metaphysical, poems or political systems, the idea of Beauty or the attributes of God. This form of philosophy is known as ontology (Greek for "the study of being"); it attempts to determine the thingness of things by exploring their true and original nature, essence, and purpose. As an ontologist, Aristotle wrote a treatise on every field of study known to his age: politics, ethics, physics, rhetoric, poetics, etc. In each of his works, Aristotle sought to define all facets of the field under study, to categorize each of those facets in accordance with a classification system, and to rank the importance of each facet against a scale of functionality and/or value.

Ontology, in its varied and sundry forms, continued to dominate philosophy throughout the classical, medieval, and early renaissance periods; however, by the time of the French Revolution, it was quickly being supplanted by a competing branch of philosophy that, though practiced by thinkers from Aristotle to Augustine to Aquinas, had previously played a relatively minor role. I speak of epistemology ("the study of knowing"), a branch of the philosophical tree that seeks to know not what things are but how are they perceived. Thus, whereas the ontological Aristotle wrote a treatise on every field of knowledge, the epistemological Kant (1724-1804) wrote a separate treatise on each of the mental faculties (or modes of thought) by which human beings perceive and interact with the world around them.

In his three great *Critiques* (of *Pure Reason*, *Practical Reason*, and *Judgment*), Kant explored the various ways in which our thoughts and perceptions of physical reality give shape, form, and meaning to those realities. In the *Critique of Judgment* (1790), Kant employed a vital distinction between the subject and the object, a distinction much used by epistemologists, especially the British Edmund Burke, whose *Philosophical Inquiry into the Origin of Our Ideas of the Sublime and the Beautiful* (1756) exerted a strong influence on Kant. Philosophically speaking, a subject is a conscious self that perceives, while an object is an unconscious thing that does not perceive but is, rather, perceived by a subject. Whereas ontologists focus their attention on the object, epistemologists focus theirs on the subject. Indeed, epistemologists go so far as to claim that when people speak of the beauty of a poem, they are not ultimately referring to the beauty of the object (the poem) but to the impact that object exerts on the eye and the consciousness of the subject (the one who reads or recites the poem).

When my daughter (the subject) looks at a flower (the object) and exclaims, "How beautiful," she is not—according to both Burke and Kant—making an objective statement about the flower itself, but a subjective statement about the mental response that is occurring in her mind. Beauty, that is, resides not in the flower itself (the object), but in the perceiving mind of my daughter (the subject). Or, to say the same thing in common parlance, beauty is in the eye of the beholder.

I would hasten to add here that when Burke and Kant defined our response to art (or nature) as a purely subjective one, they were not thereby advocating a wholesale relativism that would reduce all statements of beauty to mere expressions of personal taste. Still, their carrying of epistemology into the aesthetic realm did, one could argue, open a Pandora's Box that would pave the way for a radically interiorized and personalized view of the arts and the artist. In any case, the modern notion that the arts are first and foremost a form of self-expression, rather than an imitation of external truths and realities (whether they be natural or supernatural), does begin here with the philosophical/aesthetic shift from object to subject. Thus, in the same way that the Impressionists captured on their canvases not nature per say but the "impression" that nature made on their senses, so Blake and his Romantic heirs were less interested in faithfully recording the world around them than in projecting their own inner moods on to the surrounding world.

Picture, if you will, two female college seniors returning to their dorm rooms on the same rainy evening. The first, Mary, has just come from the most expensive restaurant in town where her boyfriend of three years has finally overcome his fears of commitment and proposed to her in a devastatingly romantic fashion. The second, Mona, has just come back from a disastrous date during which *her* boyfriend of three years has broken up with her in a devastatingly cruel and insensitive manner. When they log on to the internet to check their email, they discover that they have both received an assignment from their English professor asking them to study the storm raging outside their window and write a poem about it. Mary studies the rain and then composes a flowing, joyous paean in which she compares the storm to a universal baptism washing clean all the dirt and sorrow of the world. Mona, after gazing long on the same rain, dashes off a bitter, angry jeremiad fueled by images of fiery darts that fall from the sky and scorch the earth with their fury. Both ladies believe that they are describing the storm, when, in fact, they are describing their own inner mood, a mood which they have projected onto the rain. Mary, buoyed up by a spirit of love, joy, and harmony, discovers that same spirit in the rain. Mona, dragged down by feelings of angst, sorrow, and betrayal, equally discovers her own inner (subjective) feelings in the same (objective) rain.

Could William Blake have read their poems, he would have said that Mary was viewing the world through eyes of innocence, while Mona was viewing the (same external) world through eyes of experience. And could he have placed their two rain poems side by side, he would have found in them a succinct representation of the "two contrary states of the human soul." Mary embodies the mood of the Storming of the Bastille; Mona that of the Reign of Terror. Nevertheless, though their inner moods of innocence and experience are at variance, they both give birth to their rain poems by the same aesthetic/perceptual process—a process I like to call the externalization of the internal.

The Mind Is its Own Place

Thus far I have argued that Blake's *Songs of Innocence and Experience*, which center around speakers who externalize their inner, subjective states, embody the dual legacy of the French Revolution and aesthetic epistemology. But they also betray the influence of two English poets who left a deep and lasting mark on all the British Romantics: William Shakespeare and John Milton.

Shakespeare's *Hamlet* was never far from the minds of the Romantics. Indeed, they saw in the play's central character a young man who shared their own angst and over-self-consciousness. When Hamlet tells his treacherous friends, Rosencrantz and Guildenstern, that "there is nothing either good or bad, but thinking makes it so" (Act II, Scene 2), he voices the very thesis of the *Songs of Innocence and Experience*. It is our thoughts, whether they be sanguine or melancholy, that shape and affect the world, and not vice versa. In the same conversation, Hamlet complains that Denmark's a prison, and, when Rosencrantz and Guildenstern counter that if it be a prison, it certainly is a large and spacious one, the moody young Prince explains that size has nothing to do with it: "O God, I could be bounded in a nut-shell and count myself a king of infinite space, were it not that I have bad dreams." The imprisonment Hamlet complains of resides in his mind, not in the thick walls of the castle of Elsinore. As long as his inner state remains dark and constricting, the castle will appear equally claustrophobic.

A generation later, Milton would explore more fully the relationship between inner mood and outer world in two exquisite companion poems titled "L'Allegro" ("the happy one") and "Il Penseroso" ("the pensive one"). Both take place against the same natural landscape, but in the poems, that landscape is perceived from the point of view, first of a sanguine and then of a melancholy speaker. The first, a lover of the day, rejoices in the life, freshness, and spontaneity that surround him; the second, a creature of the night, broods on images of death, horror, and decay. The two speakers prefigure powerfully the inhabitants of Blake's twin states of innocence and experience. Blake surely cast his eye back on these two lyrical, and quite experimental, poems, but even they exerted less of an influence than did two pregnant lines from Milton's *Paradise Lost*: "The mind is its own place, and in itself / Can make a Heaven of Hell, a Hell of Heaven" (I.254-255).

Blake, as both a thinker and a poet, took seriously the idea that the mind is its own place, and used it as the framework upon which he built his *Songs of Innocence and Experience*. Those who read these unforgettable poems will remember "innocence" and "experience" as places, but those places exist less in the real world of history than in the happy or tormented mind of their speakers. In the two chapters that follow, we shall look closely at a number of Blake's *Songs* that most fully delve the twin states of innocence and experience. Here, instead, we shall consider briefly three poems from the *Songs* that help define the overall shape and import of the collection.

The first, "The Clod & the Pebble," appears in *Songs of Experience*, but Blake could equally well have used it as the frontispiece for the entire work. For, in this single poem, Blake allows us to study side by side the contrary states of innocence and experience.

> "Love seeketh not Itself to please,
> Nor for itself hath any care;
> But for another gives its ease,
> And builds a Heaven in Hell's despair."
>
> So sang a little Clod of Clay
> Trodden with the cattle's feet;
> But a Pebble of the brook
> Warbled out these metres meet:
>
> "Love seeketh only Self to please,
> To bind another to its delight;
> Joys in another's loss of ease,
> And builds a Hell in Heaven's despite."[1]

If we were to judge the lives of the Clod and the Pebble solely on the basis of their physical situation, we would clearly prefer the life of the latter. While the soft Clod lives in filth, unable to maintain even its own shape and integrity, the hard Pebble is washed clean by the cool, flowing brook. Just as most people, to paraphrase an old song, would rather be a hammer than a nail, so would most, if forced to choose, select the

---

1   Unless otherwise indicated, all quoted passages from the Romantics are taken from *English Romantic Poetry and Prose*, edited by Russell Noyes (New York: Oxford, 1956). Line numbers for poetry and page numbers for prose will be given in the body of the text. When poems are quoted in their entirety, no line numbers will be given. Noyes, like most editors of Romantic poetry, generally quotes poems in their final edited form rather than in the form of their original publication; this is particularly true for the poetry of Wordsworth and Coleridge.

protected existence of the Pebble over the utter vulnerability of the Clod. Surely, the reader concludes, the Pebble lives in the world of innocence and the Clod lives in the world of experience.

But the conclusion is too hasty. Though their external, bodily circumstances seem to suggest this categorization, the internal state of their mind/soul (psyche in Greek) reveals just the reverse. The Clod dwells in innocence, for it perceives and interacts with the world around it through "eyes" of love, mercy, and generosity. It gives of itself in the most radical way, and, because it does so, it is able to transform its hellish existence into a heaven of contentment and joyous surrender. The Pebble, on the other hand, is grasping, manipulative, and self-centered. It is incapable of moving out of itself or of taking joy in the ease of others. Blinded by selfishness, it is locked firmly in the world of experience, and thus transforms its heavenly surroundings into a hell of spite and envy.

In the contrasting psyches of the Clod and the Pebble is made manifest the truth of the passage from *Paradise Lost*: "The mind is its own place, and in itself / Can make a Heaven of Hell, a Hell of Heaven." Of course, we need neither Milton nor Blake to "prove" this truth to us. Have we not all known Clods and Pebbles? Have we not met at least one quiet, unassuming woman who, though she has suffered terrible sexual and emotional abuse, continues not only to trust in goodness but to shower compassion upon those who have suffered far less than she? Have we not met at least one privileged son of a rich father who yet looks upon the world with weariness, thanklessness, and cynicism?

The message of the poem both echoes and embodies the four blessings and woes that Jesus pronounces in the Gospel of Luke (6:20-26). Like those whom Jesus proclaims blessed in their poverty, hunger, weeping, and rejection, the Clod will laugh and be satisfied and leap for joy. And not just in the heaven to come, Blake suggests, but here, now, in the midst of its woe and oppression. The Pebble, in contrast, is like those who Jesus says are rich and well fed, who laugh and are spoken well of by men. A time will come when they shall hunger and weep, and that time, Blake again suggests, is even now. No, Blake reveals to us, it is not the Clod but the Pebble that we should pity—both in this life and the next.

I do not mean to imply that Blake is adding a new dimension to the words of Jesus. What Blake "adds" is already implicit in Jesus' teachings. Blake significantly structures his first and third stanzas around the Clod and Pebble's differing definitions of love. What the Pebble calls love is not love at all but a justification for narcissism and self-righteousness. But the Clod's true understanding of love captures fully the Christian understanding of God's unconditional and sacrificial love (*agape* in Greek; *caritas* in Latin; charity in English).

In two companions poems—one printed in *Songs of Innocence*; the other in *Songs of Experience*—that bear the same title ("The Nurse's Song"), Blake explores further the contrasting ways that love is defined by a self-giving psyche who views the world through eyes of innocence and a self-centered psyche who views the same world through eyes of experience. Let us consider first the one from *Innocence*:

> When the voices of children are heard on the green
> And laughing is heard on the hill,
> My heart is at rest within my breast
> And everything else is still.
>
> "Then come home my children, the sun is gone down
> And the dews of night arise;
> Come, come, leave off play, and let us away
> Till the morning appears in the skies."
>
> "No, no, let us play, for it is yet day
> And we cannot go to sleep;
> Besides, in the sky, the little birds fly
> And the hills are all cover'd with sheep."
>
> "Well, well, go & play till the light fades away
> And then go home to bed."
> The little ones leaped & shouted & laugh'd
> And all the hills echoed.

Blake's nurse (or nanny, as we would call her in America) perceives the world through a heart that is as innocent and carefree as those of the children she watches. She feels no envy toward them but takes delight in their simple play. Her entire being rests calmly and trustingly in a state of peace and harmony.

Suddenly, the nurse notices that twilight is beginning to fall and that it will soon be unsafe for the children. She beckons them to leave the playground and return with her to their homes, promising that they will resume their play when the sun rises anew. But the children are too excited to leave yet, and so, like countless children throughout time and culture, they beg their kind nurse for five more minutes . . . and she acquiesces.

Some mothers who read this poem might scold the nurse for her indulgence, but she neither harms nor endangers the children by giving in to their request. Rather, she shows herself capable of entering in to the joy and laughter of the children, of seeing the world through their eyes. Rather than impose her own adult worries—and *fatigue*—upon the innocent children, she allows herself to be rejuvenated by their youthful joy and energy.

Not so the nurse of experience who crushes their joy and energy, rather than allowing it to bubble up within her:

> When the voices of children are heard on the green
> And whisp'rings are in the dale,
> The days of my youth rise fresh in my mind,
> My face turns green and pale.
>
> Then come home, my children, the sun is gone down
> And the dews of night arise;
> Your spring & your day are wasted in play,
> And your winter and night in disguise.

The first thing a reader should notice when taking up this poem is that its opening line is identical to that of the previous poem. Only in the second line does the wording change—and what a sad change it is. Whereas the former nurse hears "laughing," the latter hears only "whisperings." Paranoid and mistrustful of the intentions of the children, the nurse of experience shields herself behind an "adult-versus-child" mentality that prevents her from participating in the innocent play of the children.

Indeed, their innocent play, far from rejuvenating her, inspires deeper envy and jealousy. In response, her face turns "green," a color which in the grass signifies life and health, but which in the human face signifies sickness and dis-ease. And that sickness spreads its dis-ease over the whole poem. Not only is this poem half the length of the former one, but the voices of the children are completely erased, squelched, it seems, by the bitter and warped psyche of the narcissistic governess.

There is little chance that this nanny will grant the children extra play time. Rather, she attempts to indoctrinate her innocent charges with her own spiteful view of the world. All is falseness, she teaches them, all is disguise. Play is a useless pastime that will do them no good. Her world is one of division and hypocrisy that keeps her perennially separated from the very children she claims to care for.

Neither of Blake's nurses has visited Paris, but they do not need to. The first both embodies and shares that blessed liberty, equality, and fraternity that the Storming of the Bastille promised to bestow on all of Europe. The second, imprisoned by hate and bitterness, carries the Reign of Terror within herself. She is like the demon Mephastophilis of Christopher Marlowe's *Doctor Faustus*, who, when asked by Faust why it is that he is not confined to hell, replies simply: "Why this is hell, nor am I out of it" (Scene 3, line 76).

II
The Songs of Innocence

According to the traditional, Judeo-Christian view, the problem with man is sin. It is our sinful nature, our inborn rebelliousness and disobedience, which prevents us from returning to Eden or building a utopia. That is why the role of government during the Christian Middle Ages was not to concoct and implement utopian schemes but to maintain law and order and to put a curb on human lust, greed, and pride. That does not mean that the medieval church and state were therefore callous to the plight of the poor; it simply means that they harbored few illusions about human perfectibility short of heaven.

By the eighteenth century, however, many European intellectuals had abandoned the central Christian doctrine of original sin. Inspired in part by the writings of Rousseau, such thinkers came to believe that we, by our own efforts, could remake ourselves and our world. Men *could* become angels and a pure society based on reason, rather than old medieval "superstitions," could be forged. The Reign of Terror exposed the dark side of this "optimistic" view, as Robespierre's Jacobins, considering the aristocracy to be too irredeemably corrupt to participate in the new-and-improved France, began killing them in droves. This same dark side would crop up again and again with even greater virulence throughout the twentieth century: in Stalin's Russia, where a worker's paradise seemed attainable, but only if those intractable bourgeois farmers (kulaks) could be eliminated; in Hitler's Germany, where a purified Aryan bloodline would lead Europe to greatness, but only once the "impure" blood of Jews and Slavs had been purged out; in Maoist China, where true equality would reign supreme, at least after the unenlightened counter-revolutionary landlords and intellectuals had been either properly reeducated or conveniently liquidated.

Published four years before the Reign of Terror, Blake's *Songs of Innocence* afford us a glimpse into that brief shining moment before the new fangled "doctrine" of the perfectibility of man had reveled its dark side. Not only is there a true innocence to the *Songs*; they embrace, despite their apparent rejection of original sin, a worldview that is more truly Christian in scope and tone than many a hellfire-and-brimstone sermon. Indeed, though Blake's vision would grow increasingly heterodox and ultimately gnostic, his early poems evince a profound and essentially orthodox understanding of the Incarnation and of God's self-giving love (*agape*).

For Blake's world of innocence is, at its core, an incarnational one, one where the link between God and man and man and nature either *has* been or potentially *can* be restored. Blake embodies this in part by his repeated use of two linked images: that of a child and that of a lamb. Like a pair of Wagnerian leitmotifs, these twin icons of innocence help bring a unity of theme and focus to the overall collection. When taken together, they point clearly, but not didactically, to the Incarnate Christ: he who became both a helpless child (by taking on human flesh) and an innocent lamb (by living a sinless life).

The linked images greet us immediately in the opening two stanzas of the "Introduction" to the *Songs of Innocence*:

> Piping down the valleys wild,
> Piping songs of pleasant glee,
> On a cloud I saw a child,
> And he laughing said to me:
>
> "Pipe a song about a Lamb!"
> So I piped with merry chear.
> "Piper, pipe that song again;"
> So I piped: he wept to hear. (1-8)

By mimicking the lilting rhythms and artless diction of the nursery rhymes of his day, Blake succeeds in drawing his adult readers away from the noise and confusion of the modern city toward the peace and quiet of a pastoral landscape. The speaker of the poem is neither a wandering knight nor a court wit nor a poetic craftsman; he is a simple, guileless shepherd who pipes his spontaneous songs without thought for audience or fame.

Suddenly, a laughing child appears to him on a cloud and asks him to pipe a song about a lamb. Both elements should take the reader by surprise. We expect the shepherd to be inspired, like Hesiod, by one of the nine muses; instead, his inspiration comes from a child. Likewise, though we expect the "muse" to instruct the shepherd-poet to sing of a high and serious matter—as Hesiod is instructed, in *Theogeny*, to sing of the birth of the universe and of the gods—the poet is told simply to sing about a lamb. That the song is merry yet causes the child to weep hints at the possibility that the innocent lamb (the Christ child of Christmas) will one day become a lamb for the slaughter (the crucified Christ of Good Friday).

Still, the Christmas spirit predominates, and the child encourages the shepherd-poet to transform his musical ditty first into a song with lyrics and then into a written poem:

> "Drop thy pipe, thy happy pipe;
> Sing thy songs of happy chear:"
> So I sung the same again,
> While he wept with joy to hear.
>
> "Piper, sit thee down and write
> In a book, that all may read."
> So he vanish'd from my sight,.
> And I pluck'd a hollow reed.
>
> And I made a rural pen,
> And I stain'd the water clear,
> And I wrote my happy songs
> Every child may joy to hear. (9-20)

While maintaining the utter simplicity of the first two stanzas, Blake does something here that is nothing short of stunning. By tracing the movement from playing to singing to writing, Blake provides his reader with a sort of discourse on the birth and origin of poetry. Rather than celebrate poetry as the most highly evolved genre, however, he presents it as something of a falling away from an earlier, less mediated ideal. The tune played on the pipe is far more fresh, spontaneous, and universal than either the song or the poem. With each successive movement away from pure music, art becomes both more self-conscious and more mingled with the pain, death, and decay of our material world.

But then, such was the case with the Incarnation of Christ. Through it, the invisible and eternal God entered into our physical, temporal world. The birth in the manger was hardly a clean, pristine affair. Just so, the plucking of the hollow reed and the staining of the clear water suggest the pain and "messiness" of childbirth. And yet, it is only through that pain and messiness that the Word can be made flesh (John 1:14) or the pure music be enshrined in the body of language. Further, it is in only once that embodiment has been accomplished that all can have access to it: "In a book, that all may read." The force that would bring poetry—or God!—down to earth is finally a democratizing one. The Incarnation spreads the divine covenant from one specific people group (the Jews) to, potentially, the entire world. The printing press empowers and enables the spreading of the Protestant Reformation, with its more democratic focus on the priesthood of all believers. Indeed, one might argue that Luther's most revolutionary act was not his doctrine of salvation by grace through faith, but his translating of the Bible into German.

To incarnate is to make visible what was invisible (see John 1:18); to embody is to make available what previously was limited to a few. Blake would make his songs accessible, and not just to adults, but to children as well (verse 20).

Now, those who have studied carefully the doctrine of the Incarnation might argue that Blake treads on dangerous theological ground when he links the process of incarnation to a loss of original purity . . . and they would be right. There is in Blake a pronounced streak of neo-Platonism that does not become fully manifest until *Songs of Experience* and *The Marriage of Heaven and Hell*. From the point of view of orthodox theology, Blake makes too great a distinction between body and soul. His tendency, like that of Plato, is to view the physical, particularly the body, as a mere container of the spirit. This privileging of soul over body, when taken together with the notion that perception controls reality—that things are not as they are but as they are perceived—would eventually push Blake, at least Blake the poet, outside the confines of Christian orthodoxy.

But not yet. As noted earlier, the poems that make up Blake's *Songs of Innocence*, as well as many that make up *Songs of Experience*, are not only recognizably Christian, but explore the deeper dimensions of the Incarnation and of Christian charity. Besides, in his "Introduction," Blake has a second, more personal reason for referring to the staining of the water.

Although in this book I will confine myself to Blake the poet, Blake was also an artist of prodigious talent who conceived of his poetry in conjunction with his art. Thus, rather than publish his poems as naked words on a naked page, he "incarnated" them within a visual frame. Blake was a printer by trade, and a genius in the art of illuminated printing.

On a copper plate he would engrave both the words of the poem and accompanying images, either actual images that comment on the poem or border decorations. He would then make a series of prints from the plates and finish by coloring them by hand. The process was laborious and expensive, and, ironically, it ensured that very few people would have access to poems meant for a book "that all may read." Still, the engraving process allowed Blake to realize more fully his vision, and the *Songs* are best experienced in an edition that includes both words and images.

The Marriage of Subject and Object

If the first poem in the collection introduces the twin images of child and lamb and hints at their union within the Incarnate Christ, the fourth poem in the collection ("The Lamb") makes that union clear. It is a poem that demonstrates more powerfully than any other Blake's unique gift for loading a poem of beguiling simplicity with a freight of philosophical, theological, and aesthetic meaning:

> Little Lamb, who made thee?
> Dost thou know who made thee?
> Gave thee life, & bid thee feed
> By the stream & o'er the mead;
> Gave thee clothing of delight,
> Softest clothing wooly bright;
> Gave thee such a tender voice,
> Making all the vales rejoice:
> Little Lamb, who made thee?
> Dost thou know who made thee?
>
> Little Lamb, I'll tell thee,
> Little Lamb, I'll tell thee:
> He is called by thy name,
> For he calls himself a Lamb.
> He is meek, & he is mild;
> He became a little child.
> I a child, & thou a lamb,
> We are called by his name.
> Little Lamb, God bless thee.
> Little Lamb, God bless thee.

The basic structure of the poem is simple: the first stanza asks a question; the second stanza answers it. The child, who seems fresh out of catechism class, actually asks a series of related questions: who made thee? who taught thee? who clothed thee? who gifted thee? In listing the qualities of the lamb—its feeding habits, its wooly coat, its lovely voice—the speaker seems to be reaching for the qualities of the Creator.

However, in reaching for that Creator, the child keeps his focus firmly on the real concrete world. The boy is neither a theologian nor a philosopher, and because he is not, the poem never becomes didactic or "preachy." Blake's decision to center a poem of serious theological/philosophical reflection on a child was revolutionary enough. But Blake goes even further. In addition to putting a child at the center of his song, he privileges the child-like perceptions of the child. The poem is not only *about* a child; it is seen *through the eyes* of that child. And as that child muses joyously and innocently on himself, the lamb, and the Incarnate Christ he has just learned about in Sunday school, he makes a connection that is deeply profound and yet also utterly simple and guileless.

Indeed, he arrives at the connection, as a young child might, partly through the sound and music of language. The rhyming pairs of "name" and "lamb" (lines 13-14 and 17-18) and "mild" and "child" (lines 15-16) are the very words that forge the link between the child speaker, the little lamb, and Christ, who, via the Incarnation, became both a child and a lamb. To a postmodern, deconstructed academic who has lost his faith in the meaning of language, the child's connection would seem overwhelmingly naïve, and yet, the child knows what adults too often forget: that words, and especially names, are fraught with meaning. That Christ would call himself by, and thus identify himself with, the names of "lamb" and "child," gives both those names—and those who possess them—inherent meaning, worth, and purpose. Their very existence is affirmed by the fact that the share a name with . . . with whom?

Judging by the questions he asks in stanza one, the child is seeking to know the Creator of the lamb (God the Father). Stanza two, however, shifts its attention to the Savior (God the Son). In the midst of the joining of names (God/Jesus, child, lamb), the child is discovering, without fully understanding it, a powerful theological mystery: that the pure, invisible Creator not only can name himself after one of the least parts of his creation (lamb, child); he can also, without loss of his Creator-status, actually indwell and become that name. For Jesus is not just *like* a lamb ("He is meek & he is mild"); he *is* the spotless lamb of Leviticus—the one that John the Baptist calls the Lamb of God who takes away the sins of the world.

Without understanding the full theological implications of the Incarnation, the child perceives that God both made lambs and is himself a lamb, that he is at once shepherd and sheep. Likewise, though he could not conceive abstractly the doctrine of the Trinity, he does sense in his innocence something analogous to the Trinity. The child perceives a sort of "triangulation" between himself, Christ, and the lamb, a triangulation that allows him to participate directly in the link between nature and nature's God. Child and lamb are together "called by his name," and thus, as they each draws closer to Christ, they each grow closer to each other. Through the mediation of the Word made flesh, something wonderful and magical is occurring, something that touches at the heart of one of the key Romantic yearnings.

In Chapter One, we considered the difference between the subject that perceives and the object that is perceived. Throughout most of the eighteenth century—a period referred to by historians as the Enlightenment or Age of Reason—thinkers were content to keep subject and object separated in their own discrete boxes. These lovers of reason were also lovers of logic, of analysis, of distinction. They learned by seeking out differences and by breaking things down into their constituent parts. As the century moved toward its close, however, some early Romantic thinkers—most notably, Friedrich Schiller—began to long not for analysis but synthesis. They wondered if the breach between subject and object— that is, the breach between man (the conscious, perceiving subject) and nature (the non-thinking, unconscious object)—could not somehow be healed. Could there not be some way to effect a marriage of object and subject, of nature and the mind of man? In a word, is incarnation possible?

Returning to Blake's poem with this in mind, we can quickly identify the child speaker as a subject and the lamb as an object. As such, the two are distinct from one another and cannot really communicate, despite the efforts of the question-asking boy. But magically, through the mediation of the Incarnate Christ, they are drawn together into one. In Genesis 2, God describes and defines marriage as a fusion of two distinct beings (a man and a woman) into one flesh; in the final two chapters of Revelation, heaven itself is described in terms of a Great Marriage between Christ the Bridegroom (or Lamb) and the Bride of Christ (that is, the Church or Body of Christ). Once that marriage is effected, God—who, as the great I AM, is the ultimate perceiving Subject—and his people—who, in comparison to God, are little more than an object—will be joined as one. And when they are joined, the division that began with the Fall from Eden will finally be healed.

In Blake's poem, in contrast, where the desire is not to move forward to heaven but to return to Eden, the marriage occurs less between God and man than it does between man and nature. As child and lamb are joined together in the poem, so are subject and object, perceiver (mind) and perceived (nature). Through that joining comes a sort of secular redemption that reunites what was divided and restores to wholeness what was separated and estranged.

The Movement Out of Narcissism

The healing and restoration that Blake calls for in "The Lamb" is not too difficult to come by, as it occurs against a pastoral background of peace and harmony. In "The Little Black Boy" and "The Chimney Sweeper," Blake attempts to effect a similar restoration, but this time he sets that would-be restoration against a background of intense suffering, injustice, and exploitation. It is in these two poems, more than in "The Lamb," that we realize that innocence defines an internal perception rather than an external reality—for the reality which holds the speakers of "The Little Black Boy" and "The Chimney Sweeper" in bondage lies very far away from Eden.

The former poem begins with a stanza that takes us into the mind of a child speaker who has suffered great oppression but has not lost his innocence:

> My mother bore me in the southern wild,
> And I am black, but O! my soul is white;
> White as an angel is the English child,
> But I am black, as if bereav'd of light. (1-4)

As in "The Lamb," Blake chooses not only to write a poem *about* a little black boy, but to allow that little black boy to address us directly in his own voice. By doing so, Blake does something far more revolutionary than merely register his indignation against the horrors of the British slave trade: he humanizes one of the victims of slavery. That is to say, rather than treat the little black boy as an object—as he likely would have been treated by *both* the slavers who profited from him *and* the abolitionists for whom he was nothing more than a statistic—Blake treats him as a full subject with his own unique perception of the world. Indeed, Blake increases the dignity of his speaker many fold by choosing to write this poem in a meter that is far more regal than that of the other *Songs*. This poem alone is written in iambic pentameter, a ten-syllable line with stresses on the even syllables made famous by its use in Shakespeare's soliloquies and Milton's *Paradise Lost*. Whereas most of the others *Songs of Innocence* are "sing-songy" in rhythm and tone, "The Little Black Boy" is written in stately, measured quatrains of iambic pentameter known as "heroic stanzas."

Though the outside world looks upon the black boy as dark both in face and soul, the boy himself is fully aware that one's soul cannot be read in one's face. In his case, internal and external are at odds, and the boy, despite his status as a slave, has a firm enough self image to assert his inner purity and "whiteness." The modern American who reads this stanza is likely to wince at the boy's seeming hatred of his black skin color, but the boy is actually referencing a simple, archetypal black/white dichotomy that would be universally understood by Europeans, Africans, and Asians alike. Because of its link to darkness, death, and fear, the color black has always carried with it negative connotations that do not accrue to the color white. The little black boy himself makes this clear by forging a link between his own blackness and the absence of light. The problem that the little boy struggles with is that he cannot reconcile the tension between his black outside and his white inside, and the reason that he cannot reconcile the two is that he is unable to perceive his outer blackness in a positive way.

Luckily, the boy has a mother who has retained within herself an internal state of innocence and who wishes to pass down that innocence to her son:

> My mother taught me underneath a tree,
> And sitting down before the heat of day,
> She took me on her lap and kissed me,
> And pointing to the east, began to say: (5-8)

Like the nurse of Innocence, rather than the nurse of Experience (see Chapter One), the speaker's mother neither feels envy toward her young charge nor desires to crush his youthful innocence. She provides him with what the Romantics, beginning with Rousseau, would have referred to as a natural education: one not taught through books and rote memorization but experienced more directly through intercourse with nature. Her classroom is both natural and personal, shaded by a tree and sustained by a filial bond of love and nurture.

Instead of burying her son's face in a book, the mother points his eyes toward the eastern sky and teaches him a lesson that will become a vital part of his identity:

> "Look on the rising sun: there God does live,
> And gives his light, and gives his heat away;
> And flowers and trees and beasts and men receive
> Comfort in morning, joy in the noonday.
>
> "And we are put on earth a little space,
> That we may learn to bear the beams of love;
> And these black bodies and this sunburnt face
> Is but a cloud, and like a shady grove.
>
> "For when our souls have learn'd the heat to bear,
> The cloud will vanish; we shall hear his voice,
> Saying: `Come out from the grove, my love & care,
> And round my golden tent like lambs rejoice.'" (9-20)

Despite the harshness and injustice of their situation, the mother has not lost her faith in a God of love. Indeed, she teaches her son that God's love is not just an abstraction or an emotion, but that it manifests itself in the form of action. Far more than a passive feeling, love marks an active movement out of the self toward the other. God, as a perfect and complete being, has the right to be narcissistic—to focus only on himself to the exclusion of others. Indeed, he is the only being in the universe who has that right. Yet he freely gives of himself to the world that he made. Furthermore, though the mother does not mention it directly, the poem, set as it is within the *Songs of Innocence*, reminds us that God's ultimate act of self-giving occurred at the Incarnation, when he left heaven to dwell among his creatures.

In the world of Innocence, God showers his blessings down not only on man but on nature as well. All is in harmony beneath the loving, ever watchful eyes of the divine Father. No matter how harsh the external world, both comfort and joy are available to those with eyes to see and a heart to receive. To our modern, more skeptical world, this may all sound like so much sentimental hogwash: "seeing the world through rose colored glasses," we might say, with scorn and condescension in our voice. But mother and child are both aware of the harshness of their life. They are not "idealists"; rather, like the clod in "The Clod and the Pebble" (see Chapter One), their acceptance of a self-giving "agape" love empowers them to see through their physical misery. This rare gift—the ability to give of oneself—the mother passes down to her son, but she also gives him a second gift, a lovely and poetic metaphor by which he can find a positive and special value in the blackness of his skin.

According to the mother's metaphor, most of us on this earth are unprepared to come into the presence of God in heaven. The traditional Christian reason for this unpreparedness is that our sinfulness prevents us from approaching too closely the all-consuming holiness of God. Blake suggests a slightly different reason, one that he most likely learned from Dante's *Divine Comedy*. Perhaps what we are unprepared to encounter in heaven is not God's fiery wrath but the even more fiery intensity of his love. The mother opens her son's eyes to this vital truth by encouraging him to "look on the rising sun" (9), for there God lives, and from there he shines forth his light. It is that light that the boy must learn to grow accustomed to if he is to bask some day in the pure light and love of God.

Once he emerges from hell, Dante must ascend the various levels of purgatory and paradise before he can look upon the glory of God. With each succeeding movement upward, Dante comes into contact with greater and greater light. By the time he has made it to the top of purgatory, his eyes are strong enough to allow him to gaze directly into the sun. Before that time, he must content himself with gazing first on the face, and then into the eyes of Beatrice. Until his eyes are strong enough to look into the sun, she shields them and protects them from the glare. Throughout his journey, Dante is provided with a number of such shields, the last being the Virgin Mary, whom Dante celebrates as the brightest thing in the universe outside of God himself.

In Blake's metaphor, it is our bodies that shield us from the glare. Just as a cloud or a shady grove protects us from the full might of the noonday sun, so our skin protects our soul from the bright sun-like beams of God's love. And our bodies will continue to protect our souls until they (our souls) can bear the full weight and burden of that light. At various times in church history, Christians have argued that our world is little more than a vale of tears. Blake transforms that image into a more positive one: life as a field where athletes train or a school where scholars study so that they will be physically or mentally fit to face any challenge. According to 2 Corinthians, "our light affliction, which is but for a moment, worketh for us a far more exceeding and eternal weight of glory" (4:17). According to Blake—or at least to the boy's mother—the purpose of our sojourn on earth is to give us the time and opportunity to learn to bear the full weight of the glory of God's love. Only once we have learned to bear that weight and to receive that love can our soul cast off its cloud-like body and ascend into God's direct presence.

Earlier in this chapter, I argued that even in *Songs of Innocence* Blake betrays a strong undercurrent of neo-Platonism that does not rise fully to the surface until *The Marriage of Heaven and Hell*. Here we see a second example of Blake's nascent neo-Platonism. Though the central metaphor of the poem is Dantean, the poem's treatment of the body as a mere covering for the soul is essentially Platonic. Orthodox Christian theology, on the other hand, teaches that even in heaven we will continue to be a body/soul fusion, our regenerated soul joined forever to a resurrected body of great glory and splendor. Still, the influence of Plato does not efface the greater debt to Dante and to the Christian doctrine of the Incarnation. Blake's vision of heaven is that of a restored Eden with God as a gentle shepherd who cares for his lambs (see Psalm 23). Like the Good Shepherd of John 10, God knows his sheep by name and calls them to his side. The degree of intimacy expressed in lines 18-20 exceeds that of Plato's more abstract and meditative heaven. In this perfected pastoral world, we shall, to paraphrase 1 Corinthians 13:12, know fully even as we shall be fully known.

Having shared with us the wise counsel of his mother, the little black boy goes on to share the effect that her counsel has had on him:

> Thus did my mother say, and kissed me;
> And thus I say to little English boy:
> When I from black and he from white cloud free,
> And round the tent of God like lambs we joy,
>
> I'll shade him from the heat, till he can bear
> To lean in joy upon our father's knee;
> And then I'll stand and stroke his silver hair,
> And be like him, and he will then love me. (21-28)

Just as God showers love and generosity upon his creation, and just as the boy's mother showers love and generosity upon her child, so does the boy pass on that love and generosity to the son of his slave owner. True to the two linked images that undergird all of the *Songs*, the child speaker compares himself to a lamb and expresses his hope that the master's son shall someday be a lamb as well. Only then, when they have left their differently-colored cloud-bodies behind them, will they be united in peace and harmony as fellow lambs at the feet of the One

Good Shepherd. Only then will full reconciliation be achieved, though the seeds of that reconciliation are living and growing even now in the innocent soul of the speaker.

From his mother, and from her vision of God, the little black boy has learned that our souls are all the same color, and that we are all objects of the same divine love and light. But that is not all that his mother's metaphor has taught him. Though he has come to see that his soul is the same in color as that of the master's son, he has also come to realize that his "black bod[y]" and his "sunburnt face" (15) are perhaps better equipped than those of the white boy to act as a cloud or shady grove for his soul. In fact, the speaker's pledge that he will "shade" the white boy "from the heat" (25) until he too can bear the light of God suggests that the speaker has come to see something of positive value in his black skin. Black, the speaker discovers, means something more than the absence of light (see line 4); it means shade and protection from a light and a love and a glory that most humans are not yet ready to receive in their fullness.

By the end of the poem, the little black boy has become secure enough in himself and his blackness that he can move out of himself, out of his narcissism, toward the white boy. Given the injustice and suffering that have been inflicted upon the speaker, it is nothing short of a miracle that he can respond with such Christ-like generosity. True, a slight sense of inferiority appears to remain in the closing two lines, where the speaker suggests that the white boy will not fully love him until he (the speaker) becomes like the white boy. Nevertheless, the final note of the poem is one of unity and integration, of the healing of division, of the two that were separated being fused into one.

Joy Within

In "The Chimney Sweeper," Blake extends his savage indignation and his compassionate concern from the black children of slavery to the white children of a different but no less brutal form of slavery that existed right in the heart of London. Though viewers of the wonderful Disney film *Mary Poppins* are apt to sentimentalize the life of the chimney sweeper, in Blake's day the sweeping of chimneys was anything but merry. In many cases, it was carried out by gangs of poor boys who were pressed into labor. The work was both miserable and dangerous, and many of the boys ended up dying of cancer and other diseases.

The speaker of the poem is a white boy, and yet, given that he spends most of his day working and lying in soot, he might very well have begun his poem with the words of the little black boy: "But I am black as if bereav'd of light" (4). In the opening stanza, the little chimney sweeper tells us, in simple matter-of-fact language, the sad story of his life:

> When my mother died I was very young,
> And my father sold me while yet my tongue
> Could scarcely cry "'weep! 'weep! 'weep! 'weep!"
> So your chimneys I sweep, & in soot I sleep. (1-4)

As before, Blake allows the victimized child to speak in his own voice. This time, however, he ratchets up the pathos by having his speaker make it clear that it is *our* chimney he is sweeping. Not just "the system," but the reader himself is implicated in the suffering of the chimney sweeper. Indeed, we learn, to our horror, that the boy's own father is also complicit in his suffering. Hard upon the death of his mother, before the little boy's untrained tongue could pronounce the chimney sweeper's cry of "Sweep! Sweep!" his father sold him into a life of ceaseless toil. And yet, though society has reduced the boy to nothing more than a cry ("weep! weep!"), it has proven unable to crush his spirit of innocence.

In the very next stanza, we watch in amazement as the rejected and exploited chimney sweeper reaches out with love and compassion to one of his fellow workers:

> There's little Tom Dacre, who cried when his head,
> That curl'd like a lamb's back, was shav'd: so I said
> "Hush, Tom! never mind it, for when you head's bare
> You know that the soot cannot spoil your white hair." (5-8)

As the little black boy pledges at the end of his poem to shade the master's son from the heat of God's love, so the chimney sweeper shares his own hard-won wisdom and inner reserves of strength with the weeping Tom Dacre. And poor Tom desperately needs the speaker's help. If we view this stanza from within the thematic structure of the *Songs of Innocence*, we will see that great danger looms over Tom Dacre. As in "The Lamb" and "The Little Black Boy," Blake forges a link between a child and a lamb, a link so close and intimate that the two images fuse into one. Here, however, the lamb threatens to shift its symbolic value from the spotless lamb of the Incarnation to the slaughtered lamb of the Crucifixion.

Luckily, before that shift can be effected, the speaker intercedes and offers to interpret the symbol of the shaved lamb from a different point of view: from the perspective of innocence rather than experience. When viewed/interpreted through the eyes of innocence, Tom's shaved head becomes a pledge ensuring that the black soot will not mar the whiteness of his hair. The violence of his oppressors will thus protect rather than destroy his innocence. Those acquainted with the beloved children's novel, *Pollyanna*, or the classic Disney film version, might very well accuse Blake here of indulging in Pollyanna's "glad game": that is, attempting to find some positive seed of good in every bad or negative situation. But Blake is doing something far more subtle and profound. The speaker is not advising Tom to turn a blind eye to his suffering or delude himself into believing that his life is happy and carefree. Rather, as Jesus counsels his followers to do in the Beatitudes (Matthew 5), or as the clod actually does in "The Clod and the Pebble," the speaker encourages Tom to see the world and his situation in it from a different vantage point and in a different light. There is a difference between ignoring evil and suffering and seeing through them. The Christian virtues of faith, hope, and love (*agape, caritas*) all share one thing in common: they enable those who possess them to transcend our world of sin, death, and decay and catch a glimpse both of a richer world of peace and joy and of a good and purposeful end toward which all our present suffering and evil are leading.

In the central stanzas of the poem, Tom Dacre is vouchsafed just such a glimpse:

> And so he was quiet, & that very night,
> As Tom was a-sleeping, he had such a sight!
> That thousands of sweepers, Dick, Joe, Ned, & Jack,
> Were all of them lock'd up in coffins of black.
>
> And by came an Angel who had a bright key,
> And he open'd the coffins & set them all free;
> Then down a green plain leaping, laughing, they run,
> And wash in a river, and shine in the Sun.
>
> Then naked & white, all their bags left behind,
> They rise upon clouds and sport in the wind;
> And the Angel told Tom, if he'd be a good boy,
> He'd have God for his father, & never want joy. (9-20)

By this point in the *Songs of Innocence*, readers should not be surprised to find heaven described in pastoral terms. Though no specific mention is made of shepherds or sheep, the landscape, with its green grass, its flowing river, and its shining sun, promises a return to edenic innocence. Better yet, the vision promises Tom that if he is a good boy, he will gain a heavenly Father to take the place of his absent earthly father; whereas the latter sold him into slavery, the former will redeem him from his life of misery and toil. The black soot of the chimneys will be washed away, and Tom, along with all his fellow sweepers, will be restored to naked whiteness.

The transition from earth to heaven, however, appears to be more difficult in Tom's dream than it is in the mother's Dantean/Platonic allegory in "The Little Black Boy." The chimney sweepers cannot reach their pastoral heaven simply by casting off their cloud-like bodies. They must first be pressed into and through a constrictive and horrific darkness before they can be released to live and play on the "green plain." Salvation *does* come in the form of the "bright key," but it comes *after* the suffering and bondage of the "coffins of black." Tom (and the speaker's) inner joy and innocence will sustain them until that day of their second birth, but the passage into that second birth will be at least as dark and painful as their originary journey through the birth canal.

Blake, who clearly alludes to Dante in "The Little Black Boy," is surely referencing Dante again in this poem. In the sixth ring of the inferno, Dante and Virgil encounter the damned souls of the heretics, each of which is stuffed—along with thousands of other souls—into burning coffins. When the final resurrection comes, Dante is told, an angel will visit each coffin, not to release those inside with a bright key, but to place the lids on the coffins and then nail them down for eternity. Still, though Blake surely had Dante in mind, the modern reader who encounters this dream-vision is less likely to recall the medieval Dante than a more recent thinker who lived and wrote a full century after Blake: Sigmund Freud.

Most people today hail Freud as the discoverer of the unconscious, when, in fact, it was Romantic poets like William Blake who first explored—often via the "royal road" of dreams—the internal landscape of the unconscious mind. What Freud did was to seize hold of the unconscious realm already mapped by the Romantics and give to it a scientific nomenclature. Jung would later develop that nomenclature further, attempting to identify and explore many of the same archetypal images that the Romantics had already delved in their poetry. On the literal level, the "coffins of black" are, of course, a metaphor for the black chimneys in which the sweepers toil. And yet, because of the symbolic and archetypal power of Blake's image, readers who have never looked up a chimney, much less crawled through one, can identify fully with the psychological terror and dread that the image conveys. Likewise, the image/symbol/archetype of the bright key draws together all our deepest human desires for salvation, release, and freedom.

When Tom awakes the next morning, he discovers that all is the same and yet all is different:

> And so Tom awoke; and we rose in the dark,
> And got with our bags & our brushes to work.
> Tho' the morning was cold, Tom was happy & warm,
> So if all do their duty they need not fear harm. (21-24)

The external world in which Tom lives has not changed in the least; he will continue to be oppressed and exploited by an uncaring society and will likely die young along with the speaker and the majority of his companions. His internal state, in contrast, has been transformed. Through the speaker's comforting words and his pastoral dream-vision, Tom has gained within himself a new inner life of peace and joy that will keep him warm and happy when the world outside is cold and sad. Despite the moralistic tone of the closing line of the poem, it is this inner change that will ultimately protect Tom from all harm. Unlike Marlowe's Mephastophilis, who is never out of hell for he carries it with him, Tom, by externalizing his inner state of innocence and projecting it onto the physical world, not only preserves his innocence but carries it with him even into the fiery coffins of hell.

III
The Songs of Experience

Although "The Little Black Boy" has no direct counterpart in *Songs of Experience*, Blake consciously pairs "The Chimney Sweeper" of *Innocence*, as he does "The Nurse's Song" of *Innocence,* with a poem of the same name in *Experience.* Once again, Blake expresses outrage against the plight of chimney sweepers while still providing one particular sweep with a distinct voice. This time, however, that voice is all but crushed by social, economic, and psychological forces that devour innocence and leave only death, despair, and hypocrisy in their wake. The poem begins, not with the voice of the child speaker, but with a removed, adult voice that studies the boy as if he were an object:

> A little black thing among the snow:
> Crying weep, weep, in notes of woe!
> Where are thy father & mother? say?
> They are both gone up to the church to pray. (1-4)[2]

In the world of experience, the child speaker is reduced to a "little black thing," a dehumanizing image that remains in our mind even after the poem allows the child to speak. A black stain on a white background, a smothered cry: that is all that remains of that strong and resilient child who spoke words of comfort and joy to little Tom Dacre in "The Chimney Sweeper" of *Innocence*.

The adult voice, which seems to feel a humanitarian concern for the boy even as it strips him of his individual dignity, asks the child where his parents are. Though line 3 is too short for the reader to determine clearly the tone of the adult voice, I would suggest that the tone is one

---

[2] This poem, along with "The Sick Rose" (quoted below), does not appear in Noyes's anthology. I quote both poems as they appear in William Blake's *Songs of Innocence and* Experience (Oxford: Oxford UP, 1967).

of condescension and even blame. "What are you doing here, child?" the voice seems to ask, "Why aren't you with your parents?" The child's answer should provoke a feeling of both sadness and horror in the reader. This child is neither an orphan nor even a "half orphan" as he is in "The Chimney Sweeper" of *Innocence*. Both of his parents are alive, and yet they have condemned their own son to a life of slave labor. Worse yet, as the boy toils away his childhood and his innocence, his parents are praying in church. In Blake's world of experience, church is no longer a place to draw closer to God or to learn *agape* love (as it is in the world of innocence); it is a place of repression and hypocrisy that shields sin rather than exposing it.

The final two stanzas of the poem are spoken in the voice of the chimney sweeper, but it is a voice that can only state—not overcome—its misery:

> Because I was happy upon the heath,
> And smil'd among the winters snow:
> They clothed me in the clothes of death,
> And taught me to sing the notes of woe.
>
> And because I am happy, & dance & sing,
> They think they have done me no injury:
> And are gone to praise God & his Priest & King
> Who make up a heaven of our misery. (5-12)

The words of these two stanzas should send a chill up the reader's spine; however, of all the sad and despairing words that make up the stanzas, the most chilling of all is the word "because." What that terrible word implies is that his parents have condemned him to unceasing toil not for their own profit or as a way to free them from caring for their child but *because* they saw how happy and carefree their child's life was. It is as if the parents, seeing the marks of joy and innocence in their child, consciously chose to tear them out of him by exiling him to the death-in-life existence of the black-clad chimney sweepers. In the world of innocence, life and laughter and hope bubble up from the children to inspire and rejuvenate the adults. In the world of experience, that process is reversed: death and despair and mourning pass down from the adults to crush and pervert the children.

Luckily for the child, and perhaps for some of his fellow sweeps, this process is not fully successful. Some joy and innocence remain and enable the child to express that residual happiness in the form of song and dance. But alas, the child's attempt to transform his sorrow into a song of hope only condemns him to further labor, for it convinces his oppressors—as it did many slaveholders in the antebellum South—that their child slaves must actually be enjoying themselves. Tragically, the child's songs, like the Negro spirituals of the old South, serve both to increase his bondage and to reinforce the hypocrisy of the adult world. And that hypocrisy manifests itself most powerfully and disturbingly, as it does in stanza one, in the role that the church plays in perpetuating it. Far from a friend and advocate of the poor and oppressed, the church of experience works in direct cahoots with the state to maintain the status quo. Indeed, Blake may have had Luke 23:12 in mind when he wrote line 11. Before the Crucifixion, Luke tells us, Herod (the King of the Jews) and Pontius Pilate (the Roman procurator) had been enemies; however, after they cooperated together—along with the High Priest Caiaphas, we might add—to put Christ to death, they became friends.

In the pastoral world of the *Songs of Innocence*, a gentle and life-affirming patriarchy is possible. In the hypocritical world of the *Songs of Experience*, the powerful conspire to spread misery: a misery which they—like the Satan of *Paradise Lost* or the Pebble of "The Clod and the Pebble"—transform into their own perverse version of heaven.

The Melancholy Voice of Experience

I suggested a moment ago that the voice that speaks in lines 1-3 of the "Chimney Sweeper" of *Experience* is that of a somewhat callous humanitarian. However, if we read the poem not in isolation but in the context of the *Songs of Experience*, a different identity for the speaker emerges. Just as Blake begins *Songs of Innocence* with a poem titled, simply, "Introduction" that establishes the pastoral setting and the overall mood and voice of the collection, so he begins *Songs of Experience* with a poem also titled "Introduction" that likewise establishes setting, mood, and voice:

> Hear the voice of the Bard!
> Who Present, Past, & Future sees:
> Whose ears have heard
> The Holy Word
> That walk'd among the ancient trees,
>
> Calling the lapsed Soul,
> And weeping in the evening dew;

> That might controll
> The starry pole,
> And fallen, fallen light renew! (1-10)

Whereas the "Introduction" to *Innocence* presents us with a simple shepherd-poet who, inspired by a child-muse, springs joyously and spontaneously into music, song, and poetry, the "Introduction" to *Experience* presents us with a very different poetic voice, one that is sophisticated, brooding, and world-weary. Blake calls his poet a "Bard," a word that carries with it a number of potential meanings: a national poet (like Shakespeare), a spinner of old tales (like Chaucer), an ancient Celtic singer who weaves together the legends of his tribe (like the Greek Homer).

Although Blake most likely had the third option in mind, all three meanings suggest a poet who not only exists within a wider history but who reflects, self-consciously, upon that history. Unlike the shepherd-poet of *Innocence*, who dwells in an edenic, "timeless time" of perpetual spring, the Bard of *Experience* is burdensomely aware of "Present, Past, & Future," words which Blake significantly capitalizes. Blake's Bard has seen and heard and known all things that pass in this world, and that knowledge, though it has made him wise, has also made him as melancholy and overly-self-conscious as Hamlet.

Or, to make use of the allusion implied in lines 3-6, like Adam. More than simply a member of the fallen human race, the Bard retains a clear memory of his previous, prelapsarian life in Eden. He, like Adam, has heard the voice of the Lord God walking in the garden in the cool of the day, but he, also like Adam, is aware of his nakedness and shame (Genesis 3:8). He longs to go back to Eden—which, for Blake, means also the world of innocence—but he cannot return. He knows too much; his perceptions have been colored by experience, and he can no longer *see* the world with the eyes of the shepherd-poet of *Innocence*. Because he has both seen the light that shines from Eden and the eclipsing of that light, he is doomed to yearn for a restoration that he knows can never be complete. Perpetual spring has given way to a seasonal cycle of light and darkness, life and death, fruition and decay, and neither the Bard nor the fallen Earth on which he lives can escape from that cycle.

Still, the Bard calls upon the Earth to do what he seems unable to do himself: resist corruption and decay and return to a state of innocence:

> "O Earth, O Earth return!
> Arise from out the dewy grass;
> Night is worn,
> And the morn
> Rises from the slumberous mass.
>
> "O Turn away no more;
> Why wilt thou turn away?
> The starry floor,
> The wat'ry shore,
> Is giv'n thee till the break of day." (11-20)

Thus far I have focused on the Bard as an overly-self-conscious brooder on the sadness and loss that accompany historical time. Here we see that Blake's Bard is also a poet-prophet—a common romantic type whom we will encounter again. As one who sees not only Past and Present but Future as well, Blake's prophetic Bard would speak *to* that loss and use his incantatory powers to call forth joy out of sadness. By weaving a spell of words, the Bard hopes to resurrect the dark, sullen Earth and empower her to regain the dominion that once was hers.

But his poetic powers are not strong enough. Stranded in the world of experience, both Bard and Earth are chained by their own inner despair and by an external force of repression that stifles all creativity and crushes all hope. The "Introduction" to *Experience*, which ends with the Bard's prophetic call hanging on the air, is followed immediately by a second poem ("Earth's Answer") in which the Earth responds to his call:

> Earth rais'd up her head
> From the darkness dread & drear.
> Her light fled,
> Stony dread!
> And her locks cover'd with grey despair.
>
> "Prison'd on wat'ry shore,
> Starry Jealousy does keep my den:
> Cold and hoar,
> Weeping o'er,
> I hear the father of the ancient men. (1-10)

By personifying the Earth and Sky ("Starry Jealousy") as titanic gods, Blake lifts his poem into a mythic realm that transcends both the nursery rhyme simplicity and the social-psychological commentary of the other *Songs of Innocence and Experience*. Suddenly, the reader is brought face to face with primal forces locked in deadly struggle. In Chapter Four we shall explore Blake's myth-making and his turn away from incarnational Christianity toward esoteric Gnosticism; here, let it suffice to say that the language and imagery of "Earth's Answer" is darker and more riddling than that of the other *Songs*.

In stanza two, Blake introduces "Starry Jealousy," a divine character whom he will come to name Urizen in his later, esoteric-mythic-prophetic works. Urizen holds sway over the world of experience; indeed, it is his iron rule that causes the melancholy Bard and the chained Earth to despair of ever returning to innocence, to joy, and to light. The name Urizen suggests "you reason," but not the kind of reason that frees man from fear, ignorance, and superstition. Rather, the "reason" that Urizen embodies is the kind that binds and crushes and chills ("freezing reason's colder part" to borrow a line from Tennyson). Reason bereft of emotion, of imagination, of freedom; reason that can only calculate and codify and confine.

Blake identifies Urizen in line 10 with "the father of the ancient men": a reference to the God of the Old Testament, who is described, in Daniel 7:9, as the Ancient of Days. Blake was not the first student of the Bible, nor will he be the last, to have struggled with the differing conceptions of God offered in the Old and New Testaments. Even the most orthodox of Christians cannot help but be tempted to view the God of the Old Testament as an angry, wrathful God who interacts with the world through violence and repressive commandments, while viewing the God of the New Testament as a meek and gentle God of love and mercy who accepts and forgives all people as they are. Of course, a closer reading of the Bible will give the lie to this strong, but ultimately inaccurate first impression. The God of the Old Testament (Yahweh) does display traits of love, compassion, and mercy: he abounds with covenantal love for Israel his bride; he not only accepts Gentiles like Rahab and Ruth but allows them to become part of the bloodline of David, and, through him, the Messiah; he sends Jonah the prophet to preach to Israel's brutal enemy, Assyria; he expresses many times his true desire to write the Law on the hearts of his people and to exact from them not sacrifice but loving obedience. Jesus, on the other hand, the God of the New Testament, shows his wrath, holiness, and exclusivity in his attacks on the Pharisees, his cursing of the fig tree, his cleansing of the Temple, and his far from meek appearance in the Book of Revelation.

But these things Blake did not see. To his mind, Yahweh was the God of the "thou-shalt-not," a God who binds and represses all that is natural or sexual or creative. It is a picture of God that he derived not only from the Old Testament, but from his intensely close reading of Milton's *Paradise Lost*. When Blake read that great epic, he considered its true hero to be Satan and its true villain to be Yahweh, or Jehovah as Milton calls him. In Blake's mind, Milton's Jehovah was the foe of all energy: whether physical, emotional, spiritual, or aesthetic. He was, furthermore, a jealous God who envies that which he cannot utterly control and bend to his will. In the final three stanzas of the poem, Earth describes him thus:

> "Selfish father of men!
> Cruel, jealous, selfish fear!
> Can delight,
> Chain'd in night,
> The virgins of youth and morning bear?
>
> "Does spring hide its joy
> When buds and blossoms grow?
> Does the sower?
> Sow by night?
> Or the plowman in darkness plow?
>
> "Break this heavy chain
> That does freeze my bones around.
> Selfish! vain!
> Eternal bane!
> That free Love with bondage bound." (11-25)

Those who live under the tyrannical rule of Urizen must hide their desires from his ever watchful eye. For the desires that he cannot repress he binds, and those he cannot bind he strangles. His jealousy does not spring from his intense love for his bride and his zeal for her purity, but from cruelty, selfishness, and vanity.

It is the heavy chain of Urizen that chokes out innocence, love, and joy. Earth yearns to be freed from her bondage, but the chain is too deeply laid. In Greek mythology, the Sky Father (Ouranos) continually impregnates the Earth Mother (Gaia) against her will, forcing her to give birth to a race of monsters whom he then imprisons deep within her. Blake certainly had Ouranos and Gaia in mind when writing "Earth's Answer" and when creating the figure of Urizen. In the world of experience ruled over by Urizen, sexuality and fertility are either repressed, and thus sicken and die, or grow perverse, giving way to violence and exploitation. Many of the poems that make up the *Songs of Experience* describe just such a world, one in which desire and passion are stretched and twisted out of shape on the rack of Urizen.

Youth Pined Away with Desire

One of the shortest but most terrifying poems in the collection, "The Sick Rose," affords us a frightening glimpse into a world where passion has grown violent and perverse:

> O Rose thou art sick.
> The invisible worm,
> That flies in the night
> In the howling storm:
>
> Has found out thy bed
> Of crimson joy:
> And his dark secret love
> Does thy life destroy.

Though the poem defies exact explication, it seems clear that we are dealing with the loss of innocence. The masculine worm has invaded and defiled the feminine rose in what appears to be a rape; in any case, the "secret love" of worm for rose is a "dark" one that brings destruction in its wake. And yet, the poem forces us to ask, did the rose in some way desire her defilement? Is she the victim not just of violence but of fatal curiosity? Did she perhaps yearn for the forbidden knowledge that experience promises, and then find that knowledge, as did Eve, to be destructive of life and joy?

The poem, packed as it is with a visceral intensity, catapults us, almost against our will, into a scary, arbitrary world where one is allowed no second chance. The poem plays on our deepest psychological fears—our dread and horror of encountering a force that, though we may welcome it at first, will obliterate us in the end. The embrace of Urizen corrupts and perverts all that it touches, killing its victims both from without and within.

"The Sick Rose" is indeed a terrifying poem of the dangers that accompany illicit passion. Most of the other poems in the collection, however, take as their focus not passion wrongly seized but passion wrongly repressed. Blake clearly saw far greater danger in love that is too firmly stifled than in love that is too freely given. It is the Pharisee and not the prostitute that is most destructive of natural passion. For

Urizen, as the last line of "Earth's Answer" makes clear, spreads his poison primarily through the binding of free love. As Blake himself advises in *The Marriage of Heaven and Hell* (see Chapter Four): "Sooner murder an infant in its cradle than nurse unacted desires" (212).

"Ah, Sun-flower," one of Blake's most beautiful and melancholy lyrics, captures perfectly the sorrow and frustration that befall those who nurse unacted desire.

> Ah, Sun-flower! weary of time,
> Who countest the steps of the Sun,
> Seeking after that sweet golden clime
> Where the traveller's journey is done:
>
> Where the Youth pined away with desire,
> And the pale Virgin shrouded in snow
> Arise from their graves, and aspire
> Where my Sun-flower wishes to go.

In the timeless time of the world of innocence, all is fresh, spontaneous, and immediate. In contrast, those who dwell in the world of experience are ever "weary of time." They strive and yearn, but they never achieve. Rest and refreshment lie ever just out of reach.

Blake's metaphor of the sunflower is both powerful and haunting. Drawn by a strange and mysterious instinct—by a celestial "influence" the Medievals might have said—the yellow face of the sunflower tracks the movement of the sun through the heavens. It "countest the steps of the Sun," says Blake, suggesting a slow, agonizing process that suffers the weariness of perpetual ascent without achieving its goal or its vision. It—not just the sunflower but all those who share its fruitless yearning—longs for an end, a consummation, to its journey. It can see, just barely, the "sweet golden clime" that beckons it, but it is rooted too deeply to the earth (the physical, material world) to reach that golden shore.

Like the frustrated sunflower, the pining Youth and the pale Virgin are equally unable to achieve what they seek. Their problem, however, seems tied less to earth-bound roots than to inner repression. Both have strangled their desires, have, as it were, internalized Urizen. The former dwells in a fire that gives neither light nor heat; the latter wraps herself round with a blanket of fruitless, self-protective snow. Physically, emotionally, and spiritually they are as rooted to the material world as the sunflower. Their only destiny can be the grave, to revert to the dust from which they cannot break.

Yet the poem does not leave them in utter despair. It holds out the faint hope of a future resurrection, of a life beyond the flesh. The hope is not for that glorious *bodily* resurrection promised in scripture and realized in the Resurrected Christ (again, see Chapter Four); rather, it is a hope that the binding nature of matter/flesh can be uprooted and cast off in the end. Not the world-of-innocence hope for a restored and perfected Eden in the presence of a loving shepherd-father (as in "The Little Black Boy"), but a less substantial hope for release from longing, from desire, and from over-self-conscious melancholy.

Alas, even that faint hope is denied the speaker of "The Angel," a poem which I consider to be one of the saddest in the English language:

> I Dreamt a Dream! what can it mean?
> And that I was a maiden Queen,
> Guarded by an Angel mild:
> Witless woe was ne'er beguil'd!
>
> And I wept both night and day,
> And he wip'd my tears away,
> And I wept both day and night,
> And hid from him my hearts delight.
>
> So he took his wings and fled:
> Then the morn blush'd rosy red;
> I dried my tears, & arm'd my fears
> With ten thousand shields and spears.
>
> Soon my Angel came again:
> I was arm'd, he came in vain;
> For the time of youth was fled,
> And grey hairs were on my head.

Had Blake ended the poem after line 6, it might well have made a fine addition to the *Songs of Innocence*. The relationship between the speaker and the "Angel mild" is a loving and nurturing one. If we assume that the speaker of this poem is the male Bard of the "Introduction"—and that is what Blake seems to intend us to assume for all the *Songs of Experience*—then we must first ask why the Bard chooses to take on a female form in his lyrical dream. The answer, I think, is quite clear. Throughout the Bible, God speaks of himself as Bridegroom and his people—first Israel and then the Church—as his Bride. Although Blake seems not to have understood that the biblical jealousy of Jehovah manifests itself not in petty envy but in terms of this conjugal relationship with his people, Blake certainly was aware that the Church is most properly referred to by the female pronoun. He would have been aware as well of the long standing tradition in Christian poetry of referring to the soul in feminine terms. All that is to say that by making his speaker feminine and the Angel masculine, Blake is able to add a spiritual dimension to a poem whose surface context is physical and emotional.

The male/female speaker represents all those who push off love and refuse to extend true intimacy—and, contrary to popular opinion, women are just as afraid, if not more afraid, of true intimacy as men are. We can dismiss the speaker as a prude, but that only scratches the surface of the kind of inner repression that binds all those who live beneath the sway of Urizen. The speaker conceals, suppresses, and viciously guards her true, natural desires, choosing a self-defensive and self-protective stance rather than an attitude of acceptance and thanksgiving. Perhaps she fears that she will end up like the "sick rose" discussed above, though, given the mild nature of the Angel, that fear seems unfounded. Indeed, by the time we reach the third stanza, it becomes clear that the tears she sheds in line 5 are not true tears of sorrow and longing, but manipulative tears meant to exact a tribute of pity from the Angel.

Though the Angel makes every attempt to pierce through the emotional defenses of the Queen, he is unable to reach her heart. She is too cunning for him. Like a highly educated skeptic who uses every logical loophole—and many not so logical—to escape accountability before a righteous God, the Queen plays at an elaborate "un-mating" ritual that will keep her would-be lover perpetually at bay. Her problem, as I suggested above, is finally more spiritual than emotional. Rather than allow the Angel "in," she barricades her heart and soul. Unable and unwilling to move out of her own narcissism, she refuses either to give or to receive *agape* love. Blake describes her as a "maiden" Queen, a word which links her to the "pale Virgin" of "Ah, Sun-flower" who remains "shrouded in snow." This time, however, no hope of reaching the "sweet golden clime" is offered. In the closing lines of the poem, the maiden Queen is left an old maid. Like the sick rose, she will be given no second chance. Her desolation, which stretches from the external gray hairs on her head to the internal frost that chills her heart, is both absolute and irrevocable.

The Mind-Forg'd Manacles

Thus far, we have focused on the inner repression that binds love and frustrates desire, but Urizen's deadly influence extends well beyond the hidden heart. Like a black widow, Blake's cruel, jealous deity spins his web over all of society, injecting his poison into every type and form of human relationship. In "The Garden of Love," the melancholy voice of the Bard takes us on a journey through a landscape that was once innocent but has succumbed to the corrupting power of experience:

> I went to the Garden of Love,
> And saw what I never had seen:
> A Chapel was built in the midst,
> Where I used to play on the green.
>
> And the gates of this Chapel were shut,
> And "Thou shalt not" writ over the door;
> So I turn'd to the Garden of Love
> That so many sweet flowers bore;
>
> And I saw it was filled with graves,
> And tomb-stones where flowers should be;
> And Priests in black gowns were walking their rounds,
> And binding with briars my joys & desires.

In the world of innocence, the Church functions as a fountain of faith, hope, and love, a symbol of the union between God and man. Not so in the world of experience. Here, as in "The Chimney Sweeper" of *Experience*, the Church functions as a center of hypocrisy and oppression. Rather than encourage and foster the innocence of children, this Chapel blocks their play. To borrow a line from an old song, the builders of this Chapel have "paved paradise and put up a parking lot." Having abdicated their responsibility to reconcile God and man and to show mercy to the poor, the ecclesiastical powers who commissioned the Chapel have gone a step further: they have willfully cut man off from nature and ravaged the earth over which they were commissioned by God to be stewards. Far from working to restore Eden, the Church of the poem has bulldozed over it.

The Chapel on the green was not built to glorify and spread the teachings of Christ. It is, in fact, the Chapel of Urizen—the God of the thou-shalt-not. Rather than open its doors in welcome to the poor, the lame, and the downtrodden, it keeps its doors firmly shut. Both legalistic and exclusivist, the Chapel of Urizen knows nothing of mercy or forgiveness. Turning in despair from the dark and forbidding Chapel, the Bard seeks vainly to find the Garden of Love which once stood alongside the "echoing green." (I borrow this phrase from the title of one of the *Songs of Innocence* which Blake likely meant as a contrast to "The Garden of Love.") There too, however, he finds the same capitulation to the forces of hypocrisy and oppression.

In the opening chapter of *The Scarlet Letter*, Nathaniel Hawthorne informs his readers that the first act of the Puritan settlers of Boston was the allotment of two portions of virgin soil for the building of a cemetery and a prison. So here, in the pharisaical village of Urizen, death and confinement take precedence over life and freedom. Cold, lifeless tombstones spring up where living flowers once stood, and self-righteous, black-clad priests replace the loving patriarchs and gentle shepherds of the *Songs of Innocence*. The use of internal rhyme in lines 11 and 12 (gowns/rounds, briars/desires) mimics the binding up and suppressing of all joy and desire in the name of a legalistic religiosity that hates and fears all that is natural. The poison of Urizen causes all spontaneous human impulses to sicken and die.

Such blight has Urizen inflicted upon the once pastoral landscape of the world of innocence. The peace and natural beauty of village and countryside have been stripped away and replaced by artificial, soul-crushing restriction. Still, this loss cannot match the horror of what Urizen has wrought in the cities.

For the great writers of England's Age of Enlightenment—Alexander Pope and Samuel Johnson in particular—cities like Paris and London were vital centers of life, growth, and industry. There, business and the arts could flourish side by side; there, people from different backgrounds and walks of life could mingle together and share their ideas and talents. In the city, reason triumphed, ignorance and superstition withered away, and progress and reform took root and grew. The Romantics saw things differently. For them, the city was a lonely, noisy, and impersonal place. Within its confines, nature was either tamed or eliminated, and men, having been cut off from nature, were cut off as well from each other. For the Romantics, the city signified not unity but fragmentation, not the setting free of the human spirit but the forging of fetters and the wearing of masks.

Driven by their deep pastoral desire to return to Eden, the Romantics tended to avoid contact with the city. However, none of them ever expressed so deep a repugnance for, nor painted so hellish a picture of, the city as did William Blake in "London." Having led us through the anti-pastoral wasteland of "The Garden of Love," the voice of the Bard now leads us through the nightmare world of the City of Urizen:

> I wander thro' each charter'd street,
> Near where the charter'd Thames does flow,
> And mark in every face I meet
> Marks of weakness, marks of woe. (1-4)
>
> In every cry of every Man,
> In every Infant's cry of fear,
> In every voice, in every ban,
> The mind-forg'd manacles I hear. (1-8)

Although the word "charter" generally signifies the giving of rights and privileges (as was done when King John signed the Magna Charta), the word can also signify the leasing out of a piece of property. In Blake's London, what appears to be free is, in fact, bounded on all sides. Even the free flow of the river Thames has been channeled by the city's ethos of restriction and regimentation. And that ethos not only pervades every quarter of the city but is written in the faces of those who dwell there. In their grimaces of pain and weakness, the Bard reads a silent, internalized desperation. The city has defeated them, crushed not only their bodies but their souls as well. Even infants succumb to the despair of their parents and add their cries to the din and squalor of the city.

When I read Blake's troubling description of urban angst and dis-ease, I cannot help but wonder if it inspired Norwegian artist Edvard Munch's lithograph, *The Scream* (1893). In Munch's iconic image, a small, bald-headed man dressed in black stands on a bridge. His hands are pressed to his ears, and he is screaming. His eyes are lidless, his nose flat, his cheeks sunken. Though the screaming man seems, at first, to be staring directly at us, he is actually averting his gaze: the direction of his terrified stare is inward. Though there are two other men on the bridge with him, he is totally isolated. Behind the bridge is a seaside landscape, but that landscape, like the man's face, has been reduced to a series of curving, ovular lines. Indeed, the curving lines of the landscape appear to radiate *from* the face, as though the landscape had only moments before exploded out of the tormented psyche of the screaming man. *The Scream* is a product of an artistic movement known as expressionism, a movement which took the Romantic notion of the externalization of the internal—of things being not as they are but as they are perceived—to its farthest, nearly pathological limit. In Munch's lithograph, the screaming man is trapped in a world of his own making; the horror of his surroundings ushers ultimately from his own existential terror and despair.

A full century before *The Scream*, Blake coined a phrase to describe precisely the man's internal state: "mind-forg'd manacles." The city-dwellers in Blake's "London" are, in the final analysis, their own tormenters and executioners. They wear the chains of Urizen within their own minds, and their own minds have aided in the forging of the chains. Though victims, they are also complicit in their self-imposed slavery. Unlike the Infant, the Man does not vocalize his cry, but the cry is nevertheless graven in his face. Hamlet ends his first soliloquy by cursing the fact that he must hold his tongue, but this does not prevent his internal cry from poisoning his entire being. It is not only because of the murder of his father and the hasty marriage of his mother that Hamlet considers Denmark to be a prison. The prison that holds him and the manacles that bind him are far more internal than external. So is it with the walking wounded of Blake's "London."

Of course, that does not mean that the corruption of the city exists *only* in the minds of its inhabitants. Though rooted within, the tree of experience bears its bitter fruit across the full length of the city. In the final two stanzas of the poem, Blake excoriates the external manifestations of the mind-forg'd manacles in the form of a blistering jeremiad:

> How the Chimney-sweeper's cry
> Every black'ning Church appalls;
> And the hapless Soldier's sigh
> Runs in blood down Palace walls.
>
> But most thro' midnight streets I hear
> How the youthful Harlot's curse
> Blasts the new born Infant's tear,
> And blights with plagues the Marriage hearse. (9-16)

As in "The Chimney Sweeper" of *Experience*, Blake presents us with a world in which Church and State work together to exploit the poor and defenseless. The Church remains silent as children labor to death in chimneys, while the State turns a blind eye to the heavy casualties of their soldiers. Careless alike of individual suffering, the political and religious leaders of London ignore the cries and the pain and the blood and the groans that Blake assaults our senses with in a lurid synesthesia of color and sound.

From quarter to quarter, street to street, the metaphoric poison of Urizen infects all that it touches. And as it does so, it is accompanied by a very real and literal poison known as syphilis that spreads swiftly and mercilessly from harlots to soldiers to innocent wives. When a baby passes through the birth canal of a mother infected with syphilis, it can result in childhood blindness—which is why hospital nurseries today apply antibiotics to the eyes of all newborns. For Blake, the horrific image of a child rendered blind from birth as a direct consequence of the sins of its parents marks the strongest possible contrast between the worlds of innocence and experience—stronger even than that between the two "Chimney Sweeper" poems discussed at the head of this chapter. In the former, the mother's joy and hope and life are renewed and increased through a good infection that passes upward from her child; in the latter, the mother's physical, emotional, and spiritual sickness is inflicted upon her child, blighting it from birth and casting it into lifelong darkness.

In the final two words of his poem, Blake leaves us with a stark oxymoron: "Marriage hearse." Fusing together both the joy of marriage and the despair of death, the promise of new life and the extinction of old life, Blake's ghoulish pun converts the happy strains of the wedding march into the solemn chords of the funeral procession. It is a pun that he prepares us for in line 7 when he uses the word "ban," a word that, like "charter," can be interpreted in opposing ways. The context of the line suggests the prohibitions imposed by the city on its citizens, but the word (when spelled "banns") can also refer to the announcement of an intended marriage. Weddings and births, the two events on which rest the very life and future of a family, a town, or a city, are thus compromised from their very inception and prove powerless to transcend the restrictions, hypocrisies, and plagues of Urizen.

IV
Gnostic Mythmaking

Those who leave village or town to live in the big city rarely return. Who, having seen the world, can ever go back to life on a farm? Innocence, once lost, is nearly impossible to regain. So it is with individuals—or cultures—who consciously break with the beliefs or standards or mores of the past. Once Luther decided that he would be guided not by tradition or hierarchy but by the Bible and conscience alone, it was inevitable that he, and his followers, would break from the Catholic Church. Once Protestantism in general decided to define itself against medieval "superstition," the way was paved for Enlightenment deism and its rejection of an "open" universe and a miracle-working God.

Blake the romantic revolutionary rejected in turn the over-rationalism of the Enlightenment and embraced a supernatural view of the world. Indeed, beginning at an early age, Blake himself experienced mystical visions that included encounters with God, with the prophet Elijah, with angels, with fairies, and with the soul of his dead brother. Nevertheless, his rejection of rationalism and embrace of mysticism did not therefore enable him to return to the orthodox doctrines either of Protestantism or Catholicism. Blake had, in his own mind, heart, and soul, moved forward in too radical a direction to allow for a simple return to orthodoxy. The only direction in which Blake found he could move was forward toward a new synthesis of the natural and the supernatural, the rational and the intuitive. "I must create my own system," he once wrote, "or be enslaved by another man's."

As a poet and visionary artist, Blake's new system would shape itself around a complex and highly esoteric mythology populated by a pantheon of titanic gods and goddesses. However, rather than key his deities to natural forces (wind, fire, thunder) or heavenly bodies (sun, moon, stars) or traditional abstract nouns (war, love, music), Blake used his mythic creations to explore and to embody such deeper, more subtle forces as imagination, revolution, regeneration, rationalism, desire, poetic inspiration, and spiritual beauty. His poetic eye transforms the world into a vast playground of mighty symbols whose meaning often hovers just outside the reach of comprehension. Indeed, many of Blake's later apocalyptic works—*The Four Zoas*, *Milton*, *Jerusalem*—make James Joyce's *Ulysses* seem blissfully straightforward in comparison!

Though it is impossible to pigeonhole someone like Blake into a single religious or philosophical category, I think that we can fairly identify him as a Gnostic. Beginning slowly in the second century AD and reaching their heyday in the third and fourth, the Gnostics, influenced in great part by the writings of Plato and his neo-Platonic heirs, found the orthodox teachings of Christianity to be incompatible with their conception of God, man, and the universe. Whereas the Bible taught that the problem with man was sin, rebellion, and disobedience against God's holy standards, the Gnostics saw the problem as resting elsewhere. For them, the creation of physical matter itself constituted a falling away from spiritual unity and freedom; man must seek to restore this lost unity and freedom by a change in perception. Salvation was not to be attained through faith in a crucified and risen savior—a notion that struck Gnostics as being both overly simplistic and too mired with the physical world—but by the acquisition of hidden, esoteric knowledge (gnostic in Greek means "knower"). Unlike the Arians, who argued that Jesus Christ was fully human but not fully divine, the Gnostics saw Jesus as a spiritual emanation who was not fully human, but merely wore the flesh as a garment. Indeed, the very idea that God might become incarnate, might truly take on and become flesh, was both anathema and nonsensical to the flesh-denying Gnostics.

Though the early Blake toyed with the idea of the Incarnation (see my analysis of "The Lamb" in Chapter Two), he swiftly moved away from it toward a more gnostic vision of the world. Gravitating back and forth, as Gnostics often do, between a radical dualism that sets equal and opposing forces against each other in a titanic struggle, and a radical monism that collapses all things—body and soul, physical and spiritual—into a single substance, Blake left behind the central Christian teachings of the Incarnation (that Christ was the unique God-Man) and the Resurrection (that Christ is still incarnate, even in heaven, and that the redeemed will share in his bodily Resurrection). In fact, I would suggest that much of

Blake's later work can best be summed up by a single verse from the gnostic Gospel of Philip: "When Eve was still in Adam death did not exist. When she was separated from him death came into being. If he enters again and attains his former self, death will be no more."[3] This was the kind of fusion that Blake increasingly sought—not the two-into-one of the Incarnation and Resurrection but the healing of a primal division, usually through a change in perception. Though all the Romantics believed, in one form or another, that our perceptions influence the world around us and that beauty, truth, joy, and wonder rest in great part in the eye of the beholder, nobody believed it as radically as Blake, and no philosophical-religious system adhered to it as rigidly Gnosticism.

It is my personal belief that had Blake not gone the way of Gnosticism, he would have produced a great Christian epic that fused the virtues of *Paradise Lost* with those of the *Divine Comedy*. Instead, we have *Milton* and *Jerusalem*, works of great imagination and searing genius, but which are ultimately flawed and compromised by the same obscure terminology, elitist attitudes, and desire to break down all established metaphysical, epistemological, and linguistic hierarchies that have made postmodern deconstruction such a destructive force in the world of academia. Still, in earlier works like *The Book of Thel*, *The Marriage of Heaven and Hell*, *America: A Prophecy*, *Europe: A Prophecy*, *The Book of Urizen*, and assorted shorter pieces like "The Mental Traveller" and "Auguries of Innocence," Blake speaks to his age—and ours—with a prophetic power that impels his readers to rip away veils, to look deeper, and to test the spirits. True, even the works just listed often get bogged down and border at times on the impenetrable, but when Blake's words, images, and symbols break through the obscurity and connect with the reader, they pack quite a punch.

Although *The Book of Thel* is Blake's most accessible long poem, the one that has the most relevance to modern readers, that best sums up the core of Blake's philosophy, and that can be understood without recourse to Blake's full gnostic pantheon is *The Marriage of Heaven and Hell*. Before we can explore that strange and troubling work, however, we must pause to consider one final poem from the *Songs of Experience*.

---

3   Anthologized in *The Nag Hammadi Library in English*. Third edition. General Editor, James M. Robinson (San Francisco: Harper Collins, 1988), page 150. "The Tripartite Tractate," also anthologized in this collection, bears a striking resemblance to Blake's later apocalyptic works with its complex system of divine emanations that often defy any exact explication.

Orc

In the previous chapter, I devoted much energy to exploring the many dimensions of Urizen and his baneful influence both on man and society. Indeed, much of Blake's later mythology would gain its impetus and even its raison d'être from the pressing need Blake felt to counter that influence. Blake found his "counterforce" to Urizen in the form of a god named Orc. Whereas the former embodies restriction and suppression, the latter embodies pure, unadulterated energy. At once the energy of revolution and creativity, the force that Orc unleashes has the power to shatter all fetters and boundaries. In political terms, it is the energy set loose by the French Revolution (and, Blake would have added, by the American Revolution). Aesthetically, it is the power of inspiration that overwhelms the Bard and transforms him into a poet-prophet whose words set the world on fire. Though Blake never revealed the exact etymology of Orc, he most likely based it on Orcus, another names for Hades or Pluto: that is to say, both the warden of the underworld and the underworld itself.

There is good reason to believe that Blake intended to forge a link between Orc and hell. If Urizen is linked to Milton's Jehovah, then Orc is just as clearly linked to the Satan of *Paradise Lost*. Among the most audacious quirks of Romantic poets like Blake and Shelley was their scandalous habit of reading *Paradise Lost* in such a way as to make Satan, rather than Jehovah or Christ, its hero. For Blake, Satan's unswerving resistance to the jealousy and thou-shalt-not tyranny of Jehovah made him into a revolutionary freedom fighter. Satan's refusal to bow to the will of Jehovah gave him, in Blake's mind, a touch of spiritual and even moral superiority. Now, let me hasten to add that Blake was not blind to the negative dimensions of Satan's character. He was strongly aware of the dangers of Satanic-Orcic energy and explored those dangers in nearly all of his apocalyptic works.

The problem with Orc is a natural result of the problem with Urizen. Urizen's tyranny is so absolute, so all-encompassing that only a force as wild and dangerous and uncontrollable as Orc can hope to break it. Unfortunately, once Orc is let loose to do its work, it cannot so easily be recalled. Orc is like the genie that cannot be put back into the bottle, or, to use a more apt simile from history, like the two Atom Bombs that were dropped on Hiroshima and Nagasaki. The bombs did indeed break the tyranny of imperial Japan, but they also unleashed a destructive force that could have—and still can—destroy the very civilization it was intended to save. Those familiar with J. R. R. Tolkien's *Lord of the Rings* might compare Orc to the Ring of Power, to that terrible weapon which must not be used. Better yet, those familiar with the Star Wars films might see a parallel between Orc and the Force.

Indeed, the second analogy is the more accurate one. In *The Lord of the Rings*, the Ring is clearly evil and can only be used for dark, sinister purposes. But in the Star Wars films, the Force is simply that, an energy field that can be channeled in two radically different ways. In the hands of a Jedi knight like Luke Skywalker or Obi Wan Kenobi, the Force can be used to save, to protect, and to build. In the hands of Darth Vader or the Evil Emperor, who knows how to channel and control the Dark Side of the Force, it can only be used to conquer and to destroy. I do not make these two references to popular culture merely to sound hip or "relevant." Tolkien and George Lucas, like William Blake before them, were artists who felt the need to embody the conflicts of their day (and of any day) in the form of a new "mythology." In Tolkien's case, the "myths" rested upon a solidly Catholic worldview; in the case of Lucas, the "myths" rested on the archetypal theories of Carl Jung—as filtered through the works of comparative mythologist Joseph Campbell. In the more western (Judeo-Christian) Tolkien, good and evil are preserved as separate, well-defined categories. In the more eastern (pantheistic) worldviews of Jung, Campbell, and Blake, the dividing line between good and evil is not so sharp. Rather, divinity/spirit is spread throughout the universe in a more diffuse, less "personal" way. The energy that Orc embodies is *neither* good nor evil; it is merely energy that can be channeled for different purposes.

In the midst of his *Songs of Experience*, over which the presence of Urizen hangs like a dark cloud, Blake inserted a single poem ("The Tyger") to capture the exact nature of Orcic energy. The poem, probably the best known of all Blake's works, is at once thrilling and terrifying, inspiring both awe and horror in the heart of its reader. It is a poem that needs to be read and experienced in its entirety before analysis can begin:

> Tyger! Tyger! burning bright
> In the forests of the night,
> What immortal hand or eye
> Could frame thy fearful symmetry?
>
> In what distant deeps or skies
> Burnt the fire of thine eyes?

On what wings dare he aspire?
What the hand dare sieze the fire?

And what shoulder, & what art,
Could twist the sinews of thy heart?
And when thy heart began to beat,
What dread hand? & what dread feet?

What the hammer? what the chain?
In what furnace was thy brain?
What the anvil? what dread grasp
Dare its deadly terrors clasp?

When the stars threw down their spears,
And water'd heaven with their tears,
Did he smile his work to see?
Did he who made the Lamb make thee?

Tyger! Tyger! burning bright
In the forests of the night,
What immortal hand or eye,
Dare frame thy fearful symmetry?

 Here, as in "The Sick Rose," Blake is not interested in producing a realistic portrait of something from the natural world. His Tyger is a creature of the imagination, a symbol of a force which has no name but which runs throughout nature. Were one ever to encounter Blake's Tyger, it would not be in a zoo or on a safari but in a nightmare. Just as "The Sick Rose" propels the reader into a frightening world were innocence is destroyed, so "The Tyger" opens the eyes of the reader to a different mode of being where all exists in a state of heightened energy and tension.

 In the first stanza, Blake sums up the archetypal (Orcic) power of the Tyger in a memorable oxymoron: "fearful symmetry." More often associated with the beautiful than with the sublime, symmetry connotes balance, harmony, and rest. In the symbol of the Tyger, however, the word symmetry is loaded with a new freight of meaning. Symmetry morphs into a coiled spring ready to pounce, a hinged jaw ready to devour. The Tyger inspires dread not only because it burns like a flame in the night, but because it is a thing that has been fearfully crafted and shaped by a mysterious divine hand.

 The image of fire and hand are carried into the second stanza, where together they point to the Greek myth of Prometheus. Although he was one of the immortal Titans, Prometheus, driven by his love for man, defied Zeus and stole the divine fire from Mount Olympus. For his crime, Prometheus was chained to a rock and visited by a monstrous eagle. Each day, the eagle would tear out his liver; each night the liver would regenerate, only to be devoured again on the following day. For Blake—and Shelley and Byron after him—Prometheus was the ideal hero. While possessing the rebellious energy and defiance of Milton's Satan, the Greek Titan shared Christ's love for humanity and his willingness to suffer that men might grow in knowledge and spirit. Both in the Greek myth and in Blake's reworking of it, the fire that Prometheus stole and gave to man is, at least in part, the fire of creativity. Of course creativity, like fire, like revolution, like Orc, can be used both to create and to destroy. Behind the triumph and the freedom and the light, there always lurks the dark side.

The third and fourth stanzas expand on lines 3 and 4, with their suggestion that the Tyger was not born but made. It was not a tigress but some Olympian blacksmith who gave birth to this horrific beast. Though it possesses heart and brain, the Tyger—like Darth Vader—seems more a thing of metal than of flesh. Twisted and shaped on a divine anvil, then thrust into a crucible of Promethean fire, the Tyger emerges from another realm that hovers just outside our own. The Tyger hails from that same shadowy realm whence spring inspiration and the revolutionary spark. And behind all three, stanza five suggests, lies something fierce and primeval: a Miltonic war in heaven that shook the very foundations of the universe.

"Did he smile his work to see?" the poet asks. Was God pleased by the Tyger and the fearful symmetry that it embodies? Was it truly his desire that such a force should be unleashed on the world? And then the deeper question: "Did he who made the Lamb make thee?" Is it possible that the same being who made the Lamb of *Innocence* could have made the Tyger of *Experience*? On one level, Blake is asking the age-old theological question of the origin of evil. Surely a good God (the Creator of the Lamb) could not be responsible for bringing evil (the Tyger) into the world? But Blake has something more shocking—and less orthodox—to say. The Tyger of the poem does not simply mark the opposite or contrary of the Lamb. The Tyger, and the Orcic energy it embodies, lies beyond all categories of innocence and experience, beauty and sublimity, chaos and symmetry. Though the final stanza repeats the contents of the first, it does make one small but significant change. Rather than wonder who "could" make the Tyger (line 4), the closing line wonders who, having the power to do so, would nevertheless "dare" to create a creature that shatters all boundaries and categories that would seek to contain it.

Blake, for all the debt he owed to Milton, was not ultimately concerned to "justify the ways of God to men" (*Paradise Lost*, line 26). Blake is, in fact, less a descendant of Milton than a forerunner of Nietzsche, he who called for a "superman" with the courage first to forsake and then to transcend all bourgeois notions of good and evil to assert his absolute will to power.

But now I am getting ahead of myself. The time has come to turn our attention away from the *Songs* to a work that in its very construction defies all generic categories.

Reason v. Energy

Written and engraved in 1790—only one year after the Storming of the Bastille and the *Songs of Innocence*—*The Marriage of Heaven and Hell* reads like a gnostic version of the Book of Ecclesiastes. Like those of the Teacher, the musings of Blake are conveyed in an episodic, often fragmented manner that combines poetic-prophetic prose with fanciful allegories and pithy proverbs. With mystical, apocalyptic force, Blake rips away the veil and allows us to peer into the forces that propel history forward and that underlie our little human systems of philosophy and religion. The twin targets of his half polemical/half ironic work are secular Enlightenment thinkers who privilege reason over imagination and orthodox Christian thinkers who privilege heaven over hell.

Indeed, at the very outset of his work, Blake establishes a dichotomy that underlies both Christian and Enlightenment thought:

> Without Contraries is no progression. Attraction and Repulsion, Reason and Energy, Love and Hate, are necessary to Human existence.
>
> From these contraries spring what the religious call Good & Evil. Good is the passive that obeys Reason. Evil is the active springing from Energy.
>
> Good is Heaven. Evil is Hell. (p. 210)

If the two sides of this dichotomy sound familiar, that is because Blake is in the process of identifying the opposing forces that he will soon name Urizen and Orc. Urizen, who has convinced the Western world—

particularly in the guise of Milton's Jehovah—that his vision, and his alone, is to be equated with Heaven, with Goodness, and with Love, calls on his followers to passively obey Reason. Orc, whom Western man has been taught, by Urizen and Milton, to equate with Hell, with Evil, and with Hate, calls instead for his followers to actively pursue and channel Energy. In defining the two sides of this dichotomy, Blake seeks not to endorse but to deconstruct a system upheld both by religionists and rationalists. With fervor tempered by irony, Blake will present himself, quite literally, as the devil's advocate. He will speak on behalf of that Satanic, Orcic Energy that refuses to remain passive in the face of Urizen's heavenly propaganda.

Blake begins his legal brief by listing three Urizenic errors and their Orcic contraries:

> All Bibles or sacred codes have been the causes of the following Errors:
>
> 1. That Man has two real existing principles: Viz: a Body & a Soul.
>
> 2. That Energy, call'd Evil, is alone from the Body; & that Reason, call'd Good, is alone from the Soul.
>
> 3. That God will torment Man in Eternity for following his Energies.
>
> But the following Contraries to these are True:
>
> 1. Man has no Body distinct from his Soul; for that call'd Body is a portion of Soul discern'd by the five Senses, the chief inlets of Soul in this age.
>
> 2. Energy is the only life, and is from the body; and Reason is the bound or outward circumference of Energy.
>
> 3. Energy is Eternal Delight. (210)

Adding on to the dichotomy he has already established, Blake argues that we have been falsely taught to view the Soul as the source of both Reason and Goodness and to degrade and dismiss the Body as the exclusive dwelling place of both Energy and Evil. Further, we have been taught to believe that God—that is, the Old Testament, thou-shalt-not God—will punish all those who seek after and make use of Energy. In contrast to this view, Blake asserts that the body is but the sensual part of the soul, that energy animates *both* body and soul, and that reason is but the outward boundary of energy. Although Blake may seem here to be championing the orthodox Christian view of man—that he is not a soul trapped in a body but an incarnational fusion of both—he is actually working within a gnostic framework. Just as the Gnostics accepted Jesus' divinity but denied his humanity, Blake envisions not an incarnation of body and soul but a collapsing of the two: an energized soul swallowing up the body even as the body, throwing off the bounds of reason, devours the soul. Rather than an incarnation effected by divine love, we get a shattering of all distinctions driven by hell-born Energy. For those taught by Urizen, such Energy is but another name for evil, sin, and madness; for those taught by Orc, it is Eternal Delight—at once the consummation of sensual desire, the revolutionary spark that tears down established hierarchies, and the Promethean fire of genius that makes men into gods.

Why then do all people not embrace this Energy and revel in its Eternal Delight? In answering this question, Blake anticipates by a century Nietzsche's famous—or perhaps infamous—critique of religion as a slave ethic:

> Those who restrain desire, do so because theirs is weak enough to be restrained; and the restrainer or reason usurps its place & governs the unwilling.
>
> And being restrain'd, it by degrees becomes passive, till it is only the shadow of desire. (210-211)

Because the weak and self-enslaved fear energy, they allow their desires to be restrained by reason. In doing so, however, they turn reason into a tyrant that crushes their desires and demands of them total passivity. As reason grows ever more powerful and the weak ever more passive, the weak insist that the desires of even the strong should be restrained as well by reason. By reason, of course, Blake does not mean intelligence or the ability to think critically. He means something far closer to what Nietzsche would denigrate as bourgeois standards of good and evil, right and wrong, virtue and vice. Both Blake and Nietzsche, in their own idiosyncratic way, would call for the overthrow of these artificial, Urizen-made standards: the former by way of a poetic genius inspired by Orcic Energy; the latter by way of a bold and charismatic leader (the *Übermensch* or "overman") who would assert his power to move beyond the narrow confines of good and evil. Both poet and superman bear a striking, if troubling resemblance to Blake's Tyger.

Having diagnosed the problem, Blake goes on to argue, in a way unique to himself, that most of the poets and mystics before him have only served to further the problem. Whereas the name Satan in Hebrew means "accuser"—the role he plays in the Book of Job—in *Paradise Lost*, Blake asserts, it is the Messiah (Christ) who plays the role of accuser. In a later passage of great visionary force that takes not only Milton but the mythmakers of the West to task, Blake suggests that the same dichotomy between Energy and Reason, Satan and Jehovah, Orc and Urizen can be traced in the mythic war between the Giants (or Titans) and Jupiter/Zeus:

> The Giants who formed this world into its sensual existence, and now seem to live in its chains are in truth the causes of its life & the sources of all activity; but the chains are the cunning of weak and tame minds which have power to resist energy; according to the proverb, the weak in courage is strong in cunning. (213)

Blake's Giants, treated in Greco-Roman mythology as forces of chaos, are here transformed from proud rebels and fierce destroyers into primal sources of Orcic energy. They are chthonic ("of the earth") powers, volcanoes of energy that once animated the world but are now chained by slavish-minded men and gods who use religion and philosophy as weapons. Such men Blake labels Devourers; they seek to stem the Prolific energy of the Giants.

I mentioned in my analysis of "The Tyger" that Zeus put Prometheus in chains for stealing the fire of heaven and giving it to man. But that is not the full story; many years earlier it had been Prometheus who had helped Zeus overthrow the Titans and establish his rule over Olympus. That is to say, Zeus was responsible for binding and punishing the very god who gave him his throne. For Blake, this terrible irony is replayed every time the slavish-minded chain Energy and thus betray the very source of their life and power. 100 years later, Nietzsche would argue that it was chiefly through religion that this chaining and betrayal were carried out. In "London," Blake identifies as the chief culprit the internalization of the state of experience via what he calls the "mind forg'd manacles." In *The Marriage of Heaven and Hell*, he intimates the same by explaining that to the angels—the passive lackeys of Milton's Jehovah—the "enjoyments of Genius . . . look like torment and insanity" (211).

Once again, Blake lays much of the blame at the feet of Milton . . . or does he? In one of his boldest and most shocking moves, Blake first deconstructs and then reconstructs the author of *Paradise Lost*:

> NOTE: The reason Milton wrote in fetters when he wrote of Angels & God, and at liberty when of Devils & Hell, is because he was a true Poet and of the Devil's party without knowing it. (211)

Blake here offers more than merely a new "spin" on *Paradise Lost*. He suggests that although the internal censors of Urizenic morality compelled Milton to privilege heaven, angels, goodness, and reason over hell, devils, evil, and energy, the true poet within revolted against the mind-forg'd manacles that chained his inner mind. This revolt, though too weak to allow Milton to write *The Marriage of Heaven and Hell*, impelled him to imbue his Satan with a kind of tragic heroism and fearless tenacity that made him, at least in Blake's mind, more interesting and more noble than Jehovah or Christ. Indeed, so sure was Blake of Milton's true poetic desires and energies that he wrote his epic *Milton*, in part, as a vehicle for freeing Milton from the chains that bound him.

States of Mind

Blake clearly saw himself as a poet of liberation, though the freedom he sought to offer was more perceptual than political. He hoped to teach his readers to see in a radically new way, a hope that was tied inextricably to his insistence on engraving rather than printing his poetry. As he explains it in *The Marriage of Heaven and Hell*, his "infernal method" of printing is central to his poetic program: for Blake the medium truly *is* the message. Before man can achieve that "improvement of sensual enjoyment" that Blake calls for,

> . . . the notion that man has a body distinct from his soul is to be expunged; this I shall do by printing in the infernal method, by corrosives, which in Hell are salutary and medicinal, melting apparent surfaces away, and displaying the infinite which was hid.
>
> If the doors of perception were cleansed every thing would appear to man as it is, infinite.
>
> For man has closed himself up, till he sees all things thro' narrow chinks of his cavern." (213)

For Blake the acids he used in the engraving process were not only a metaphor but an actual enactment of the fire of Prometheus and the crucible of Orc. Only by burning away the surface can we reveal the hidden (cryptic) and secret (esoteric) truths that lie beneath. In what may rank as the most radical expression of the Romantic belief that things are as they are perceived and that beauty and truth rest in the eye of the beholder, Blake prophesies that man will achieve the infinite through a change in perception. It is not faith in the Incarnation, Atonement, and Resurrection that will bring about the beatific vision, nor even a change in our moral and ethical behaviors, but a cleansing of our physical and spiritual perceptions. It is not improper beliefs or immoral actions but flawed seeing that prevents us from perceiving and embracing the truths about ourselves and our universe.

Anticipating quantum physics by two centuries, Blake the Romantic poet-prophet proclaims that human beings directly influence the reality of nature and even the cosmos (ontology) by our perceptions *of* that reality (epistemology). And Blake carries his epistemology-determines-ontology theorem from our world to the next. Heaven and Hell, he boldly asserts, are not so much places as they are states of mind. "An Angel came to me," he writes in the third of four allegorical sections to which he gives the subtitle "A Memorable Fancy,"

> and said, "O pitiable foolish young man! O horrible! O dreadful state! consider the hot burning dungeon thou art preparing for thyself to all eternity, to which thou art going in such a career."
>
> I said, "Perhaps you will be willing to shew me my eternal lot, & we will contemplate together upon it, and see whether your lot or mine is most desirable."
>
> So he took me thro' a stable & thro' a church & down into the church vault, at the end of which was a mill: thro' the mill we went, and came to a cave: down the winding cavern we groped our tedious way, till a void boundless as a nether sky appear'd beneath us . . .
>
> By degrees we beheld the infinite Abyss, fiery as the smoke of a burning city; beneath us, at an immense distance, was the sun, black but shining; round it were fiery tracks on which revolv'd vast spiders, crawling after their prey, which flew, or rather swum, in the infinite deep, in the most terrific shapes of animals sprung from corruption; & the air was full of them, & seem'd composed of them: these are Devils, and are called Powers of the air. I now asked my companion which was my eternal lot? he said, "between the black & white spiders. . . ."
>
> My friend the Angel climb'd up from his station into the mill. I remain'd alone; & then this appearance was no more, but

> I found myself sitting on a pleasant bank beside a river by moonlight, hearing a harper, who sung to the harp; & his theme was: "The man who never alters his opinion is like standing water, & breeds reptiles of the mind."
>
> But I arose, and sought for the mill, & there I found my Angel, who, surprised, asked me, how I escaped?
>
> I answered, "All that we saw was owing to your metaphysics: for when you ran away, I found myself on a bank by moonlight hearing a harper. . . ." (213-214)

The message here, though cloaked in fanciful allegory, is quite clear: hell is not an intrinsically terrible place; it is only because our perceptions have been shaped by a rationalistic and religious (pro-reason, anti-energy) paradigm that we see it that way. If we could only free ourselves from these ancient taboos and superstitions—as the hippie culture tried to do in the 1960's and 70's through the use of "mind-expanding" drugs—we would see that hell is a place of peace and beauty. Heaven and hell are not to be defined as the presence or absence of God; that is to afford them an ultimate reality that can rest only in what the phenomonologists of the twentieth century would call acts of perception. For Blake, it is cognition that defines reality, not vice versa, and the best kind of cognition, the kind that sets us free and makes all appear infinite, is dynamic, volatile, ever shifting and shaping anew. As the harper in the allegory sings, "The man who never alters his opinion is like standing water, & breeds reptiles of the mind."

Of all the great poets of our tradition, Blake was certainly one of the most visionary; he *saw*, and in the most radical way. For Blake, seeing is an end in itself; it defines its own reality. In that sense, Blake would claim, only *he* fully understood those two lines spoken by Satan in *Paradise Lost* that we have encountered before: "The mind is its own place, and in itself / Can make a Heaven of Hell, a Hell of Heaven" (I.254-255). While "The Clod and the Pebble" demonstrates the spiritual truth behind these lines, Blake's "Memorable Fancy" brings them literally to life. Even when the stakes are as high as heaven, salvation, and eternity, Blake holds true to his faith in the power of perception to shape both physical and metaphysical reality.

Like Nietzsche after him, Blake never shied away from making bold and even scandalous statements, and, like Nietzsche as well, he often couched those statements in the form of aphorisms. Thus, jumbled together with his cryptic sayings and memorable fancies, Blake presents us with the "Proverbs of Hell." Here are some samples:

> The road of excess leads to the palace of wisdom.
> He who desires but acts not, breeds pestilence.
> The lust of the goat is the bounty of God.
> The wrath of the lion is the wisdom of God.
> The cistern contains; the fountain overflows.
> The tygers of wrath are wiser than the horses of instruction.
> You never know what is enough unless you know what is more than enough. Sooner murder an infant in its cradle than nurse unacted desires. (211-212)

Forsaking the balance and temperance taught by Pythagoras, Plato, Aristotle, and most of their philosophical and theological heirs, Blake advocates excess and indulgence. We cannot hope to triumph over Urizen unless we are willing to shatter all internal restraints and set free our inner passions. Only when our desires flow, strong and unimpeded, from our inner psyche to the outer world will our internal perceptions and external senses be truly cleansed.

In the closing lines of his *Marriage*, Blake drives this point home by calling for a final end to all those forces that would damn up the river of our desires:

> Let the Priests of the Raven of dawn no longer, in deadly black, with hoarse note curse the sons of joy. Nor his accepted brethren—whom, tyrant, he calls free—lay the bound or build the roof. Nor pale religious letchery call that virginity that wishes but acts not!
> For every thing that lives is Holy. (216)

Though I disagree, on a personal level, with much that Blake teaches in his philosophical epics, I cannot help but find in Blake, even at his most gnostic, something . . . well . . . healthy. Despite the heterodoxy of his opinions, I believe that Blake understood dimensions of Jesus that more orthodox Christians have often missed. I can think of few poets who hated hypocrisy more than Blake or exposed with greater force how asceticism destroys body and soul and pharisaism causes life, joy, hope, and love to sicken. Like Jesus, Blake shows a greater concern for inner motivation than outer action and understands that it is what comes out of a man, rather than what goes in, that corrupts him. And he not only understood but *saw* the potential holiness in all things. That new type of seeing—that ability to "see a World in a Grain of Sand / And a Heaven in a Wild Flower" ("Auguries of Innocence," lines 1-2)—was the greatest gift that Blake passed down to his readers/viewers and his poetic heirs.

\#

A full century and a half would pass before Blake received a direct challenge to his vision of the afterlife. The challenge would come from a fellow Englishman, who would proclaim not the marriage of heaven and hell, but their divorce. In his brief, but profound work, *The Great Divorce* (1946), C. S. Lewis takes his readers on a magical bus ride from hell to heaven. As Lewis imagines it, the damned are allowed to take trips to heaven—really the valley before heaven—where the souls of the blessed meet them and try to convince them, even now, to see, embrace, and enter heaven. Most stubbornly refuse, shutting their eyes to the glories before them and to the grace of God being offered, but a few accept and enter heaven.

Lewis, who, in a dream vision, accompanies the damned souls on their journey, is shocked by what seems to his Protestant mind to be a second, post-mortem chance for salvation. But his guide in heaven (George MacDonald) calms his anxieties and says that this is not really a "second chance": those who accept and enter heaven will, when they look back on their time in hell, see it rather as time in Purgatory; those who reject the offer, will imagine that they have always been in hell. To this explanation, Lewis responds, with Blake heavy in his mind: "'Then those people are right who say that Heaven and Hell are only states of mind?'" But MacDonald hushes him again and says:

> "Do not blaspheme. Hell is a state of mind—ye never said a truer word. And every state of mind, left to itself, every shutting up of the creature within the dungeon of its own mind—is, in the end, Hell. But Heaven is not a state of mind. Heaven is reality itself. All that is fully real is Heavenly. For all that can be shaken will be shaken and only the unshakable remains."[4]

Lewis—who had already, four years earlier, published a scholarly work (*A Preface to Paradise Lost*) in which he exposed as untenable Blake's argument that Milton was of the devil's party without knowing it—here reveals a thunderous Christian truth about heaven and hell that exposes the weak-kneed Gnosticism that underlies Blake's vision. Yes, heaven and hell are states of mind, but they are two very different states. The vision which sees and enters heaven is outwardly directed and yearns <u>upward for realit</u>y and truth; the vision which sees death and enters hell is

4 C. S. Lewis, *The Great Divorce* (New York: MacMillan, 1946), 68-9.

inwardly directed and solipsistic. It is profoundly narcissistic and cannot see beyond itself and its own petty concerns. Such a vision does not—as Blake and his Gnostic heirs and predecessors would have it—open up the doors of perception and reveal everything as infinite; rather, it closes the doors, "shutting up the creature within the dungeon of its own mind." The vision which saves is drawn toward the light; the vision which damns turns inward to hide and sulk in the darkness.

That is the dark side of Romantic solipsism that Blake, for all his genius and insight and mystical joy, was never quite able to escape.

PART TWO

NATURE AND SUPERNATURE

V
Lyrical Ballads

Had William Blake chosen to print rather than engrave his *Songs of Innocence*, future generations would likely have hailed 1789 as the birth year of British Romanticism. As it turned out, Blake's refusal to publish his poems apart from his art and designs—a refusal born out of a healthy dose of artistic integrity and a less healthy dose of artistic stubbornness—made the cost of the *Songs*, not to mention the other works that followed, prohibitive to all but a few patrons who knew of Blake's genius. It also meant that Blake could only afford to produce small, limited runs of his work.

The upshot of Blake's relative obscurity was that the laurels for "inventing" British Romanticism fell instead on the heads of two younger poets who were as galvanized as Blake by the promise of the French Revolution. Their names were William Wordsworth (1770-1850) and Samuel Taylor Coleridge (1772-1834), and their personal and literary friendship turned out to be as famous, fruitful, and age-defining as those between Emerson & Thoreau, Van Gogh & Gauguin, Stravinsky & Diaghilev, Hemingway & Fitzgerald, Dali & Buñuel, and C. S. Lewis & J. R. R. Tolkien. Together they would publish a slim collection of poems titled *Lyrical Ballads* that would help to redefine the language, subject matter, and purpose of poetry. 1798, the year of its publication, is generally accepted as the birthday of the Romantic Age in England.

Wordsworth and Coleridge's friendship began one year earlier, when the former was 27 and the latter just shy of 25. Both had already been touched by the progressivist spirit of the age—with Wordsworth swearing a temporary allegiance to French republican ideals and Coleridge nearly emigrating to America as part of a utopian socialist scheme—and both had begun their lives as poets with some promising though as yet unsuccessful work. It was the swift but deep intimacy of their friendship—an intimacy shared with Wordsworth's beloved sister, Dorothy—that brought the creative genius of the two men to the surface. For Wordsworth it initiated a prolific ten-year period (rightly referred to by Wordsworth scholars as the "great decade"), during which he produced a body of poetry whose collective beauty, insight, and brilliance more than merit it a place in the literary pantheon. Coleridge's period was far less prolific and only lasted five years, but the poems it produced are among the greatest in the language.

Two decades after that memorable year, Coleridge published his autobiography, *Biographia Literaria* (1817); in it, he records the mysterious process by which his friendship with Wordsworth blossomed into *Lyrical Ballads*. By 1817, Coleridge had shifted from being one of the poetic architects of Romanticism to one of the keenest and sagest literary theorists of the nineteenth century. He had also become one of the few critics who could explain to his fellow countrymen the subtleties of German philosophy, theology, and aesthetics—particularly the shift from object to subject and ontology to epistemology that we discussed in Part One. As a result, his recollections of the genesis of *Lyrical Ballads* are suffused with an analysis of what exactly he and Wordsworth were "up to" when they planned and wrote their poems.

Tearing Back the Veil

The opening two paragraphs of Chapter XIV of *Biographia Literaria* read as follows:

> During the first year that Mr. Wordsworth and I were neighbours our conversations turned frequently on the two cardinal points of poetry, the power of exciting the sympathy of the reader by a faithful adherence to the truth of nature, and the power of giving the interest of novelty by the modifying colours of imagination. The sudden charm, which accidents of light and shade, which moonlight or sunset diffused over a known and familiar landscape, appeared to represent the practicability of combining both. These are the poetry of nature. The thought suggested itself (to which of us I do not recollect) that a series of poems might be composed of two sorts. In the one, the incidents and agents were to be, in part at least, supernatural; and the excellence aimed at was to consist in the interesting of the affections by the dramatic truth of such emotions as

> would naturally accompany such situations, supposing them real. And real in *this* sense they have been to every human being who, from whatever source of delusion, has at any time believed himself under supernatural agency. For the second class, subjects were to be chosen from ordinary life; the characters and incidents were to be such, as will be found in every village and its vicinity, where there is a meditative and feeling mind to seek after them, or to notice them when they present themselves.
>
> In this idea originated the plan of the *Lyrical Ballads*; in which it was agreed, that my endeavours should be directed to persons and characters supernatural, or at least romantic; yet so as to transfer from our inward nature a human interest and a semblance of truth sufficient to procure for these shadows of imagination that willing suspension of disbelief for the moment, which constitutes poetic faith. Mr. Wordsworth, on the other hand, was to propose to himself as his object, to give the charm of novelty to things of every day, and to excite a feeling analogous to the supernatural, by awakening the mind's attention from the lethargy of custom, and directing it to the loveliness and the wonders of the world before us; an inexhaustible treasure, but for which, in consequence of the film of familiarity and selfish solicitude we have eyes, yet see not, ears that hear not, and hearts that neither feel nor understand. (424-425)

In this thrilling memoir, we catch the poets on the very cusp of a new era of poetry. Behind them lies an eighteenth century desire to record faithfully and accurately the beauty and sublimity of nature. Before them lies a nineteenth century desire to remake nature through the power of the imagination. Interestingly, Coleridge explains that it was nature herself who taught them how to shift and modify reality. When a familiar landscape is seen again through a bank of fog or a flood of moonlight, it takes on a sudden charm and strangeness which the viewer had not previously seen. Just so, when familiar objects are perceived afresh through the eyes of a poet, they take on a mystery and a wonder that they did not previously possess. Though neither Wordsworth nor Coleridge took things quite as far as Blake ("If the doors of perception were cleansed every thing would appear to man as it is, infinite."), they did believe—as poets at least—that perception does affect reality and that we half-create the world around us. Indeed, both came to believe that it was one of the duties of the poet not only to see with new eyes but to bestow new eyes on his reader as well.

As the two friends discussed together the nature of perception and the power of the imagination to alter reality, they conceived the idea of composing a series of poems of two distinct but complementary kinds. The former kind would select its objects from nature, from the common, mundane, everyday world of the countryside and its inhabitants. The latter would select its characters and agents from the realm of the supernatural. However, rather than merely copy or record these things, the poets would throw over them an imaginative coloring that would allow their readers to perceive them in a fresh new way. Thus, the former would present its natural objects in such a way as to stimulate an almost supernatural response, while the latter would present its supernatural tales in such a way as to render them almost natural. Wordsworth took up the former task and composed a series of poems centered around such humble, rustic characters as Simon Lee, Goody Blake, and the Idiot Boy. Coleridge took up the latter and produced the truly strange and yet somehow strangely true "Rime of the Ancient Mariner."

The key to appreciating Wordsworth's contribution to *Lyrical Ballads* is to realize that when an object or a place or a person becomes too familiar to us, it tends to become invisible. The man who ceases to notice the beauty of his wife and the woman who ceases to be impressed by her husband are not necessarily bad or even inattentive spouses—they have simply lost the fresh perception they had on their honeymoon. Two clichés express the lesser and greater dangers of this loss of freshness: because we do not "stop and smell the roses," we miss the magic that lies all about us; because "familiarity breeds contempt," we end up treating with scorn that which initially filled us with the joy of revelation. One of the reasons that the Romantics celebrated childhood was because they envied the child's ability to see everything around it as if for the first time. No matter how many times a boy sees the moon, the vision never ceases to fill him with excitement and awe; no matter how many times a girl holds a puppy or a kitten, the experience never ceases to provoke in her feelings of warmth and delight.

In *Orthodoxy* (1908), G. K. Chesterton suggests that this childlike quality is also one of the qualities of God. Attempting to refute Enlightenment-minded, anti-Romantic materialists who claim that the clockwork nature of our universe precludes the existence of a personal Creator, Chesterton argues that the fact that the sun has risen and set in a fixed pattern since time began does not, in itself, indicate an empty, mechanical cosmos. To the contrary, it may mask a dynamic divine activity that our weary, adult eyes fail to perceive. When we play a new game with our children, he explains, they will ask us to repeat it again and again until we are bored, exhausted, or both. For you see, counsels Chesterton, we grown-ups "are not strong enough to exult in monotony."

> But perhaps God is strong enough to exult in monotony. It is possible that God says every morning, "Do it again" to the sun; and every evening, "Do it again" to the moon. It may not be automatic necessity that makes all daisies alike; it may be that God makes every daisy separately, but has never got tired of making them. It may be that He has the eternal appetite of infancy; for we have sinned and grown old, and our Father is younger than we. The repetition in Nature may not be a mere recurrence; it may be a theatrical *encore*.[5]

That "eternal appetite of infancy" which Chesterton sees alike in children and in God the Father is the same quality that Romantic poets like Wordsworth hoped to instill in their readers. If we could only revive our child-like sense of wonder, Wordsworth hoped, we could all perceive the mystery that lurks behind the everyday.

This hope, shared by both poets, might be seen as their less radical, more orthodox version of Blake's Gnosticism. Rather than cleansing our "doors of perception" via some hidden, esoteric wisdom, we need simply to reawaken our dormant capacity for wonder. What is needed is not a new theology of heaven and hell, but a willingness to put aside our self-absorbed anxiousness ("selfish solicitude") and to rip away that "film [or veil] of familiarity" that blinds us to the "inexhaustible treasure" of nature's loveliness. Though Coleridge was, by 1817, an orthodox Christian, in the closing sentence of the passage quoted above, he offers something of a secularization or aestheticization of some of Jesus' key spiritual teachings. In the Sermon on the Mount (Matthew 5-7), Jesus counsels his followers both to put aside their anxieties and to rip away the veil. The former counsel is heard in the well-known exhortation to imitate the lilies of the field and to seek first God's kingdom (6:25-34); the latter is heard in the Beatitudes (5:3-12), with their call to look through mourning and persecution to see the comfort and reward that wait on the other side.

The more vital biblical reference, however, comes at the very end of the quote, when Coleridge warns that until we put aside our anxieties and

---

5   G. K. Chesterton, *Orthodoxy* (New York: Image Books, 1990), 60.

rip away the veil, we will "have eyes, yet see not, ears that hear not, and hearts that neither feel nor understand." Coleridge is here paraphrasing two verses from Isaiah 6:9-10 that Jesus himself quotes to explain why he speaks in parables (Mark 4:9-12). Despite what children are taught in Sunday School, Jesus, by his own admission, did not speak in parables so that he would be understood, but so that only those with ears to hear might understand, believe, and follow his teachings. That, of course, is not to say that Jesus was a Gnostic teacher peddling secret wisdom meant only for an elite coterie. To the contrary, he broadcast his message freely and openly for any to see or hear—and, significantly, while the poor and the outcasts did see and hear in great numbers, most of the elite corps of Pharisees, Scribes, and Sadducees refused to do either.

Just as the Jewish leaders willfully blinded and deafened themselves to Jesus' spiritual message, so most of us close our eyes and ears to the natural wonder around us. Enter Wordsworth who, by ripping away the veil of familiarity, forces us to see the familiar as though it were, for a moment, unfamiliar. By thus "defamiliarizing" the world that we have grown accustomed to, Wordsworth restores to us the original freshness of that familiar world, thus empowering us to see it as if for the first time. A similar experience of defamiliarization can be gained by someone who, having grown up among sunflowers and gazed on their beauty hundreds of times, gets the chance to study one of Van Gogh's sunflower paintings in a museum. The reaction that such people tend to have when they look upon one of these painting is akin to a spiritual revelation. "Yes," they will often exclaim to themselves, "I don't think I have ever looked, *really* looked at a sunflower before. Now I truly know what a sunflower *is*." What Van Gogh did for sunflowers—and wheat fields and crows and starry nights—Wordsworth did for the common objects and people who populated the countryside of England. By forcing us to look again—as if for the first time—Wordsworth infuses his rustic characters and their rustic world with dignity, power, and mystery.

Coleridge, on the other hand, used a slightly different poetic process to make supernatural tales like "The Rime of the Ancient Mariner" seem natural. As he explains in the passage quoted above, Coleridge accomplishes this poetic feat by uncovering behind the supernatural veil of his tale dramatic and emotional truths that all readers can identify with. Our recognition of the psychological truth of, say, the Mariner's sea voyage compels us to give to the poem what Coleridge calls the "willing suspension of disbelief." By this famous phrase, Coleridge signifies our ability to temporarily suspend the claims of reason and logic and to enter, through the power of the sympathetic imagination, into the life and heart of a poem. To inspire in its readers this moment of "poetic faith," the poem must invite them into a higher realm of illusion rather than merely delude them with fanciful images and events. Filmgoers who watched the original Star Wars trilogy (Episodes 4-6) willingly suspended their disbelief and followed the characters on the screen to that magical, illusory place "a long time ago, in a galaxy far, far away." Alas, with the second trilogy (Episodes 1-3)—where character, plot, and theme played second fiddle to special effects—many viewers who had willingly accepted the illusion of the first left the theater feeling deluded by a once cinematic poet who had morphed into a hollow showman.

On the surface, Wordsworth and Coleridge may seem to be writing two very different kinds of poems about two very different kinds of subject matter. But if we look a bit deeper, we will see that they are engaged in the same poetic task. Nature, or "supernature," is merely the occasion for the poem; the poetic act itself is the real point. Or, to put it another way, it is not the subject matter but the imaginative vision of the poet that determines the shape and purpose of the poem. In both cases, Wordsworth and Coleridge act as Romantic poet-prophets engaged in an apocalyptic enterprise. Whether it is Coleridge ripping away the veil of mystery or Wordsworth ripping away the veil of familiarity, the result is the same—a poetics of transformation that allows the reader to pierce through the many-layered, usually artificial coverings that prevent us from seeing the truth and the wonder that lie concealed beneath. Both poets, that is, attempt to mix together the natural and the supernatural, the real and the ideal: not that we might confuse the two but that we might see the natural *in* the supernatural and the real *in* the ideal.

When Wordsworth and Coleridge published *Lyrical Ballads* in 1798, they referred to it as an "experiment." Indeed, perhaps worried or even embarrassed by the highly personal vision that the poems embodied, they chose (somewhat ironically) to publish it anonymously. The book sold well, and soon requests rose up from the reading public that the poets would explain in an essay of some sort what exactly their motives were in writing these unique poems. By rights, the more theoretical Coleridge, who had just gotten back from studying language, literature, and philosophy in Germany, should have written the essay. But Coleridge, one of the most learned and brilliant men of the nineteenth century, was also an inveterate procrastinator. And so, the duty of writing a preface to their second edition of *Lyrical Ballads* (1800) fell to the normally non-theoretical Wordsworth.

In the third paragraphs of Chapter XIV of *Biographia Literaria*, Coleridge has this to say of Wordsworth's preface:

> To the second edition [Wordsworth] added a preface of considerable length; in which, notwithstanding some passages of apparently a contrary import, he was understood to contend for the extension of this style to poetry of all kinds, and to reject as vicious and indefensible all phrases and forms of style that were not included in what he (unfortunately, I think, adopting an equivocal expression) called the language of *real* life. From this preface, prefixed to poems in which it was impossible to deny the presence of original genius, however mistaken its direction might be deemed, arose the whole long continued controversy. (425)

If Coleridge is right, and I believe that he mostly is—despite his somewhat mixed motives in attacking a preface that he knew he should have written himself—then we may need to emend our birthday for British Romanticism from 1798 to 1800. For, whichever date we finally settle on, the fact remains that Wordsworth's Preface to the second edition of *Lyrical Ballads* was as revolutionary in the aesthetic world as the Storming of the Bastille was in the political!

The Language of Real Men

In his Preface, Wordsworth does nothing less than redefine the nature and status of both poetry and the poet. He begins by positing a new subject matter for poetry and a new kind of language for the poet:

> The principal object, then, proposed in these Poems was to choose incidents and situations from common life, and to relate or describe them, throughout, as far as was possible in a selection of language really used by men, and, at the same time, to throw over them a certain colouring of imagination, whereby ordinary things should be presented to the mind in an unusual aspect; and, further, and above all, to make these incidents and situations interesting by tracing in them, truly though not ostentatiously, the primary laws of our nature: chiefly, as far as regards the manner in which we associate ideas in a state of excitement. Humble and rustic life was generally chosen, because, in that condition, the essential

passions of the heart find a better soil in which they can attain their maturity, are less under restraint, and speak a plainer and more emphatic language; because in that condition of life our elementary feelings co-exist in a state of greater simplicity, and, consequently, may be more accurately contemplated, and more forcibly communicated; because the manners of rural life germinate from those elementary feelings, and, from the necessary character of rural occupations, are more easily comprehended, and are more durable; and, lastly, because in that condition the passions of men are incorporated with the beautiful and permanent forms of nature. The language, too, of these men has been adopted (purified indeed from what appear to be its real defects, from all lasting and rational causes of dislike or disgust) because such men hourly communicate with the best objects from which the best part of language is originally derived; and because, from their rank in society and the sameness and narrow circle of their intercourse, being less under the influence of social vanity, they convey their feelings and notions in simple and unelaborated expressions. Accordingly, such a language, arising out of repeated experience and regular feelings, is a more permanent, and a far more philosophical language, than that which is frequently substituted for it by Poets . . . (358)

Not only in *Lyrical Ballads* but throughout his poetic career, Wordsworth turned often to such rustic subjects for inspiration and raw material. In this passage, he makes clear his motive for doing so. Wordsworth turned to the countryside, not because it made him "feel good," but because he believed that in such a setting men were more in touch with elementary feelings and durable truths. It was these essential passions, this emphatic, unmediated kind of life that Wordsworth wanted to capture and embody in his poetry.

For Wordsworth, as for Blake, the city life of the eighteenth-century poet was artificial, insincere, and out of touch with the well-springs of our humanity. Wordsworth looked to the freer and simpler life of the country for the same reason that he looked within his own heart: only in such places did he encounter passion and truth in their purity. The reason I belabor this point is my desire to clear Wordsworth's name of some of the blame for the present state of poetry and the arts. Yes, as the true father of British Romantic Poetry and as the author of what is arguably the world's first poetic autobiography (*The Prelude*), Wordsworth must bear part of the responsibility for the current ubiquitous belief that poetry—not to mention the other arts—is nothing more than a form of self-expression. Still, it must be made clear that Wordsworth never intended for self-expression to be an end-in-itself; rather, it was both a vehicle and a road for reaching that which is most permanent and universal. The American Romantic Ralph Waldo Emerson likely had Wordsworth in mind when he asserted: "The poet, in utter solitude remembering his spontaneous thoughts and recording them, is found to have recorded that which men in crowded cities find true for them also."[6]

In the country, as in his own heart, Wordsworth sought that which lasts, and he found it not only in the lives and passions of the rustics but in their simple, direct language as well. Wordsworth rejected what he saw as the phony poetic diction of the eighteenth century, with its purposely contorted syntax and its artificial poeticisms. In its place, he adopted a more natural, less mannered style that mimicked the syntax of good prose. He dubbed this authentic, unelaborated style the "language really used by men," a phrase that Coleridge would later find cause to quibble with (see the passage from *Biographia Literaria* quoted directly above). But Coleridge, who otherwise understood Wordsworth's strengths and weaknesses better than anyone of his day, is a bit unfair in his criticism. In the passage from the Preface quoted above, Wordsworth clearly advises that the poet should not slavishly imitate the rustic, but, through a process of selection, purge his natural speech of its defects and its grossness. Wordsworth was not a "dialect writer" like Mark Twain or even, like the Edmund Spenser of *The Faerie Queene*, a poet who purposely used archaisms and obsolete words to establish mood and atmosphere. Wordsworth's goal was a language of the heart and soul—rather like the vernacular Italian that Dante used for his *Commedia*—and he fashioned that language by first "channeling" the felt and lived speech of the countryside and then using his poetic craft to shape that speech into a purer, more permanent, more *emphatic* language than that used in the fashionable, ever-changing city.

Wordsworth makes a similar distinction between "inspiration" and "art" later in his Preface in the form of a definition that is still frequently quoted today:

> For all good poetry is the spontaneous overflow of powerful feelings: and though this be true, Poems to which any value can be attached were never produced on any variety of subjects

---

6   Ralph Waldo Emerson, "The American Scholar," *The Selected Writings of Ralph Waldo Emerson*, edited by Brooks Atksinson (New York: Modern Library, 1950), 57.

but by a man who being possessed of more than usual organic sensibility, had also thought long and deeply. (358)

On the one hand, Wordsworth's definition of poetry as an externalization of the internal emotions, moods, and perceptions of the poet is strongly, if not excessively romantic. But Wordsworth, unlike Blake, immediately reigns in that excess by reminding his reader that true poetry is written by a poet who *both* feels robustly and spontaneously *and* thinks "long and deeply." Still, though Wordsworth never became quite so wild or primitive or crude as his critics liked to claim, he played a central role in tilting the scales of poetry away from reason and logic toward emotion and intuition. He even went so far as to replace the traditional Aristotelian focus on plot and action with a new focus on mood and feeling. In his poems, Wordsworth asserts, it is the feeling that "gives importance to the action and situation, and not the action and situation to the feeling" (359).

Wordsworth, even more than Blake, would thrust feeling to the very heart of the poetic enterprise, a move that would compel him to redefine not only the nature of poetry but of the poet as well. "What is a poet?" asks Wordsworth, and then answers his own question:

> He is a man speaking to men: a man, it is true, endowed with more lively sensibility, more enthusiasm and tenderness, who has a greater knowledge of human nature, and a more comprehensive soul, than are supposed to be common among mankind; a man pleased with his own passions and volitions, and who rejoices more than other men in the spirit of life that is in him; delighting to contemplate similar volitions and passions as manifested in the goings-on of the Universe, and habitually impelled to create them where he does not find them. To these qualities he has added a disposition to be affected more than other men by absent things as if they were present; an ability of conjuring up in himself passions, which are indeed far from being the same as those produced by real events, yet (especially in those parts of the general sympathy which are pleasing and delightful) do more nearly resemble the passions produced by real events, than anything which, from the motions of their own minds merely, other men are accustomed to feel in themselves:—whence, and from practice, he has acquired a greater readiness and power in expressing what he thinks and feels, and especially those thoughts and feelings which, by his own choice, or from the structure of his own mind, arise in him without immediate external excitement. (361)

Wordsworth, together with Coleridge, believed strongly that the questions "What is a poem?" and "What is a poet?" are synonymous. Just as poetry is to be written in the "real language of men," so is the poet to be a "man speaking to men." The poet, Wordsworth and Coleridge insisted, was not to be viewed as a different kind of creature, as he often was in the cities and courts of eighteenth century England and France. No, the poet is of the same *kind* as all other men, though he does differ in *degree*. The poet possesses a *more* organic, comprehensive soul than do other men. He has *more* lively sensibilities and is more in touch with his feelings. Far from needing gross stimulation to experience deep emotion, he is able to feel absent pleasures as though they were present. The true Romantic poet rejoices in his own spirit of life and seeks to discover that joy in the world around him; if it is not there, he will create it. He possesses a rich store of memories he can tap for poetic inspiration, and the ability to relive those memories and the emotions attached to them through recourse to an inner mood of tranquility and pleasure.

The Grand Elementary Principle of Pleasure

Most poets and critics of the past had argued, in one form or another, that the role of poetry was to teach and to please: more specifically, to teach *through* pleasing. What Wordsworth adds to this classic formulation is not only a greater emphasis on the pleasing part, but a defense of the necessity *of* pleasure to the human enterprise. Wordsworth argues in his Preface that the poet who cultivates pleasure within himself and then labors to spread that pleasure to others through his poetry performs a noble task:

> Nor let this necessity of producing immediate pleasure be considered as a degradation of the Poet's art. It is far otherwise. It is an acknowledgment of the beauty of the universe, an acknowledgment the more sincere, because is not formal, but indirect; it is a task light and easy to him who looks at the world in the spirit of love: further, it is a homage paid to the native and naked dignity of man, to the grand elementary principle of pleasure, by which he knows, and feels, and lives, and moves. (362)

It is through pleasure that the poet and his poetry—remember that the two are virtuously synonymous for Wordsworth—draw us back into touch with our world, our fellow man, and ourselves. The pleasure that poetry gives is no mere entertainment and is not to be scorned; it is the very spirit through which we feel and know and live.

Just as Coleridge ends paragraph two of Chapter XIV of *Biographia Literaria* by paraphrasing Jesus quoting Isaiah, so here, Wordsworth ends the passage by paraphrasing St. Paul quoting a pagan poet ("In him we live and move and have our being"; Acts 17:28). Paul quotes the Cretan poet Epimenides to try to convince a group of Athenian Stoics and Epicureans that even their own (Gentile) poets understood something of the true nature of the God of the Bible and his relationship to the humans he created. As in *Biographia Literaria*, Wordsworth is not so much making a spiritual statement as he is offering a secularization or aestheticization of a biblical truth. Just as the God who created the universe and raised Christ from the dead is the one toward whom and in whom all the yearnings of mankind, Jew and Gentile alike, meet and find their consummation, so Wordsworth's "grand elementary principle of pleasure" is the prism through which all men can perceive the beauty around them and the dignity within them. Through pleasure—not mere happiness, but deep and abiding joy—the poet strips away all that is mechanical and artificial to reveal a truly humanistic vision that is authentic and lasting.

Later in the Preface, Wordsworth develops further this noble view of the poet by making an incisive distinction between the poet and the man of science:

> The Man of Science seeks truth as a remote and unknown benefactor; he cherishes and loves it in his solitude: the Poet, singing a song in which all human beings join with him, rejoices in the presence of truth as our visible friend and hourly companion. Poetry is the breath and finer spirit of all knowledge; it is the impassioned expression which is in the countenance of all Science. Emphatically may it be said of the Poet, as Shakespeare hath said of man, "that he looks before and after." He is the rock of defence of human nature; an upholder and preserver, carrying everywhere with him relationship and love. In spite of difference of soil and climate, of language and manners, of laws and customs, in spite of things silently gone out of mind, and things violently destroyed; the Poet binds together by passion and knowledge the vast empire of human society, as it is spread over the whole earth, and over all time. (363)

Unlike the eighteenth century poet (Alexander Pope, Jonathan Swift, Samuel Johnson), who tends to be a public man-about-town, the Romantic poet spends his days in isolation, away from the city and the crowds. And yet, paradoxically, the Romantic poet is supremely a man of the people. His goal is to use his poetry to uphold, preserve, edify, and draw together all men. True, the Romantic poet will withdraw and sequester himself, but his solitude is vastly different from that of the man of science. The latter's solitude comes from the fact that he studies his formulas and conducts his experiments apart from the joys and sorrows and loves and desires of humanity; for him, truth is more an abstract idea than something lived in the flesh. The poet's solitude, on the other hand, allows him to pierce more deeply to the inner sanctum of the human heart that he might touch those perennial human truths that bind the ancient Greek to the nineteenth-century Brazilian, the Tibetan monk to the modern city dweller, the law-abiding civil servant to the rogue samurai, the emotional artist to the logical engineer.

Most people today think of poets as sensitive types who experience both joy and sorrow at a higher pitch than their non-artistic friends. That we think so, even in cases when it is not true, shows that we are all, whether we realize it or not, heirs of Wordsworth and his fellow Romantics. Wordsworth's Preface places on the poet's shoulders a unique burden: to be so sensitive to all that passes around him that he can, via his inspiration and his art, humanize all knowledge. It is an ongoing burden and call to which Wordsworth sets no limit. "If the time should ever come," he writes, "when what is now called science, thus familiarized to men, shall be ready to put on, as it were, a form of flesh and blood, the Poet will lend his divine spirit to aid the transfiguration, and will welcome the Being thus produced, as a dear and genuine inmate of the household of man" (363). In the end, Wordsworth asserts, it will be the poet, not the scientist, who will transform science into a kindred spirit with which we can commune and through which we can enhance our fellowship, our passion, and our joy.

There are some who might consider Wordsworth's definition of the role of the poet to be quaint and old-fashioned, of little real or practical use in a modern, technological age. And yet, as Wordsworth explains in an earlier passage in the Prelude, the ministry of the Romantic poet is more, not less necessary in an industrialized age than in a rural, pastoral one:

> For the human mind is capable of being excited without the application of gross and violent stimulants; and he must have a very faint perception of its beauty and dignity who does not know this, and who does not further know, that one being is elevated above another, in proportion as he possesses this

> capability. It has therefore appeared to me, that to endeavour to produce or enlarge this capability is one of the best services in which, at any period, a Writer can be engaged; but this service, excellent at all times, is especially so at the present day. For a multitude of causes, unknown to former times, are now acting with a combined force to blunt the discriminating powers of the mind, and, unfitting it for all voluntary exertion, to reduce it to a state of almost savage torpor. The most effective of these causes are the great national events which are daily taking place, and the increasing accumulation of men in cities, where the uniformity of their occupations produces a craving for extraordinary incident, which the rapid communication of intelligence hourly gratifies. . . . When I think upon this degrading thirst after outrageous stimulation, I am almost ashamed to have spoken of the feeble endeavour made in these volumes to counteract it . . . (359)

In this remarkable passage, that accurately describes Wordsworth's Age—the dawn of the Industrial Revolution—while eerily prophesying our own, the poet catalogues the ill effects of urbanization. The massing of men into cities and the repetitive drudgery of their jobs, he warns, produces in them an ignoble "craving after extraordinary incident" and "a degrading thirst after outrageous stimulation." Their senses grown dull by the inhuman pace of the city, they find themselves in need of grosser, more violent, and more scandalous stimulants to satisfy their blunted psyches. Wordsworth's London, like the Manhattan and Los Angeles of today, had its own versions of MTV, "The Enquirer," intrusive and insistent advertisers and media moguls, and public entertainment fueled by gratuitous sex, violence, and special effects.

Wordsworth uses the powerful oxymoron "savage torpor" to describe this state of emotional and spiritual deadness, this loss of the ability to be moved by simple beauty and truth. Wordsworth saw it as the chief role of poetry to restore to its readers this lost ability. By enlarging and refining our sensibilities, poetry has the power to re-humanize us, to bring us back into the human community. By restoring our child-like wonder, it revives our ability to take joy and delight in the natural world and in the quiet beatings of our heart.

Let us not be tempted to think that because Wordsworth insists on linking poetry to pleasure that he therefore takes poetry less seriously than his eighteenth-century forebears. On the contrary, Wordsworth takes poetry very seriously, ascribing to it not only the maintenance of the human heart and soul but the continuation of the human race itself.

VI
Wise Passiveness

Near the end of "Simon Lee," Wordsworth offers an aside to his reader that embodies the central theme not only of the poem but of the collection to which it belongs:

> O Reader! had you in your mind
> Such stores as silent thought can bring,
> O gentle Reader! you would find
> A tale in everything.
> What more I have to say is short,
> And you must kindly take it:
> It is no tale; but, should you think,
> Perhaps a tale you'll make it. (65-72)

If I were asked to sum up in a few words the overarching goal that Wordsworth and Coleridge set themselves when they wrote *Lyrical Ballads*, I would require only two: to see. We need not look to Ancient Greece or Imperial Rome or the Middle Ages to find the matter for a song. The raw material for a thousand tales lies all about us—if only we had eyes to see, ears to hear, and a heart prepared to receive. As a sensitive Romantic poet possessed of a comprehensive soul and an ability to experience absent things as though they were present, Wordsworth carried within him vast stores of memories, observations, and interactions which, in moments of silence, he could draw on for inspiration.

But he also believed that all people, potentially at least, carry around such stores. In sharing his recollections, Wordsworth hoped not only to bring pleasure but to encourage his readers to imitate him. Indeed, in the second half of the stanza, he invites them to participate with him in realizing his poem. Wordsworth will tell what he knows, but he leaves it up to his readers to shape that telling into a tale. Despite their simple diction, the *Lyrical Ballads* are anything but simple: they call upon their reader to work hard at understanding, to focus their attention on those things which often go unseen and to find meaning and even mystery in the most ordinary of tales. In the majority of the poems he contributed to the collection, Wordsworth studies closely a number of marginalized characters who eke out their existences invisible to most of society. However, those poems in which Wordsworth is himself more directly involved tend to be of greater interest and to make their points in a more subtle fashion. In what follows, we shall consider four such poems, poems that take us to the very heart of Wordsworth's Romantic vision.

Out of the Mouth of Babes

Rather than follow his usual method of plunging directly into his poem, Wordsworth begins "We are Seven" by making a somewhat abstract comment on the nature of childhood:

> ---------A simple Child,
> That lightly draws its breath,
> And feels its life in every limb,
> What should it know of death? (1-4)

I have already mentioned in previous chapters that Romantic poets privileged the perceptions of children, in particular, their ability to see the world continually afresh, as though they were gazing on it for the first time. Here, Wordsworth explains that this childlike freshness and wonder is tied in part to the indomitable life within them. The child, as Blake would say, still lives in a world of innocence; though aware that death exists, it nevertheless views all things from the point of view of the young and vital life that flows through its entire being. Just as the little black boy and the chimney sweeper of *Innocence* are aware of their oppression even as their vision allows them to transcend that oppression and find inner freedom and joy, so the child protagonist of "We are Seven," rather than closing her eyes to the reality of death, uses her vision to look through it.

Wordsworth begins by describing for us this unremarkable—and yet, for those who have eyes to see, remarkable—child:

> I met a little cottage Girl:
> She was eight years old, she said;
> Her hair was thick with many a curl
> That clustered round her head.

> She had a rustic, woodland air,
> And she was wildly clad:
> Her eyes were fair, and very fair;
> —Her beauty made me glad. (5-12)

The way Wordsworth describes her, the girl seems almost an embodiment of nature and of the rural countryside that the poet so loved. In place of the frightening oxymoron that Blake uses to capture the Orcic energy of the Tyger ("fearful symmetry"), Wordsworth offers a quieter more subtle oxymoron (the girl is both "wild" and "fair") that captures the active and primal beauty of childhood innocence. At first, the speaker of the poem, who is clearly Wordsworth the poet—the poem is based on an actual incident in which the poet met such a girl—displays his "Romantic credentials" by taking gladness in her rustic beauty. Rather than dismiss her as a vagabond, he perceives a unique spirit and value in her.

From this point on, however, the poem takes an uncharacteristic turn. Whereas in all the other poems in the collection Wordsworth's voice remains that of a devotee of and an apologist for the Romantic ethos, in this poem, he sets himself in opposition to that ethos, allowing the girl instead to take on (unselfconsciously) the role of devotee and apologist. In hopes of learning more about the girl, Wordsworth asks her how many siblings she has. The girl replies that there are seven children in her family and then goes on to explain that two live in Conway, two are gone to sea, and the other two

> "... in the church-yard lie,
> My sister and my brother;
> And in the church-yard cottage, I
> Dwell near them with my mother." (21-4)

The adult speaker, realizing that two of the girl's siblings are dead, spends the rest of the poem trying to convince her that if two "in the church-yard lie," then there must be only five, not seven, of them. But the girl will have nothing to do with the man's arithmetic or logic. Over and over she repeats the locations of her six siblings, and then insists again that "we are seven."

The man, desperate to talk some sense into the little girl, reminds her that while she is alive and runs about on the grass, her two siblings are laid in the graveyard. But his explanations prove incapable of disrupting her firm faith and belief that her two dead siblings are still a part of her family. She tries again to explain it to the incredulous adult:

"Their graves are green, they may be seen,"
The little Maid replied,
"Twelve steps or more from my mother's door,
And they are side by side.

"My stockings there I often knit,
My kerchief there I hem;
And there upon the ground I sit,
And sing a song to them.

"And often after sunset, Sir,
When it is light and fair,
I take my little porringer,
And eat my supper there.

"The first that died was sister Jane;
In bed she moaning lay,
Till God released her of her pain;
And then she went away.

"So in the church-yard she was laid;
And when the grass was dry,
Together round her grave we played,
My brother John and I.

"And when the ground was white with snow,
And I could run and slide,
My brother John was forced to go,
And he lies by her side." (37-60)

The girl is no fool. She knows and accepts that her brother and sister are dead and that their bodies are under the ground. What she will not accept is the utter finality of death or its power to sever her living connection with her siblings. As far as she is concerned, they are still a part of her family and a part of her life. She eats and works and plays by their graves, and even sings songs to them.

Viewing death from the perspective of innocence, the girl sees it as a natural process, one that brings an end to pain and suffering. It is significant that when the girl recalls the death of her brother John, she remembers it as occurring in conjunction with winter. In her own simple, intuitive way, the girl understands the nature of the seasonal cycle of life, death, and rebirth. All is a part of the circle of life, of the line of sentience and continuity that links parent to child and brother to sister.

Aside from the first and last stanza, Wordsworth employs an ABAB rhyme scheme: that is, the first and third and second and fourth lines of each stanza rhyme. Midway through the poem, however, in lines 37-40, he breaks this pattern. While lines two and four rhyme ("replied/side"), lines one and three each make use of a pair of internal rhymes ("green/seen" and "more/door"). When a poet of Wordsworth's caliber sets up a pattern and then deliberately breaks it, he generally has a good reason for doing so. Here that reason becomes clear once we study carefully the two pairs of internal rhymes. Taken by themselves, the four words—green, seen, more, and door—sum up powerfully the girl's Romantic vision. *Seen* from her eyes, all is *green*, brimming with life and growth; death to her is not a wall, but a *door* that opens on to *more*, to a fuller and richer form of existence.

But the adult seems incapable of perceiving that life and that existence, and so he tries one final time to force the girl to see the "truth" of the situation:

> "How many are you then," said I,
> "If they two are in Heaven?"
> Quick was the little Maid's reply,
> "O Master! we are seven."
>
> "But they are dead; those two are dead!
> Their spirits are in heaven!"
> 'Twas throwing words away; for still
> The little Maid would have her will,
> And said, "Nay, we are seven !" (61-69)

Try as he might, the adult cannot kill the girl's certainty of her siblings' continued participation in the life of her family. Death may have had the power to force her brother John into the grave, but the man's logic lacks a similar power to force her innocent perceptions into the "grave" of experience. All his efforts to do so are quite literally thrown to the wind.

As if to award the final victory in the debate to the girl, Wordsworth the poet, as opposed to Wordsworth the speaker, breaks his rhyme scheme a second time. The final stanza, which is five lines long rather than four, boasts a peculiar ABCCB rhyme scheme: a rhyme scheme that has the effect of detaching the first line of the stanza from the succeeding four. That Wordsworth intends for us to effect such a detaching in our mind becomes apparent when we consider what that line says: "'But they are dead; those two are dead.'" The line, which sums up the adult view, can have no intercourse with the girl's lively and indefatigable faith. The two views are as incompatible as darkness and light, despair and hope, death and life. To further emphasize his point, Wordsworth makes use in line 65, as he does in lines 37 and 39, of internal rhyme; but this time the rhyme is somewhat peculiar: "death/death." Death, at least as the adult perceives it, rhymes only with itself—it has no echo, no "green," no "more."

By mounting such a debate between adult and child, Wordsworth not only draws a distinction between what Blake terms experience and innocence but dramatizes the wider debate between Enlightenment rationalism and Romantic feeling. Whereas the adult relies solely on reason and logic in his assessment of the situation, the child bases her conclusions on emotion and intuition. The adult arrives at his position by a process of separation, by categorizing the living and the dead into two neat, air-tight compartments. The child, in contrast, looks at life and death holistically as participating in a single flow. Of course, the distinction I am here drawing between the rational and the emotional, the logical and the intuitive, the compartmental and the holistic is also descriptive of the distinction between masculine and feminine—thus making Wordsworth's decision to set a *male* adult against a *female* child particularly appropriate.

To help further clarify this vital distinction—one that all the Romantic poets were aware of—we might consider as well one of the key differences between Protestant and Catholic devotion. If there is one aspect of Catholicism that Protestants find hard not only to accept but to understand, it is the practice of praying to the saints. Though all traditional Protestants believe firmly that the dead in Christ are alive eternally in heaven, they balk at the notion that we on earth can have any form of communication with the "dead." Most Catholics, in contrast, have little trouble bridging the gap between earth and heaven through their prayers to Mary, Peter, or one of the other saints. Indeed, Greek Orthodox Christians, who share with Catholics a strong liturgical focus, believe that when the Mass (Liturgy) is performed on earth it is simultaneously performed in the throne room of God. For the more systematic rational-minded Protestant heaven is heaven and earth is earth and never the twain shall meet; for the more holistic mystical-minded Catholic or Orthodox these two realms, bridged by the Incarnation, continue to be bridged through the sacraments, especially the Eucharist, and the intercession of the saints.

Within the many denominations that make up the Protestant world, we can find a similar distinction played out between Baptists and Presbyterians on the one hand and Pentecostals and Charismatics on the other. While the former tend to draw near to God through a close and disciplined study of the Scriptures, the latter seek a more emotional and intuitive connection with the divine through ecstatic worship and the exercise of such spiritual gifts as tongues and prophecy. If your typical Protestant looks upon Catholic prayers to the saints as nothing more than pious superstition, then your typical conservative Baptist will often look upon the Pentecostal openness to continual revelation from God as borderline heresy. Of course, the dangers of superstition and of heresy *do* lurk behind both practices, but then the dangers of intellectual pride and bibliolatry lurk with equal menace behind a too-narrow focus on systematic theology and Bible-only exclusivism.

For all those whose fear or suspicion of emotion, intuition, and logic-defying mystery keeps them from embracing the full beauty and wonder of both this world and the next, Wordsworth's "child philosopher" speaks a message of inner hope, joy, and connection. Throughout the Catholic Middle Ages, poets and philosophers like Dante understood that while the number four represented the human realm—not just the four seasons, but the four classical virtues which the pagans knew apart from revelation—and the number three represented the divine—the Trinity as well as the three theological virtues that were revealed only through the New Testament—the combined number (seven) represented wholeness and completion, the integration of pagan and Christian, human and divine.

We are Seven indeed!

The Poet in His Bower

Close your eyes and try to picture an eighteenth-century poet like Alexander Pope at work. If you have read Pope's poetry and know something of his Age, then you should have pictured a well-dressed man sitting at a desk with quill in hand. Now close your eyes again and picture a Romantic poet at work. Suddenly, the desk, the study, and the house disappear and you are left with the picture of a man stretched out on the grass or kneeling in an orchard or sitting on a stone by the side of a lake. The former poet is an artisan, his desk a workshop; he goes there daily to practice and hone his craft. Not so the latter poet, who cannot simply enter a room and begin to create. He must first be inspired, and so he seeks out a bower, a rustic retreat where he can find rest and peace and can commune silently with the beauties of nature. It is in just such a bower that we discover Wordsworth in the opening stanzas of "Lines Written in Early Spring":

> I heard a thousand blended notes,
> While in a grove I sate reclined,
> In that sweet mood when pleasant thoughts
> Bring sad thoughts to the mind.
>
> To her fair works did Nature link
> The human soul that through me ran;
> And much it grieved my heart to think
> What man has made of man. (1-8)

The sound the poet hears as he reclines in his bower is the music of nature in harmony with herself. As he listens to it, he feels one not only with the world around him but with all humanity. Nature does more than merely inspire him; she draws out his soul and connects it to the trees, to the stones, to the rivers, to the sky.

The poet longs to join fully with that harmony, but two things hold him back. First, his own sensitivity betrays him. The sudden feelings of pleasure that fall upon him set in motion a shift in mood that sends him spiraling downward into a state of sadness and melancholy. Though we must temper our modern inclination to interpret lines 3 and 4 as a bipolar episode, it is nevertheless true that all the Romantics record such mood swings in their poetry. Those who live closely in touch with their feelings experience moments of intense joy, but with the joy comes ever the shadow of pain. Second, the poet is prevented from joining fully in the blended harmony of nature by the very fact that he is a member of the human race His perception of the unity within nature only serves to remind him of the division within man.

Saddened by this division, the poet turns away from himself and his melancholy thoughts to study in detail his isolated bower:

> Through primrose tufts, in that sweet bower,
> The periwinkle trailed its wreathes;
> And 'tis my faith that every flower
> Enjoys the air it breathes.
>
> The birds around me hopped and played,
> Their thoughts I cannot measure:
> But the least motion which they made,
> It seemed a thrill of pleasure.
>
> The budding twigs spread out their fan,
> To catch the breezy air;

> And I must think, do all I can,
> That there was pleasure there. (9-20)

Though the references are somewhat subtle, in these three stanzas we catch a glimpse of a philosophical-theological belief system that all of the Romantic poets toyed with: pantheism. Unlike polytheism, the belief in many gods, pantheism teaches that god is everything and everything is god ("pan" in Greek means "all"). The god of the pantheists is not a being or even a personality; it is simply a force or spirit. For the pantheist, all of nature is alive, pervaded by a presence that is beside all and in all and through all. The flowers and the twigs and the breezy air of Wordsworth's bower respond to and interact with one another, for the same spirit animates all parts of nature and makes them one.

The distinction I made above between masculine-rational-logical-compartmental and feminine-emotional-intuitive-holistic can also be seen here in Wordsworth's partial embrace of pantheism. In contrast to the West, where philosophers and theologians have typically posited a transcendent Creator who is separate from the world he made, the sages and gurus of the East have tended to worship an immanent deity who, far from dwelling outside of the world, is identical with it. In yearning to commune with such a pervading spirit, the Romantics betray an almost Eastern sensibility, one that seeks wisdom not through analysis but through synthesis, not by breaking things down into their constituent parts but by straining to see the invisible threads that connect and unite all things.

Those who suffer from back trouble and seek the advice of an orthopedic surgeon and a chiropractor will be treated not only to two competing prognoses but to two radically different visions of how the body works and what constitutes health. The former, raised on a Western compartmentalized model of medicine, will sequester the backbone from the rest of the body and treat it in isolation, usually by some form of invasive surgery. The latter, raised on an Eastern holistic view of the body, will consider the backbone in interaction with the rest of the body, and seek, through readjustment and realignment, to restore equilibrium. When Romantic poets look out on nature, they seek to discern a similar holistic vision of unity and equilibrium. Indeed, in keeping with the Romantic belief that things are as they are perceived, Wordsworth suggests in lines 19-20 that he must participate in achieving this equilibrium by projecting his own inner pleasure onto nature

In the final stanza, Wordsworth, having drawn himself part way into the life of the bower, is pulled back again into the human world of division and strife:

> If this belief from heaven be sent,
> If such be Nature's holy plan,
> Have I not reason to lament
> What man has made of man? (21-24)

Still, the poet leaves the bower, and the poem, having glimpsed, if briefly, a secularized edenic vision of what the world might be like could that division and strife be healed and man live at peace with nature and the spirit that pervades her.

Sparring Partners

In "Expostulation and Reply," Wordsworth returns to the dialogue structure of "We are Seven," but this time it is Wordsworth ("William") who embodies the Romantic ethos. Set over against William is his friend Matthew, who embodies the Enlightenment ethos of the Age of Reason. Ironically, though the poem will favor William's less structured, less systematic view, the poem itself is structured like a formal debate. Matthew goes first and is given three stanzas to present his case:

> "Why, William, on that old grey stone,
> Thus for the length of half a day,
> Why, William, sit you thus alone,
> And dream your time away?
>
> "Where are your books?—that light bequeathed
> To Beings else forlorn and blind!
> Up! Up! and drink the spirit breathed
> From dead men to their kind.
>
> "You look round on your Mother Earth,
> As if she for no purpose bore you;
> As if you were her first-born birth,
> And none had lived before you!" (1-12)

What initiates the debate between the two friends is Matthew's consternation at the seemingly lackadaisical attitude of William. From Matthew's perspective, William has wasted away his entire morning daydreaming on a rock when he could have been learning valuable lessons.

Matthew, like a good classics professor, or like a good Southern Baptist, believes that the reading and studying of old books (or Book, in the case of the Baptist) marks the only safe and proper road to truth and illumination. The analyzing, interpreting, and critiquing of authoritative texts, not the seeking of inspiration from who knows what source, are the methods that rational scholars use to gain wisdom and understanding. So passionate does Matthew become in his defense of these methods that, in his zeal, he comes very close to parodying his own position. "[D]rink the spirit breathed / From dead men to their kind," he counsels William, forgetting that dead men cannot breathe and that to seek the living among the dead is to follow a path of folly and frustration.

Perhaps realizing that he has made a tactical error, Matthew shifts his approach in the third stanza and takes William to task for his relaxed and careless approach to life. "You act," says Matthew, "as if you were the special child of Mother Earth, as if you were made merely to enjoy life and spend your days in idleness." Though William never responds directly to this criticism, he would likely agree with Matthew: not out of pride, but out of faith that he is indeed a child of nature meant to take solace and pleasure in the beauties of the natural world.

Rather than shift directly from Matthew's "expostulation" to William's "reply," the poet inserts a transitional stanza which introduces the two participants in the debate.

> One morning thus, by Esthwaite lake,
> When life was sweet, I knew not why,
> To me my good friend Matthew spake,
> And thus I made reply: (13-16)

In addition to identifying Matthew as his "good friend"—thereby making it clear that they are engaged in a friendly debate—the stanza gives insight into the character of William. Despite Matthew's good-natured taunts, William remains in a state of peace and joy. Life is sweet, the poet tells us, but he does not know why it is sweet nor does he seem interested in figuring out why it is sweet. Any husband who has spent a frustrating hour trying to get a logical explanation out of his wife for why she is depressed will recognize immediately that William's seeming lack of interest in establishing a clear cause for his mood is more a feminine trait than a masculine one. Unmolested by the masculine need to assign logical causes to all things, most women (and all Romantic poets!) are generally content to accept their present mood.

Once we realize that William possesses this traditionally feminine—and Eastern—capacity to receive passively, rather than pursue actively, the feelings and experiences that come his way we will be in a better position to understand his reply to Matthew:

> "The eye—it cannot choose but see;
> We cannot bid the ear be still;
> Our bodies feel, where'er they be,
> Against or with our will.
>
> "Nor less I deem that there are Powers
> Which of themselves our minds impress;
> That we can feed this mind of ours
> In a wise passiveness.
>
> "Think you, 'mid all this mighty sum
> Of things for ever speaking,
> That nothing of itself will come,
> But we must still be seeking? (17-28)

Whereas Matthew would gain knowledge by active study, William would gain it by passive embrace. After all, he asserts, we cannot prevent our senses from taking in the myriad splendors that surround us. Sensations rush upon us from all directions, enough to fill eye and ear to overflowing. So often, the things that really matter come to us not after long and arduous study but in a flash of insight: direct, spontaneous, unpremeditated.

Flirting again with pantheism, William speaks to Matthew of invisible Powers that press themselves upon us, Powers which we must open our minds to receive. We do not need to seek them, only be ready to receive them when they appear. We need to stop and listen, to cease doing and commence seeing. In a sense, what William advocates in his reply is a kind of active passivity—or "wise passiveness" as he paradoxically puts it—an active focusing of the mind so that it will be prepared to receive passively when the sensations come. To Matthew and his fellow rationalists, William's "pedagogical methods" would seem strange indeed, but they would not seem so to either a Christian or a Buddhist monk. In the mystical branches of all religions, intense prayer and meditation generally precede moments of mystical insight. The final goal is for the soul to open itself to the Presence of the divine, but the soul needs first to be in a state of equilibrium—and to achieve that state takes focused, concentrated effort.

Now that William has had his three stanzas to reply to Matthew, we expect that Wordsworth will end his poem with a concluding stanza (#8) to balance the transitional stanza (#4) that followed Matthew's expostulation. Instead, he gives William a fourth stanza in which he moves, ironically, from passive defense to an active claim of victory:

> "—Then ask not wherefore, here, alone,
> Conversing as I may,
> I sit upon this old grey stone,
> And dream my time away." (29-32)

By no means is William dreaming his time away as Matthew claims in the opening stanza. His quest for knowledge is as serious and intentional as Matthew's; it is merely carried out in a different manner. In fact, Matthew is even wrong in his assertion that William is alone. Though he may seem alone to those who lack eyes to see and ears to hear, he is, in reality, engaged in an actively passive dialogue with the whole mighty sum of speaking things.

Buoyed up by this victorious conclusion to his reply, William rushes headlong into a second poem titled "The Tables Turned" and subtitled "An Evening Scene on the Same Subject." This time around, William takes the offense and, quite literally, turns the tables on Matthew. In stanza two of "Expostulation and Reply," Matthew had rebuked William with the following words: "Up! Up! and drink the spirit breathed / From dead men to their kind." With a smile on his face and his tongue firmly in his check, William begins "The Tables Turned" by quoting Matthew's words against him:

> Up! up! my Friend, and quit your books;
> Or surely you'll grow double.
>
> Up! up! my Friend, and clear your looks;
> Why all this toil and trouble? (1-4)

If William needed to get off his old grey stone and pick up a book, then Matthew is in even greater need of a break from his studies. Bent over his desk for hours on end, the overly studious Matthew is in danger of becoming a hunchback. Too many long nights burning the midnight oil have left him with a pale and chalky complexion and given him a permanent expression of worry and dis-ease.

For such unnatural behavior, William advises, there can be only one remedy. Leave your study and go outside!

> The sun, above the mountain's head,
> A freshening lustre mellow
> Through all the long green fields has spread,
> His first sweet evening yellow. (5-8)

William, falling back again into a mild pantheism, speaks of the sun not as an "it" but as a "him." As in the bower of "Lines Written in Early Spring," sun, mountain, and field all exist in mutual harmony. The sun spreads out its lazy evening rays like the fingers of a hand stretched out to embrace the long green fields. William invites Matthew to be embraced as well.

Besides, argues William, nature has things to teach Matthew that he cannot find in books:

> Books! 'tis a dull and endless strife:
> Come, here the woodland linnet,
> How sweet his music! on my life,
> There's more of wisdom in it.
>
> And hark! how blithe the throstle sings!
> He, too, is no mean preacher:
> Come forth into the light of things,
> Let Nature be your Teacher. (9-16)

For the last two centuries, Wordsworth has been both criticized and parodied for making such statements—statements that, if taken too literally, are nothing short of ludicrous. Does Mr. Wordsworth really mean us to believe that a bird makes a finer preacher than a minister or that the whistling of a linnet can instruct us in wisdom better than Milton, Shakespeare, or the Bible? Well, of course that is not what Wordsworth means. The poet uses hyperbole—as Jesus does when he instructs us to pluck out the eye that offends us—in order to make his point. And his point is not that the song of a bird can take the place of a sermon or a textbook, but that wisdom and truth and beauty are not to be found *only* in books. Nature offers us a more direct, unmediated kind of wisdom that goes straight to the heart.

If we will only stop, look, and listen, if we will only open our eyes and ears, we will discover a whole new world of meaning.

> She [nature] has a world of ready wealth,
> Our minds and hearts to bless—
> Spontaneous wisdom breathed by health,
> Truth breathed by cheerfulness.

> One impulse from a vernal wood
> May teach you more of man,
> Of moral evil and of good,
> Than all the sages can. (17-24)

Joy, health, and spontaneity: all of these are commingled with the lore of nature and are what make that lore so fit for assimilation—nay, consumption—by human beings. Nature offers us an embarrassment of riches, a treasure trove of truth than cannot be horded, only enjoyed. The very trees of the forest cry out their knowledge of humanity, of the good and the evil in man that they have witnessed for ages untold. Yes, lines 21-24 are particularly easy to parody—they were, in fact, lampooned by many of Wordsworth's contemporaries—but the poet means them to convey a deeply felt passion for truths that are permanent, that transcend the little lives of men.

Most important for the poet, however, is the wholeness and integrity of the truths that nature teaches:

> Sweet is the lore which nature brings;
> Our meddling intellect
> Mis-shapes the beauteous forms of things:—
> We murder to dissect. (25-28)

Here we see the Romantic privileging of synthesis over analysis in its most extreme form. Too often our meddling (Enlightenment) intellect thinks that it can only know a thing after it has dissected it. Behind Wordsworth's lines I hear the words of a man who lived a century later but who knew well the lore of trees: "he that breaks a thing to find out what it is has left the path of wisdom."[7] In nature, Wordsworth found a truth that dwelled side by side with beauty and that therefore did not require the misshaping of beauty as a prerequisite for extracting truth.

In the final stanza of the poem, William calls directly upon Matthew, and through him the reader, to take a step of faith and open himself to truths that can't be contained in books:

> Enough of Science and of Art;
> Close up those barren leaves;
> Come forth, and bring with you a heart
> That watches and receives. (29-32)

Wordsworth's pun on the word leaves—both the leaves of a tree and the leaves of a book—is a clever one that helps to drive home his

---

[7] J. R. R. Tolkien, *The Lord of the Rings* (New York: Houghton Mifflin, 2005), 259.

argument. When the pages of a book grow faded and old, they cannot be rejuvenated, but the leaves that fall from autumn trees will be born anew in the spring. In the same way, the lore that nature brings is ever young, ever fresh, ever spontaneous. When that lore surrounds us and knocks on the door of our heart, we need only to receive it passively. But until that mystical moment arrives, we must actively decide to close our books, come forth into the light, and instruct our eyes to watch . . .

VII
The Willing Suspension of Disbelief

Perhaps the best known Romantic poem, the one that provokes immediate recognition in most people, is Samuel Taylor Coleridge's *The Rime of the Ancient Mariner*. As we saw in Chapter Five, Coleridge, in composing the *Ancient Mariner*, set himself the task of transforming a strange and fantastic tale into a poem whose psychological and dramatic truths would win from the reader "that willing suspension of disbelief for the moment, which constitutes poetic faith." Unlike Wordsworth's contributions to *Lyrical Ballads*, which were intended to rip away the veil of familiarity and allow the reader to see natural objects as though they were supernatural, Coleridge's *Ancient Mariner* seeks to present its supernatural tale in such a way as to lend it a reality and a truth that can speak to the ordinary, everyday life of its reader.

That Coleridge was concerned about issues of perception, about how we apprehend and comprehend the natural and supernatural world around us, is made plain in the Latin epigraph he chose to append to later editions of his poem. When translated into English, the epigraph reads:

> I readily believe that there are more invisible than visible beings in the universe. But who will tell us the families, the ranks, the relationships, the differences, the respective functions of all these beings? What do they do? Where do they dwell? The human mind has circled around this knowledge, but has never reached it. Still, it is pleasant, I have no doubt, to contemplate sometimes in one's mind, as in a picture, the image of a bigger and better world; lest the mind, accustomed to the details of daily life, be too narrowed and settle down entirely on trifling thoughts. Meanwhile, however, we must be on the lookout for truth and observe restraint, in order that we may distinguish the certain from the uncertain, day from night. (392)

On the simplest level, Coleridge's epigraph prepares us for the supernatural machinery that we will encounter in the poem. Birds of good omen, vengeful and benevolent spirits, ghost ships piloted by spectral fiends and animated corpses: all these and more greet us as we journey alongside the Mariner. Coleridge's epigraph, however, serves a second, deeper purpose, and that is to exhort us to open our eyes and ears to "a bigger and better world," to lift our sights from the narrow confines of our "daily life" and "trifling thoughts" to catch a glimpse of truths we too often overlook.

Though Coleridge uses various poetic techniques for accomplishing this, his overall method for tearing down the veil and allowing his reader to gain both insight and discernment (to "distinguish the certain from the uncertain, day from night") is to invite his reader to join him on a dual journey. The primary journey is an external, geographical one—the journey taken by the Mariner as he crisscrosses the globe. The secondary journey is an internal, psychological one—the journey into and through the Mariner's tormented psyche as he first breaks and then restores his fellowship with God, man, and nature. Though the reader experiences pleasure mingled with horror, wonder, and awe as he accompanies the Mariner on his primary journey, his participation in the secondary journey brings with it a different kind of delight and fear. As we travel along the internalized landscape of the Mariner's unconscious mind—as Freud would term it a century later—we are impelled to peer into our shared human capacity for sin, despair, and isolation and our equally shared need for redemption, penance, and self-knowledge.

In orchestrating this dual journey, Coleridge works in the tradition of Dante, he whose pilgrim takes his own parallel journey along the geographical landscapes of hell, purgatory, and paradise and the spiritual landscapes of repentance, purgation, and glorification. Though the *Divine Comedy* will no doubt exert its fullest impact upon Christian readers who believe in the reality of heaven and hell, Dante's epic still retains its force when it is read by those who do not believe in a literal afterlife and who may not even believe in God. That is because Dante simultaneously explores the theological and psychological consequences of sin: sin not only cuts us off from God and robs us of heaven, but it snares us in a cycle of futility and imprisons us—as *both* the orthodox C. S. Lewis and the heterodox William Blake would agree—in a hell of our own making. Just so, *The Rime of the Ancient Mariner* works on various levels, speaking with equal power and conviction to those who believe in a supernatural realm and to those who do not. As long as we are prepared to give our willing suspension of disbelief and enter into the journey of Coleridge's pilgrim, we will have our eyes and ears opened to a type of beauty and terror that we spend most of our lives blind and deaf to.

We Cannot Choose But Hear

Like the great epics of Homer and Virgil, *The Rime of the Ancient Mariner* begins not at the beginning but *in medias res* ("in the middle of things"). Without warning or preparation, we are cast headlong into the poem and left to find our own bearings—a task rendered even more difficult by Coleridge's use of deliberately obscure diction in his opening stanza:

> It is an ancient Mariner,
> And he stoppeth one of three.
>
> "By thy long grey beard and glittering eye,
> Now wherefore stopp'st thou me?" (1-4)

The stanza is so well known that we risk missing the strangeness of the first line. It is simply not proper to use "it is" when referring to a human being. We would not say "it is an old professor" or "it is a preacher's daughter." We might use "there was" or "she is," but not "it is." That Coleridge nevertheless uses the phrase to introduce his Mariner has the effect of transforming him from a man of flesh and blood into something akin to a force of nature. And yet, at the same time that the phrase sinks the Mariner below human consciousness, it also raises him above it. The starkness, simplicity, and eternality of the phrase cannot help but remind us of the name of God: "I am that I am." Coleridge's Mariner is a figure who endures, godlike, without change.

And the first action we see him perform is itself godlike—that of choosing or calling an individual in a way that seems arbitrary to us yet clearly conceals some deeper purpose known only to the chooser. In actuality, the Mariner has come upon a party of three young wedding guests and detains one of them, but the phrasing of the second line seems to refer to a grander, apocalyptic form of divine election that will one day sift the nations. The confusion and tension into which the first two lines catapult the reader are shared by the one whom the Mariner chooses. He too is knocked off his guard by the suddenness and strangeness of the Mariner's actions, and insists that his outlandish "abductor" explain the reason for his behavior.

When the Mariner makes no reply to his question, the wedding guest pleads the urgency of his situation:

> "The Bridegroom's doors are opened wide,
> And I am next of kin;
> The guests are met, the feast is set:
> May'st hear the merry din."
>
> He holds him with his skinny hand,
> "There was a ship," quoth he.
> "Hold off! unhand me, grey-beard loon!"
> Eftsoons his hand dropt he. (5-12)

The wedding guest yearns to join the feast, but the Mariner holds him fast on the threshold of the banqueting hall. In the same way, Coleridge will hold his reader, for the duration of his poem, on the threshold between the real and the fantastical, the natural and the supernatural, innocence and experience. Both Mariner and poet will *compel* their listeners to hear their tale. Terrified by the single-minded intransigence of the Mariner, the wedding guest demands that he release him, and the Mariner immediately complies.

But the wedding guests' victory is a short lived one. No sooner does the Mariner release his physical grip on the wedding guest than he exerts a stronger mental/psychological grip:

> He holds him with his glittering eye—
> The Wedding-Guest stood still,
> And listens like a three years' child:
> The Mariner hath his will.
>
> The Wedding-Guest sat on a stone:
> He cannot choose but hear;
> And thus spake on that ancient man,
> The bright-eyed Mariner. (13-20)

By the power of his eye, and the overwhelming, if tormented self-consciousness that lies behind it, the Mariner so mesmerizes the wedding guest as to covert him into a passive receptacle of the Mariner's tale. The bright-eyed Mariner not only gains "his [the Mariner's] will," but controls "his [the wedding guest's] will" as well. From our own modern point of view this may seem a bad thing, a stripping away of the wedding guest's "rights" as an autonomous individual, but for the Romantics the state into which the wedding guest is lulled by the hypnotic powers of the Mariner is not necessarily a negative one.

If line 18 sounds somewhat familiar, that is because we have heard it before in stanza 6 of Wordsworth's "Expostulation and Reply":

> "The eye—it cannot choose but see;
> We cannot bid the ear be still;
> Our bodies feel, where'er they be,
> Against or with our will." (17-20)

In this stanza of the poem, Wordsworth defends the pedagogical efficacy of his sitting on a stone (compare lines 1 and 31 of "Expostulation and Reply" with line 17 of the *Ancient Mariner*) and communing with the natural world around him. As we saw in the previous chapter, the Romantics not only privileged emotion over reason and intuition over logic, but the passive over the active. There are things in nature—and, as we saw above, the Mariner is himself something of a force of nature—that we must hearken to and receive in an actively passive manner. If the wedding guest is "reduced" to a "three years' child," it is not because he has been "infantilized" by the Mariner but because he gains for a moment the child-like innocence and receptivity of the child protagonist of Wordsworth's "We are Seven." That Wordsworth himself wrote lines 13-16 of the *Ancient Mariner* (in its earliest stages, the poem was planned as a collaborative effort) makes the connection to "We are Seven" even stronger. That lines 17-20, which so directly mimic "Expostulation and Reply," were *not* written by Wordsworth, makes clear how actively passive the two poets-friends were in absorbing each other's words and ideas.

As the Mariner begins his tale, the weddings guest, who hears nearby the sounds of the feast, twice "beat[s] his breast" (31, 37) and longs to join the revelers, but he is held fast by the glittering eye of the teller and the mesmerizing power of the tale. He "cannot choose but hear" (38) . . . and neither can we.

Medieval Romance and Allegory

The Mariner explains to his rapt audience how his ship sailed south past the equator only to be caught by a storm that drove it further southward toward the Pole. His description of the frozen desert that greets the crew immediately establishes that his tale will occupy a literary no man's land between natural realism and supernatural fantasy:

> And now there came both mist and snow,
> And it grew wondrous cold:
> And ice, mast-high, came floating by,

> As green as emerald. . . .
>
> The ice was here, the ice was there,
> The ice was all around:
> It cracked and growled, and roared and howled,
> Like noises in a swound! (51-54, 59-62)

Though Coleridge was clearly influenced by the sea voyages of the *Odyssey* and *Aeneid*, his *Rime*, written in a medieval folk stanza known as ballad rhythm rather than in the stately blank verse of Milton's *Paradise Lost*, is modeled less on the epics of antiquity than on the popular romances of the Middle Ages. Though medieval romances tend to be set within a historical period—that of Alexander the Great or King Arthur or Charlemagne—their heroes nevertheless journey through exotic landscapes that are as strange, beautiful, and deadly as the one described above. While journeying through these imaginative spaces, they participate in marvelous adventures that lie outside the ken of everyday life but which never fully lose their connection with real human struggles. At times, their journey will take the form of a quest, often for a sacred or magical object like the Holy Grail; in such cases—the Arthurian romances of Chrétien de Troyes, for example—there will often be a heightened awareness of spiritual realities and a deeper exploration of psychological states. Though strongly plot driven and obsessed with details that are likely to provoke a yawn from most modern readers, romances shun pragmatism, rationalism, and materialism in favor of an instinctual life of courage, idealism, and imagination.

This would be as good a time as any to clarify a point of common confusion. The Romantic poets are not called "romantics" because they specialize in love poems or are particularly good at wooing women (though Byron and Shelley were, admittedly, experts in that field). They are called "romantics" because they sought, in part, to revive both the forms and the preoccupations of medieval romance. Though neither Wordsworth nor Coleridge were particularly interested in chivalry or the historical subject matter of the romances, they did share with their medieval forebears a desire to affirm the centrality of love, joy, beauty, and passion, to restore harmony between man and nature, and to delve the emotional and mystical sides of human existence. All of this Coleridge accomplishes in the *Ancient Mariner*, while ratcheting up the spiritual and psychological elements to a level rarely reached by the Medievals.

And he does so by working through his own unique version of a medieval allegory or morality play. As the ice floes grow more menacing and the crew begins to lose heart, an albatross appears out of the fog. No sooner does the bird appear than the ice breaks around them, and a strong, steady wind pushes the stalled ship northward. The Mariner's shipmates, their spirits lifted, treat the albatross as an honored guest aboard their ship. But the Mariner reacts in a different manner. Rather than hail the bird as a gift from God, he takes up his crossbow and shoots the albatross. Neither the Mariner nor Coleridge supplies us with a reason for this heinous and unnatural crime. His act of murder is as senseless as Adam and Eve's eating of the forbidden fruit.

In later editions of the *Ancient Mariner*, Coleridge, perhaps fearing that readers would misinterpret the allegorical aspects of his poem, added marginal glosses, three of which offer important insight into the meaning of the Mariner's crime. The Mariner recounts that after his shooting of the albatross the crew initially attacks him for his foul deed:

> And I had done an hellish thing,
> And it would work 'em woe:
> For all averred, I had killed the bird
> That made the breeze to blow.
> Ah wretch! said they, the bird to slay,
> That made the breeze to blow! (91-96)

However, when the weather changes, they change their attitude:

> Nor dim nor red, like God's own head,
> The glorious Sun uprist:
> Then all averred, I had killed the bird
> That brought the fog and mist.
> 'Twas right, said they, such birds to slay,
> That bring the fog and mist. (97-102)

Lest we miss the point of these two stanzas, Coleridge explains his purpose in the form of two glosses, one appended to each of the stanzas: "His shipmates cry out against the ancient Mariner, for killing the bird of good luck."; "But when the fog cleared off, they justify the same, and thus make themselves accomplices in the crime." According to the Christian doctrine of original sin, all human beings after Adam participate in his act of rebellion against God and thus share in his guilt. So here, the crew, in becoming "accomplices in the crime," share equally in the guilt of the Mariner and can thus be punished fairly alongside him.

However, if we read as well the gloss that Coleridge appends to lines 79-82, in which the Mariner confesses to the wedding guest that he shot the albatross, we will see that the poet meant to imbue the killing of the bird with a second level of significance. "The ancient Mariner," the gloss reads, "inhospitably killeth the pious bird of good omen." In the moral and aesthetic writings of Greece and Rome, a high value was placed upon the relationship between guest and host. If this guest/host relationship was breached by either party, vengeance and destruction generally followed. Two of the best known examples of this in ancient literature are the abduction of Helen by Paris while he was a guest in the home of Menelaus (an act that precipitates the Trojan War), and the murder of Agamemnon by his wife/hostess Clytemnestra (which sets in motion the tragic cycle of Aeschylus's *Oresteia*). When he "inhospitably" kills the albatross, who is a guest aboard his vessel, the Mariner breaks the guest/host relationship. As understood in both the biblical (Judeo-Christian) and classical (Greco-Roman) sense, the Mariner's crime constitutes not only a morally reprehensible act but a rupture in the delicate weave that binds man to God, man to man, and man to nature.

That is why when the Mariner's punishment begins, it manifests itself in the form of utter isolation and despair. Not only does the corrupt soul of the Mariner begin to wither within him; the very sea itself falls prey to corruption:

> Water, water, every where
> And all the boards did shrink;
> Water, water, every where,
> Nor any drop to drink.
>
> The very deep did rot: O Christ!
> That ever this should be!
> Yea, slimy things did crawl with legs
> Upon the slimy sea. (119-126)

In the Old Testament, leprosy is understood not only as a punishment for sin, but as an external illustration of what sin does internally. As leprosy devours the skin, so sin devours the soul. Just so, the putrefaction of the water manifests physically what is happening within the tormented psyche of the Mariner. His punishment, in fact, is as much psychological as it is physical. In addition to beholding with his bodily eyes the externalization of his inner depravity, the Mariner must face the exquisite mental torment of dying of thirst while being surrounded by water.

And he must face as well the condemnatory looks of the crew who take it upon themselves to mark him with their own version of Hawthorne's scarlet letter:

> Ah! well a-day! what evil looks
> Had I from old and young!
> Instead of the cross, the Albatross
> About my neck was hung. (139-142)

Too conscious of his own guilt to refuse, the Mariner agrees to bear the symbol of his shame and is transformed into a living scapegoat—an object lesson of the dread consequences that must follow when the moral law and the guest/host relationship are breached.

Life-in-Death

Baked by the merciless sun, with nary a drop of water to quench their parched throats, all give way to despair and a veil of silence shrouds the ship. Suddenly, in the distance, the Mariner catches sight of a sail. He yearns to share the news, but is at first unable to do so:

> With throats unslaked, with black lips baked,
> We could nor laugh nor wail;
> Through utter drought all dumb we stood!
> I bit my arm, I sucked the blood,
> And cried, A sail! a sail! (157-161)

Coleridge likely intended the Mariner's sucking of his own blood to function as a metaphor for the Romantic poet who speaks out of his own anguish and pain—an image to which he will return with a vengeance in the closing section of his poem. However, this lurid example of "self-vampirism" serves a second function, that of preparing us for the greater horror to come.

Far from bringing rescue, the sail that the Mariner spies belongs to a ghost ship piloted by a two-person crew whom Coleridge identifies (in his gloss to lines 185-189) as a "Spectre-Woman and her Death-mate." Coleridge describes the former thus:

> *Her* lips were red, *her* looks were free,
> Her locks were yellow as gold :
> Her skin was as white as leprosy,
> The Night-mare LIFE-IN-DEATH was she,
> Who thicks man's blood with cold. (190-194)

In contrast to the Mariner's sucking of his own blood, the Spectre-Woman feeds on the blood of others. She carries in her wake not death itself but a perverse anti-life that dooms its victim to wander hopelessly, cut off from redemption, regeneration, and resurrection. She is the spiritual mother not only of undead monsters like Dracula, Frankenstein, and the Golem, and cursed creatures like mummies, zombies, and werewolves, but of the cold and treacherous femme fatales ("fatal women") who have lured men to inner destruction and despair in countless film noir movies. The life-in-death that she inflicts upon her victims imprisons them in their own anguished, guilt-ridden psyches so that they become, quite literally, their own tormentors and executioners.

In the poem the male and female fiends cast dice for the soul of the Mariner, and Life-in-Death wins the game. Shortly after, her sinister mate claims his ownership over the remaining crewmembers, who succumb, each in his turn, to a swift death:

> One after one, by the star-dogged Moon,
> Too quick for groan or sigh,
> Each turned his face with a ghastly pang,
> And cursed me with his eye.
>
> Four times fifty living men,
> (And I heard nor sigh nor groan)
> With heavy thump, a lifeless lump,
>
> They dropped down one by one.
> The souls did from their bodies fly,—
> They fled to bliss or woe!
> And every soul, it passed me by,
> Like the whizz of my cross-bow! (212-223)

Two hundred men die as the Mariner looks on helplessly; each curses the slayer of the albatross with his eye until the weight of guilt becomes almost unbearable. One by one, the souls fly to their final judgment and from there to heaven or hell. In the whizzing sound made by their fleeting souls, the Mariner fancies that he hears the sound of his crossbow. His eyes and ears, controlled now by the inner torment of his soul, interpret all they perceive in terms of his own shame and remorse. The full measure of his life-in-death punishment has begun.

As the wedding guest listens to the Mariner's tale, a sudden fear seizes him. Perhaps the man who speaks to him is not a man at all, but a dark spirit sent to drive him mad and lure him to his doom:

> "I fear thee, ancient Mariner!
>
> I fear thy skinny hand!
> And thou art long, and lank, and brown,
> As is the ribbed sea-sand.

> I fear thee and thy glittering eye,
> And thy skinny hand, so brown."—
> Fear not, fear not, thou Wedding-Guest!
> This body dropt not down. (224-231)

Unlike the Mariner, the wedding guest still dwells in the world of innocence; he is ignorant of, and therefore fears, the danger and horror that lurk in the world of experience. It is as if one of the shepherds from Blake's *Songs of Innocence* were to hearken to the voice of Blake's melancholy Bard and suffer the terror of having his eyes and ears opened to a world he has, until now, only glimpsed in nightmares. But the Mariner assures the wedding guest that he is no ghost but a living man. He alone of the crew of that ill-fated vessel did not succumb to death.

Instead, he lived on to experience the profound alienation that is the fate of all those who are cursed with life-in-death:

> Alone, alone, all, all alone,
> Alone on a wide wide sea!
> And never a saint took pity on
> My soul in agony.
>
> The many men, so beautiful!
> And they all dead did lie:
> And a thousand thousand slimy things
> Lived on; and so did I. (232-239)

Cut off utterly from the life of men, abandoned to his own existential torment and despair, the Mariner is left with none to commune with but the loathsome vermin of the sea. So isolated and companionless is he that he finds he cannot even lift a prayer to God:

> I looked to heaven, and tried to pray;
> But or ever a prayer had gusht,
> A wicked whisper came, and made
> My heart as dry as dust. (244-247)

Like Shakespeare's Claudius, who, though he feels some remorse over his unnatural murder of his brother Hamlet, finds that he cannot connect with God in prayer, the Mariner finds that he too is trapped within the confines of his own guilty soul and cannot move outward in prayer. His heart, chilled by the curse of the Spectre-Woman, has been left physically, emotionally, and spiritually dry. His inner fountains of joy and restoration have ceased to flow.

And then something miraculous occurs:

> Beyond the shadow of the ship,
> I watched the water-snakes:
> They moved in tracks of shining white,
> And when they reared, the elfish light
> Fell off in hoary flakes.
>
> Within the shadow of the ship
> I watched their rich attire:
> Blue, glossy green, and velvet black,
> They coiled and swam; and every track
> Was a flash of golden fire.
>
> O happy living things! no tongue
> Their beauty might declare:
> A spring of love gushed from my heart,
> And I blessed them unaware:
> Sure my kind saint took pity on me,
> And I blessed them unaware. (272-287)

The water snakes that the Mariner first gazes upon and then blesses are not in themselves natural symbols of beauty, love, or delight—as lambs are of innocence or tigers are of fear. The elfin magic and sinuous charm that accrue to them in the quoted stanzas come ultimately from within the Mariner who, by divine aid, is enabled to perceive them through new eyes. Understood on a physical, ontological level, their sudden and mystical beauty is the simple result of an optical illusion, a trick of light and shadow, line and color. Understood on an aesthetic, epistemological level their beauty is not innate but has been projected on to them—"the externalization of the internal"—by the Mariner.

Granted new eyes by his "kind saint," the Mariner is able to move out of himself toward the water snakes and even to feel a harmony and kinship with them—something he had not previously felt toward the albatross. Community, though it be with the lowliest of God's creatures, is restored, and the Mariner is freed, if only for a moment, from his egocentric focus on himself and his guilt. If, as I argued in my analysis of Blake's "The Little Black Boy," love is best defined as the movement out of narcissism, then the Mariner's blessing of the water snakes must be accounted an act of love and even of worship. Its results are immediate and profound:

> The self-same moment I could pray;
> And from my neck so free
> The Albatross fell off, and sank
> Like lead into the sea. (288-291)

"The spell," explains Coleridge in his gloss to this stanza, "begins to break," and indeed, though the Mariner's penance is far from over, from this point on the crushing weight of his guilt is lifted from his soul. If the albatross be interpreted as a symbol of original sin, and Coleridge seems, at least in part, to intend this, then the Mariner is here saved from both the direct and ultimate consequences of his crime. Still, we must be careful not to confuse—either aesthetically or theologically—salvation with sanctification. The Mariner, like the protagonist of Bunyan's *Pilgrim's Progress*, still has many miles to tread if he is to reach the celestial city. As we shall see in a moment, the indirect and ongoing consequences of his sin will continue to pursue him throughout his journey and his life thereafter.

For now, however, salvation has been gained through the gracious intervention of his "kind saint," a gift of heaven that is marked by two events that occur in quick succession:

> Oh sleep! it is a gentle thing,
>
> Beloved from pole to pole!
> To Mary Queen the praise be given!
> She sent the gentle sleep from Heaven,
> That slid into my soul.
>
> The silly buckets on the deck,
> That had so long remained,
> I dreamt that they were filled with dew;
> And when I awoke, it rained. (292-300)

First, rescued from his internal imprisonment to narcissism and despair, the Mariner trades in his life-in-death over-self-consciousness for several hours of peaceful, angst-free sleep. Second, the physical thirst that has tormented him as greatly as his internal dryness is brought to an end when a shower of rain falls upon the ship and fills up its empty ("silly") buckets. According to the Mariner, both of these ministries are performed by the Virgin Mary, an allusion that lends the poem a distinctly Catholic sensibility which increases its supernatural, sacramental aura.

Significantly, Coleridge links together these two divine ministrations by having the Mariner dream of rain and then wake to find it true. I say significant because in Milton's telling of the creation of Eve out of the side of the sleeping Adam, he adds a detail not mentioned in Genesis: Adam dreams the creation of Eve and then wakes to find his dream a reality. John Keats famously alludes to this memorable detail from *Paradise Lost* while attempting, in one of his letters, to define the imagination: "The

Imagination may be compared to Adam's dream—he awoke and found it truth" (1210). Could there be any greater or more mystical instance of the externalization of the internal than this: that someone could dream a thing and then find that very thing materialized in the "real" world? That the Mariner experiences such a rare Romantic "wish fulfillment" bodes well for his healing and restoration.

The Circular Journey Home

Over the next 150 lines of poetry, the Mariner recounts his further adventures, recording as he goes moments both of ghastly horror and scintillating beauty. Out there, in that strange and terrifying world that lies beyond the borders of innocence, dwell wonders untold, but to see the angelic visions one must face as well the darkness that chills the bones. The same Dante who hears the heavenly choirs in Paradise hears first the groaning of the damned.

In the end, after his ship has been driven northward by benevolent spirits, the Mariner looks up from the deck to see—wonder of wonders—that he has returned home:

> Oh! dream of joy! is this indeed
> The light-house top I see?
> Is this the hill? is this the kirk?
> Is this mine own countree?
>
> We drifted o'er the harbour-bar,
> And I with sobs did pray—
> O let me be awake, my God!
> Or let me sleep alway. (464-471)

His journey has been a circular one, but, like Odysseus returned to Ithaca or a questing knight returned to Camelot, it has left him on a higher level of wisdom and understanding. Even so, the human race had to lose Eden that they might, after millennia of weary searching, find a new, but surpassingly greater Eden that the book of Revelation calls the New Jerusalem. Or, as T. S. Eliot explains it near the end of *Little Gidding* (the fourth of his *Four Quartets*): "And the end of all our exploring / Will be to arrive where we started / And know the place for the first time."

Coleridge's *Rime* is divided into Seven Parts. His first sight of home occurs midway through Part 6, but it is not until Part 7 that his ship nears the harbor and he sets foot again on his "own countree." In both the Judeo-Christian and Greco-Roman traditions the number seven is imbued with great spiritual significance. Indeed, as I argued in my analysis of "We are Seven," the number often represents wholeness and completion. For the Mariner, whose supernatural journey has not only brought him self-knowledge but opened his eyes to the mystical cords that bind the natural, the human, and the divine, his homecoming marks his attainment of the final, culminating level of wisdom.

But his special penance is such that he cannot stop there. The man whose crime it was to destroy fellowship and exacerbate the alienation between both man and beast and the natural and supernatural realms must not be allowed to hoard his hard-won knowledge. He must share that knowledge, must become, like the prophet Ezekiel, a living, breathing allegory (see Ezekiel 12). The teller must *become* his tale.

The moment the Mariner sets foot on land, he turns to a hermit who lives by the sea and ministers to sailors and begs the holy man to hear his confession, to absolve him of guilt, and to set forth his penance:

> "O shrieve me, shrieve me, holy man!"
> The Hermit crossed his brow.
> "Say quick," quoth he, "I bid thee say—
> What manner of man art thou?"
>
> Forthwith this frame of mine was wrenched
> With a woful agony,
> Which forced me to begin my tale;
> And then it left me free.
>
> Since then, at an uncertain hour,
> That agony returns:
> And till my ghastly tale is told,
> This heart within me burns.
>
> I pass, like night, from land to land;
> I have strange power of speech;
> That moment that his face I see,
> I know the man that must hear me:
> To him my tale I teach. (574-590)

Henceforth, the Mariner will live the life of a pilgrim, wandering from land to land and telling his cautionary tale to all who have ears to hear. Partly like Abraham, partly like the Israelites in the wilderness, and party like Cain, he shall live as a stranger and a sojourner, a border figure belonging to no one and no place. He shall endure what Coleridge, in his gloss to lines 574-577, calls "the penance of life," but his endurance shall prove a blessing to mankind. As the apostles at Pentecost (Acts 2) were granted the power to speak in other languages that they might share the good news with the whole world, so the Mariner is gifted with a "strange power of speech" that allows him to communicate his tale to those in distant lands.

Earlier, I argued that the scene in which the Mariner sucks his own blood that he might free his lips to speak was meant by Coleridge to function in part as a metaphor for the Romantic poet who writes out of his pain. Here, in detailing the Mariner's life-long penance, Coleridge clarifies and develops this metaphoric link. Neither an artisan nor a patronized member of the court, the Romantic poet creates because he *must* create, because the feelings and passions within him *compel* him to create Just as the word of God burns like fire in the bones of the prophet Jeremiah (Jeremiah 20:9), so does the fire of inspiration rage within the breast of the Romantic poet-prophet. The Romantic poet's ability to externalize in words his internal struggles and moods is, in some senses, a blessing and a gift. But it is a gift that is also a curse, for it drives him relentlessly to relive and re-experience his deepest and most personal anguish. At times, he, like the Mariner, is verily possessed by the inspiration that seizes him and drags out of him the words he may not always wish to speak.

Nevertheless, he *must* speak, and as he must speak, so we must listen, mesmerized, as the wedding guest is by the Mariner. His tale complete, the Mariner explains the simple yet profound lesson that his journey—both external and internal—has taught him:

> O Wedding-Guest! this soul hath been
> Alone on a wide wide sea:
> So lonely 'twas, that God himself
> Scarce seeméd there to be.
>
> O sweeter than the marriage-feast,
> 'Tis sweeter far to me,
> To walk together to the kirk
> With a goodly company!—
>
> To walk together to the kirk,
> And all together pray,
> While each to his great Father bends,
> Old men, and babes, and loving friends
> And youths and maidens gay!
>
> Farewell, farewell! but this I tell
> To thee, thou Wedding-Guest!
> He prayeth well, who loveth well

> Both man and bird and beast.
>
> He prayeth best, who loveth best
> All things both great and small;
> For the dear God who loveth us,
> He made and loveth all. (597-617)

Though this "moral" may seem somewhat trite to modern readers, and even a bit anti-climactic, it does flow quite naturally out of the Mariner's crime and penance. As Coleridge explains in his gloss to lines 610-613, the Mariner's poetic-prophetic commission is "to teach, by his own example, love and reverence to all things that God made and loveth." Or, to express it another way, his calling is to proclaim what Blake proclaims in the last line of *The Marriage of Heaven and Hell*: "For every thing that lives is Holy" (216).

In killing the albatross, the Mariner violated the sacred relationship between guest and host and breached the delicate balance between God, man, and nature. In fulfilling his calling, he witnesses to the need for unity, fellowship, and mutual regard and respect for all forms of life. And he witnesses to something else, something more personal that his trials have taught him: that a congregation at prayer can be a more joyous thing than a wedding feast; that when people of all ages join hands to praise the great Father in heaven their unified voice composes a hymn that surpasses in beauty, sweetness, and resonance even the marriage song of bride and groom.

So shares the Mariner his high Romantic vision of fusion and synthesis; then, like a phantom or a dream, he disappears into the night:

> The Mariner, whose eye is bright,
> Whose beard with age is hoar,
> Is gone: and now the Wedding-Guest
> Turned from the bridegroom's door.
>
> He went like one that hath been stunned,
> And is of sense forlorn:
> A sadder and a wiser man,
> He rose the morrow morn. (618-625)

Through the vicarious ministry of the Mariner, the wedding guest has passed safely from innocence to experience without having to suffer the pain that such a transition usually entails. In that sense, the Mariner truly functions as a scapegoat, as one who bridges the gap between death and renewal and who buys us wisdom at a terrible price. And in that sense too, the Romantic poet is himself something of a scapegoat, subjecting himself to the terrors and the anguish of human passion that he might bring back to the world a message of hope, of beauty, and of joy.

VIII
The Dark Side of Inspiration

Though most readers are familiar with the title of Coleridge's poem "Kubla Khan," far fewer could tell you the full title that Coleridge gave to his strangely beautiful (and beautifully strange) lyric: "Kubla Khan, Or, A Vision in a Dream. A Fragment." Each of the three nouns that make up Coleridge's subtitle is vital, not only for a proper understanding of the poem but of Romanticism itself. For each word points to the link between poetry and prophecy that lies at the heart of so many of the great Romantic poems. Whether it be in the melancholy Voice of the Bard that narrates the *Songs of Experience*, in the apocalyptic fervor that proclaims the *Marriage of Heaven and Hell*, in the naïve faith of the child protagonist of "We are Seven" who sees the unbroken connection between the living and the dead, in the joyous, natural mysticism that encourages us to cultivate wise passiveness and to let nature be our teacher in "Expostulation and Reply" and "The Tables Turned," or, supremely, in the penance of life that compels the Mariner to tell his tale again and again, the essentially prophetic nature of Romantic poetry is everywhere evident in the work of Blake, Wordsworth, Coleridge, and their fellow poets.

It is certainly evident in all its fullness in "Kubla Khan," and not only in the poem itself.

The Ultimate Romantic Fantasy

When Coleridge published "Kubla Khan" in 1816, nearly two decades after he had composed it in1797 (or perhaps 1798), he appended a note to it that must, I would argue, be accounted, and read as, an integral part of the poem. I quote the note at some length for it helps provide us with the key to understanding the relationship of the words "Vision,"

"Dream," and "Fragment" in Coleridge's subtitle:

> In the summer of the year 1797 the Author, then in ill-health, had retired to a lonely farm-house between Porlock and Linton, on the Exmoor confines of Somerset and Devonshire. In consequence of a slight indisposition, an anodyne had been prescribed, from the effects of which he fell asleep in his chair at the moment he was reading the following sentence, or words of the same substance, in Purchas's *Pilgrimage*: "Here the Khan Kubla commanded a palace to be built, and a stately garden thereunto: and thus ten miles of fertile ground were inclosed with a wall." The Author continued for about three hours in a profound sleep, at least of the external senses, during which time he has the most vivid confidence, that he could not have composed less than from two to three hundred lines; if that indeed can be called composition in which all the images rose up before him as *things*, with a parallel production of the correspondent expressions, without any sensation or consciousness of effort. On awakening he appeared to himself to have a distinct recollection of the whole, and taking his pen, ink, and paper, instantly and eagerly wrote down the lines that are here preserved. At this moment he was unfortunately called out by a person on business from Porlock, and detained by him above an hour, and on his return to his room, found, to his no small surprise and mortification, that though he still retained some vague and dim recollection of the general purport of the vision, yet, with the exception of some eight or ten scattered lines and images, all the rest had passed away like the images on the surface of a stream into which a stone has been cast, but, alas! without the after restoration of the latter! (391)

The anodyne to which Coleridge refers is opium, a drug whose harmful properties and addictive nature were not fully understood at the time. According to Coleridge, the opium cast him into a state which he describes as "a profound sleep, at least of the external senses." But what exactly was the nature of this state? The poet seems sure that his external senses were asleep, but what of his mind: was that asleep, awake, or in some strange middle state? Did Coleridge have a "Vision" or a "Dream"? Are the two things the same or different?

The great prophets of the Bible seem themselves to have been unclear as to the exact nature of the prophetic state. Surely when we read the writings of Isaiah or Ezekiel or John, it is not easy to say whether the

Lord spoke to them while they were awake, asleep, or in some kind of a waking trance. For Romantic poets (and their heirs) the exact state of the inspired bard is itself a difficult thing to determine. In what category shall we place the poet who conceives his poem in a fit of inspiration? Is he active or passive, conscious or unconscious, awake or asleep? One thing at least is clear. Those who receive their images from vivid dreams or prophetic visions or drug-induced reveries or flashes of inspiration do not themselves have control over those images. That is why those who rely upon visions and dreams—whatever their source or the nature of their transmission—often end up producing "Fragments": either unfinished poems or works that, like Isaiah and Revelation, are fragmentary in nature. Or both. When Coleridge is interrupted by the businessman from Porlock, his reverie leaves him, and his would-be poetic masterpiece is put down, never to be taken up again. It will remain but the shadow of what might have been, in a disjointed, fragmentary form that has frustrated the attempts of two centuries of students and critics to arrive at a definitive interpretation.

The poet-artisan, guided by the rules of decorum and his own sense of balance and harmony, works away at his poem until it has achieved the desired shape and form. The poet-prophet, guided by inspiration and by his own willingness to be a vessel *of* that inspiration, awaits the longed-for arrival of the vision (or dream) and then creates feverishly until it departs. The former trusts to his skill, while the latter trusts to his imagination; but it is an imagination that dwells in close proximity with the visionary states of the poet, the dreamer, the prophet, and, at least in "Kubla Khan," the opium eater. For the Romantic poet, imagination is more than a tool for fashioning similes and metaphors; it is, rather, a kind of sacred energy: both a spell by which to conjure images from the depths of the soul, and a conduit for channeling, shaping, and fusing these images into new forms. Likewise, the poet is more than a dedicated craftsman; he is an intoxicated visionary, drunk on the spirit—whether that spirit be man-made or God-made. Just as the Oracle of Delphi breathed in the vapors from the earth before going into her prophetic trance, so the Romantic poet must open himself to the shattering force of the imagination before he can enter that visionary, dream-like state that is the very womb of poetry.

Having said all this, I must now pause and make a somewhat stunning confession. I do not think that we can necessarily believe everything that Coleridge says in his note to "Kubla Khan." In saying that, I no more accuse Coleridge of bald-faced lying than I would a romantic lover who tells everyone that he and his wife fell madly in love at first sight when that really was not the case. The question is not one of sincerity but of the power of illusion and wish-fulfillment to shape our memories of past events. For you see, whether or not the composition of "Kubla Khan" occurred in exactly the way Coleridge says it did, what he does describe in his note is nothing less than the ultimate Romantic fantasy. Any of the Romantic poets would have sacrificed much to experience firsthand a "composition in which all the images rose up before him as *things* . . . without any sensation or consciousness of effort." Which is not to say that Romantic poets are like lazy college students who hope and pray that inspiration (or God!) will write their paper *for* them. It was because the Romantics valued so highly fresh, direct, unmediated spontaneity that they yearned to break forth in unpremeditated song and to feel the force of inspiration flow through them in all its purity.

And they yearned for something else as well, something that Coleridge claims to have experienced in composing "Kubla Khan." Not only did "all the images [rise] up before him as things"; they rose up "with a parallel production of the correspondent expressions." What Coleridge is here suggesting is that inspiration fashioned through him an at once mystical and aesthetic incarnation of image and word, content and form. In a series of three essays known collectively as "Essays Upon Epitaphs," Wordsworth seeks for just this kind of incarnation, for a language that will not be "what the garb is to the body but what the body is to the soul." Indeed, Wordsworth goes so far as to assert that if "words be not . . . an incarnation of the thought but only a clothing for it, then surely will they prove an ill gift."[8]

As it offers direct insight into the nature of Coleridge's Romantic fantasy, Wordsworth's subtle but incisive distinction is worth drawing out. Before I headed to work this morning, I covered my body with a red shirt and a pair of navy slacks. Both the shirt and the slacks were so designed as to conform to the rough contours of my arms, legs, and torso. There exists, however, no organic relationship between my body and my clothes. Before going to bed, I tossed both articles of clothing into the hamper without compromising in any way my arms, legs, or torso. Not so the relationship between my body and my soul. My flesh is more than a mere covering for my soul. My soul expresses itself through my flesh even as my flesh is animated—and, I hope, guided—by my soul. What is

---

8   William Wordsworth, "Essays Upon Epitaphs," in *The Prose Works of William Wordsworth*, edited by W. J. B. Owen and J. W. Smyser (Oxford: Clarendon Press), Volume I, page 84.

so wonderful about Coleridge's description of the composition process of "Kubla Khan" is that he suggests that flesh-like words rose up together with soul-like images to produce, albeit in fragmented form, a perfect incarnation of the two. So often when a poet attempts to write a poem, his words prove a woefully inadequate medium for embodying his thoughts, feelings, and images. But what if he could find words that would not only express but externalize and give concrete shape to those thoughts, feelings, and images? That is what Coleridge celebrates in his note to "Kubla Khan," what Wordsworth calls for in his "Essays Upon Epitaphs," and what all Romantic poets yearn to achieve as the end product of their dream-visions, their visionary dreams, and their prophetic utterances.

He on Honeydew hath Fed

The opening lines of "Kubla Khan" possess the rare, incantatory power to instantly sweep us away from the mundane world of our daily lives to the dream world of the imagination:

> In Xanadu did Kubla Khan
>
> A stately pleasure-dome decree:
> Where Alph, the sacred river, ran
> Through caverns measureless to man
>
> Down to a sunless sea. (1-5)

The strange yet somehow familiar names and places, the flow of the verse, the sound of the words: all work on us their fairy magic and make us feel as though we have been physically transported to Xanadu. We are invited not so much to read Coleridge's poem as to participate in his reverie.

At first we enter willingly into Coleridge's vision, but as we move through the poem, we become confused and unsettled. Things are not what they seemed at first to be:

> So twice five miles of fertile ground
> With walls and towers were girdled round:
> And there were gardens bright with sinuous rills,
> Where blossomed many an incense-bearing tree;
> And here were forests ancient as the hills,
>
> Enfolding sunny spots of greenery.
>
> But oh! that deep romantic chasm which slanted
> Down the green hill athwart a cedarn cover!
> A savage place! as holy and enchanted

> As e'er beneath a waning moon was haunted
> By woman wailing for her demon-lover! (6-16)

I argued above that the author of "Kubla Khan" is a poet, dreamer, and prophet in one, and indeed, the passage just quoted shares the vivid, disjointed, symbol-laden qualities of those enigmatic, often terrifying episodes that populate both the prophetic books of the Bible (Daniel and Revelation in particular) and our own personal nightmares. The symbols and episodes of the poem come at us, as they do in our dreams, in a swirl of sights and sounds that defy logical arrangement. As the poem proceeds, all sense of continuity and transition breaks down: opposites are juxtaposed and fused; places and figures appear, disappear, then appear once again. It is as if the binding of a book had snapped and the leaves, like those of the prophetic Sibyl in Virgil's *Aeneid*, had become loosened and detached, left to scatter and float on the wandering breeze. The critic who would make sense of "Kubla Khan" must, like a Freudian psychoanalyst, reassemble the fragments of the poem into a psychic narrative whose structural key is more emotional than intellectual, more intuitive than rational. We must leave behind the walled and ordered polis of Apollo (the "Enlightenment" god of order, balance, and harmony) and enter into the holy, savage forest of Dionysus (the "Romantic" god of intuition, intoxication, and excess).

Still, the poem does seem to be leading us somewhere. Past the encircling walls, the fragrant gardens, and the ancient forests, we are led inexorably to the "deep romantic chasm," a sacred, primal place haunted by man's deepest passions and fears. The chasm is a volcano, but it is also, like one of Blake's earth goddesses, a titan in labor:

> And from this chasm, with ceaseless turmoil seething,
> As if this earth in fast thick pants were breathing,
>
> A mighty fountain momently was forced:
> Amid whose swift half-intermitted burst
> Huge fragments vaulted like rebounding hail,
>
> Or chaffy grain beneath the thresher's flail:
> And 'mid these dancing rocks at once and ever
> It flung up momently the sacred river. (17-24)

Coleridge's fragmentary dream-vision carries us to the very birthing-place of Orcic energy, to the fiery abyss out of which inspiration flows like a mighty fountain. Here, we learn, is the source of all that the poet most desires; here may we gaze with awe and dread on the imagination in its rawest form.

But there is a dark side:

> Five miles meandering with a mazy motion
> Through wood and dale the sacred river ran,
> Then reached the caverns measureless to man,
> And sank in tumult to a lifeless ocean:
> And 'mid this tumult Kubla heard from far
> Ancestral voices prophesying war! (25-30)

Just as the phantasmagoric burst of creativity that opium inspires in its user is quickly followed by an almost existential deadness of emotion and spirit, so the poet who opens himself too fully to the power of Orc may find himself in the end drained of all will and desire, his dreams and visions sunk in a "lifeless ocean." Those who are lifted most high by inspiration suffer the most when inspiration leaves them. With the joy, the vision, the rapture, there comes as well the danger of slipping into the abyss. We may at first think it odd that when Kubla hears the tumultuous explosion of the chasm he does not hear in it the sound of imagination or inspiration but the dread prophecy of a coming war. That is, until we recall that Orc embodies both the healing, life-giving power of creativity and the destructive, apocalyptic force of revolution. The Storming of the Bastille and the Reign of Terror, we must remember, both sprang from the same Orcic crucible.

For a moment, all seems lost. Inspiration and its attendant vision have been swallowed by the lifeless ocean, leaving the poet empty and dry. And then, softly, gently, like the still, small voice that Elijah hears when the wind and earthquake and fire have died away (see 1 Kings 19:11-13), an image of pure beauty and romance drifts before the mind's eye of the poet:

> The shadow of the dome of pleasure
> Floated midway on the waves;
> Where was heard the mingled measure
>
> From the fountain and the caves.
>
> It was a miracle of rare device,
> A sunny pleasure-dome with caves of ice! (31-36)

For both Coleridge and Wordsworth one of the key functions of the imagination was to discover similitude in the midst of dissimilitude and thus effect a new incarnation out of previously discordant elements. Something similar happens in our dreams when we find ourselves in the bedroom of our home, but, when we look out the window, we see not the landscape behind our house but the backyard, say, of our grandmother's house. Or perhaps we meet people or visit places that are a combination of various people and places we have known in our lives. In the world of logic and rationality, there can be no traffic between sunny domes and caves of ice, but in the beautiful and terrible world of Orcic inspiration such things can happen and such things can *be*.

Fast on the heels of this lovely if paradoxical vision, there arises a second vision that seems to have no logical connection to the first:

> A damsel with a dulcimer
> In a vision once I saw:
> It was an Abyssinian maid,
> And on her dulcimer she played,
> Singing of Mount Abora. (37-41)

Coleridge is probably alluding to one of the nine muses that the ancient Greeks believed inspired poetry and the arts, but he defamiliarizes this well-worn allusion by his use of magical place names and the delicious liquidity of his phrasing and diction. Through our participation in Coleridge's fragmented reverie, we catch a glimpse of an ethereal, Apollonian inspiration to balance the violent, Dionysian energy of the deep romantic chasm.

As quickly as the two visions come, they depart from before the eyes of the poet. But not before he gives voice to a desire that all Romantic poets nurture within their hearts:

> Could I revive within me
> Her symphony and song,
> To such a deep delight 'twould win me,
>
> That with music loud and long,
> I would build that dome in air,
> That sunny dome! those caves of ice!
> And all who heard should see them there . . . (42-48)

What if, the poet asks, I could "revive within" myself that initial burst of inspiration in all its freshness and purity? What if I could hold on to it until it yielded up all its wonder-working powers? Then, truly, could I build poetic castles in the air; then could I bring to shimmering life whatever lurks in the caverns of my mind's eye.

In his "ultra-Romantic" essay, "A Defense of Poetry," Percy Bysshe Shelley, while expressing the same desire as the speaker of "Kubla Khan," explains why such a desire cannot be realized in our world:

> Poetry is not like reasoning, a power to be exerted according to the determination of the will. A man cannot say, "I will compose poetry." The greatest poet even cannot say it; for the mind in creation is as a fading coal, which some invisible influence, like an inconstant wind, awakens to transitory brightness; this power arises from within, like the color of a flower which fades and changes as it is developed, and the conscious portions of our natures are unprophetic either of its approach or its departure. Could this influence be durable in its original purity and force, it is impossible to predict the greatness of the results; but when composition begins, inspiration is already on the decline, and the most glorious poetry that has ever been communicated to the world is probably a feeble shadow of the original conception of the Poet. (1109)

The problem, laments Shelley, is that we have no control over the winds of inspiration; we cannot even say for sure when they will come or when they will depart. The creation of poetry is not something we can will into existence as a carpenter might a table or a potter a vase. We must simply wait for the inspiration to fall, knowing all along that even when it does fall, the poem that results will be but a shadow of what was intended. Worse yet, when the power comes and inspiration begins to burn like fire in our bones, the very act of tapping that fire will hasten its extinction. Like a "fading coal," the more fiercely it burns, the more quickly it burns out.

There is, however, one thing of which both Shelly and Coleridge are sure. *If* they could hold on to that inspiration in its "original purity and force," then would they be able to do and create anything they desired. Then could they build in air a true dome of poetry that all would see and all would praise. Then would they truly become Romantic poet-prophets. But, of course, they cannot, and that "cannot" lies at the core of so much Romantic angst and despair.

Here then, we expect, Coleridge will end his poem with frustration at his inability to sustain the intensity of inspiration. But instead he surprises us with an ending that takes Romantic wish-fulfillment to its final, triumphant, dreadful extreme. As the poem rushes to its close, the poet suddenly gets what he has so long desired. He builds that dome in air, and the people who hear his words see the dome for themselves. But their reaction, far from one of praise, is one of sheer panic and horror:

> And all who heard should see them there,
> And all should cry, Beware! Beware!
> His flashing eyes, his floating hair!
> Weave a circle round him thrice,
> And close your eyes with holy dread,
> For he on honey-dew hath fed,
> And drunk the milk of Paradise. (48-54)

For the second time in the poem, the dark side of Romantic inspiration snares the poet. Too late he learns a terrible truth: if someone could embody in himself all the force of inspiration, if he could truly evolve into a divine poet-prophet, then would he become an outcast, a contagion to the earth. People would shun his wild eyes and his mad gaze. He would become, at best, a border figure like the ancient Mariner, unable to join in the life around him, condemned to wander, lonely and isolated, from land to land. At worst, he would cease to be human.

As far back as ancient Greece and Rome, Plato and Horace had warned against the dangers of divine madness. In his dialogue, *Ion*, Plato has Socrates assert that poets do not write by art or skill. Far from understanding (rationally) what they create, they are carried away (irrationally) by a divine inspiration that literally possesses them:

> For all good poets, epic as well as lyric, compose their beautiful poems not by art, but because they are inspired and possessed. And as the Korybantian revelers when they dance are not in their right mind, so the lyric poets are not in their right mind when they are composing their beautiful strains: but when falling under the power of music and meter they are inspired and possessed; like Bacchic maidens who draw milk and honey from the rivers when they are under the influence of Dionysus but not when there are in their right mind. . . . the poet is a light and winged and holy thing, and there is no invention in him until he has been inspired and is out of his senses, and reason is no longer in him: no man, while he retains that faculty, has the oracular gift of poetry.[9]

Though Coleridge's references to "honeydew" and "milk of paradise" in the last two line of his poem are meant, I would argue, to refer to opium (hence the necessity of reading the note as an integral part of the poem), I believe that they also allude to this passage from Plato's *Ion*. Of course, whereas Plato—he who kicked the poets out of his ideal Republic—meant

---

9   Plato, *Ion*, in *Critical Theory Since Plato*, Revised Edition, edited by Hazard Adams (New York: HBJ, 1992), 14.

his words as a critique of poetry, Coleridge, as a Romantic poet, celebrated the fact that poetry relied more on inspiration than on reason and was essentially oracular, or prophetic, in nature.

Still, both Plato and Coleridge were aware of the dangers of Dionysus. The Bacchic maidens to whom Plato refers—known also as Bacchae or Maenads—were wild women who followed in the train of the Greek god of the grape. Intoxicated by the physical and spiritual wine of Dionysus, they abandoned the polis and lived in the woods among ferocious beasts. They represent the breakdown of Apollonian order and rationality and the primal, enthusiastic embrace of instinct and intuition. On one level they embody the very heart and soul of nature; in Euripides' play, *The Bacchae*, they are even described as offering their breasts to suckle fawns. But here too there is a dark side. When the protagonist of Euripides' play (Pentheus) spies on their Bacchic rites, they go insane and, with the superhuman strength given them by the god, tear him limb from limb. Those who feed on wild milk and honey, whether they be Maenads or Romantic poets, cannot simply return to the farm when the fit of intoxication leaves them.

Nearly four centuries after the Greek Plato compared the poet to a Bacchic reveler, the Roman Horace added his own touch to Plato's portrait of the mad poet. In Horace's more satirical *Art of Poetry*, he playfully describes the reaction that such poets elicit from society:

> As people avoid someone afflicted with the itch, with jaundice, the fits, or insanity, so sensible men stay clear of a mad poet. Children tease him and rash fools follow him. Spewing out verses, he wanders off, with his head held high, like a fowler with his eyes on the blackbirds: and if he falls into a well or ditch, he may call, out, "Help, fellow citizens!"—but no one cares to help him.... He is mad, at any rate; and like a bear that has been strong enough to break the bars of its cage, he frightens away both the learned and the ignorant by reciting his verses. If he catches a victim, he clings to him and reads him to death, like a leech that will not leave the skin until it is filled with blood.[10]

This remarkable passage, the last sentence of which reads like a parody of the opening stanzas of *The Rime of the Ancient Mariner*, adds to Plato's portrait a sense of the poet as one who is so diseased that people must avoid him lest they be infected themselves. One can almost hear

---

10   Horace, *Art of Poetry*, in *Critical Theory Since Plato*, 74.

Horace advising his readers to "Weave a circle round him thrice / And close [their] eyes with holy dread." However, what Horace says mostly in jest, Coleridge echoes with gravity and fear. He understands the risks of playing with fire.

Aside from the beauty of its lyricism and the power of its images, "Kubla Khan" must be read as both an invitation and a warning to the would-be Romantic poet. Orcic energy offers gifts most precious to the poet-prophet, but beneath its divine promises lurk satanic dangers. Let us not, in seeking to rise above our human capacity for wisdom and understanding find that we have sunk below it. Let us not, in seeking to become an angel, find we have become a beast. Let us not tread the path of Satan and of Nebuchadnezzar (see Daniel 4). That way madness lies.

The Byronic Hero

The story is told a hundred different ways in a hundred different cultures. The young, untested hero travels blissfully along the road in search of adventure and meets, instead, the devil. And there, at the crossroads, he sells his soul for a "year at the top." It matters little what his dearly-bought year will bring him—fame, fortune, desire, talent. It matters even less if his initial motivation seems honorable: to unlock the secrets of immortality (like Dr. Frankenstein) or to release mankind from his bestial side (like Dr. Jekyll) or to bring about world peace (like Captain Nemo). Indeed, he may not even meet the devil himself. What he encounters at the crossroads may simply be the lure of forbidden knowledge . . . and of the power that such knowledge always promises to bring.

These Faustian anti-heroes have always been with us, but their numbers vastly increased, and have continued to increase, since Rousseau and the French Revolution proclaimed throughout Europe their belief that man's potential is unlimited and that he is the maker of his own destiny. In the wake of the Revolution, the Romantic poet Lord Byron wrote a dozen or so popular verse romances about passionate young men who commit an unforgivable sin; as a result, they—like the ancient Mariner and the speaker of "Kubla Khan"—become lonely wanderers and outcasts who can no longer dwell within the circle of humanity. Though these "oriental tales" have been all but forgotten today—their exotic titles include *The Prisoner of Chillon, The Corsair, Lara, The Giaour, The Bride of Abydos*, and *The Siege of Corinth*—their moody, passionate, tormented protagonists captured the imagination of Europe and ensured that such figures would henceforth bear the generic title of Byronic hero.

The life-cycle of the Byronic hero always begins with the breaching of some type of taboo (Adam eating the forbidden fruit; Cain killing his brother; Prometheus stealing the fire; Oedipus marrying his mother; the Ancient Mariner shooting the albatross), an act that, whether nobly or basely motivated, manifests itself ultimately as an act of rebellion and defiance. They soon discover that the fruit is sour, that their action has made them both a curse and a contagion, but they have progressed too far in their sin to go back and, in any case, are too proud to seek forgiveness (Macbeth, Heathcliff, Ahab, Dorian Gray, etc.). For Christians, the ultimate example of this figure is Satan, the fallen archangel who is not only himself the great Byronic hero but who would—in accordance with the ethos of hell: misery loves company—tempt all of us to become little byronic heroes. For those who do not accept the literal existence of the Devil, the Byronic hero reaches its fullest embodiment in Satan's legendary, mythopoeic counterpart: Count Dracula, the Prince of Darkness who lives on the borders of society, feeds on human blood, and fears the Cross. Indeed, popular culture in America is overrun with Byronic heroes: from the Mummy and the Wolfman to the Highlander and Darth Vader to the innumerable dark, vigilante-like superheroes who populate the pages of comic books and graphic novel and who have come to dominate movie screens since the late 1990's. It is not too much to say that our modern—and now postmodern—age is obsessed with the Byronic hero, with his willingness to risk all for forbidden knowledge, his self-inflicted torment and agony, his tragic greatness.

My decision to keep the focus of this book on short, lyrical poetry prevents me from considering either Byron's oriental tales or his two truly great and lasting embodiments of the Byronic hero: *Childe Harold's Pilgrimage* and *Manfred*; in any case, the subject of the Byronic hero requires its own book-length study. Still, as this subject does have bearing on the themes of this book, and as the Byronic hero represents, to my mind at least, Byron's central contribution to Romanticism (*Don Juan* is more an eighteenth century work than a Romantic one), I would like to look briefly at what is surely Byron's finest short treatment of the subject, "Prometheus."

As I explained in my analysis of Blake's "The Tyger," the Romantics tended to look upon the Greek Titan who stole the fire from Zeus and gave it to man as a combination of Satan (the rebel who defies the authority of God) and of Christ (the willing scapegoat who suffers that man might gain wisdom and truth). In his poem, Byron presents his hero as one whose kindness and whose capacity for suffering are matched only by his monumental pride:

> Titan! to whose immortal eyes
> The sufferings of mortality,
> Seen in their sad reality,
> Were not as things that gods despise;
> What was thy pity's recompense?
> A silent suffering, and intense;
> The rock, the vulture, and the chain,
> All that the proud can feel of pain,
> The agony they do not show,
> The suffocating sense of woe,
> Which speaks but in its loneliness,
> And then is jealous lest the sky
> Should have a listener, nor will sigh
> Until its voice is echoless. (1-14)

Ironically, Prometheus's theft of the "forbidden fruit" has cut him off from the very humans he risked all to save. With great pity he looked upon the "sufferings of mortality," but the deed he performed to alleviate those sufferings has condemned him to a lonely, silent, and agonizing penance, enacted in total isolation from all human life. The wisdom Prometheus has filched from Zeus has not enhanced his fellowship with man; it has ended it. Just so the poet-prophet of "Kubla Khan," in seeking to bring before mortal eyes the vision of the "sunny dome" and "caves of ice," finds himself the object, not of love and thankfulness, but of fear and even horror.

Prometheus, the Mariner, and the speaker of "Kubla Khan" have all learned, in their own way, the hard truth that Solomon learned so long ago: "For in much wisdom is much grief: and he that increaseth knowledge, increaseth sorrow" (Ecclesiastes 1:18). Or, to borrow an old adage: "Be careful what you wish for; you may have the misfortune to get it." Romantics suffer from perpetual melancholy because they cannot surpass the limits of reason, of mortality, of brute matter. They yearn with every fiber of their being to be special, to have prophetic insight, to be bearers of the divine word. And yet, if they achieve their goal, their melancholy is only increased. In the end, their last refuge is pride, pride that they alone can bear what they bear and suffer what they suffer. Thus, Prometheus refuses to show his agony and is "jealous lest the sky /

Should have a listener." The extreme Romantic wears his specialness as a badge of honor; he will not be pitied nor turned from his course. He will be his own executioner.

According to Byron, the greatest pain that Zeus inflicts upon his victim is to refuse him "even the boon to die: / The wretched gift eternity / Was thine" (23-25). Prometheus will know no rest either from the external pain of the vulture who feeds on his liver or the internal pain of his own tormented self-consciousness. Nevertheless, Byron exults, "thou hast born it well" (25). Prometheus' consolation comes from the fact that he alone can carry the burden laid upon him. Though the analogy may strike some readers as odd, we may label as an extreme Promethean Romantic the 1960's radical icon, Timothy Leary. Leary, and others like him, truly believed that by experimenting with LSD and other "mind-expanding" drugs, he could open his psyche to higher levels of consciousness. Through subjecting his body to the "discipline" of a whole range of modern opiates, he hoped to gain access to knowledge that he could then share with his fellow mortals. In the end, Leary, though he brought back precious little wisdom, did much harm to his body and mind. Still, like Prometheus, like the Byronic hero, like many of the Romantic poets themselves, Leary bore to the end his "penance of life," never recanting his choice to feed on honeydew, to drink the milk of paradise, and to take into himself the full energy of Orc.

In the third and final stanza of his poem—a stanza composed of one single labyrinthine sentence whose tortured syntax twists and turns through twenty five lines of verse—Byron takes us to the core of the Promethean spirit, holding it up as a symbol and sign of Man himself:

> Thy Godlike crime was to be kind,
> To render with thy precepts less
> The sum of human wretchedness,
> And strengthen Man with his own mind;
> But baffled as thou wert from high,
> Still in thy patient energy,
> In the endurance, and repulse
> Of thine impenetrable Spirit,
> Which Earth and Heaven could not convulse,
> A mighty lesson we inherit:
> Thou art a symbol and a sign
>
> To Mortals of their fate and force;
> Like thee, Man is in part divine,
> A troubled stream from a pure source;

> And Man in portions can foresee
> His own funereal destiny;
> His wretchedness, and his resistance,
> And his sad unallied existence:
> To which his Spirit may oppose
> Itself—and equal to all woes,
> And a firm will, and a deep sense,
> Which even in torture can descry
> Its own concenter'd recompense,
> Triumphant where it dares defy,
> And making Death a Victory. (35-59)

Though guilty of a crime, Byron asserts, his crime was "Godlike," motivated by kindness and a desire to lessen the "sum of human wretchedness." Though that desire is "baffled" by the tyranny of Zeus, Prometheus bears it with patience and endurance. His triumph comes not so much in his success as in the defiance of his "impenetrable Spirit," which cannot be bowed by all the forces of earth and sky. Trapped by a dark fate and by divine powers that transcend his own, Prometheus nevertheless asserts his dignity and nobility. In this he is a type of Man, whom Byron describes hauntingly as a "troubled stream from a pure source." Though, from a Christian standpoint, Byron is as heterodox as Blake, the vision of Man that he offers in this line is not far removed from the orthodox belief that Man was created good (in the image of God) but that he is now fallen, his life subjected to sadness and futility.

For the traditional-minded reader, whether his traditionalism rests on Jewish or Christian doctrine or on an adherence to secular Enlightenment rationalism, Romanticism is something of a mixed blessing. In their courageous desire to press the boundaries and to access wisdom heretofore untapped by man, the Romantics are heroic indeed. But in their strange defiance and pride, in their insistence on lifting veils that were perhaps not meant to be lifted, and in their severing of the very fellowship they so desperately long for, the Romantics are like tempests that stir the still waters or nightmares that trouble our most peaceable dreams.

#

Ironically, although our age remains fixated on the seductive qualities of the Byronic hero, its creator managed, in the three years following "Prometheus," first to internalize him (*Childe Harold's Pilgrimage*, Cantos III and IV), then to perfect him (*Manfred*), and finally, through the healing power of satire, to exorcise him for good (*Don Juan*). Whether or not our age will do the same remains to be seen.

PART THREE

CRISIS AND RESOLUTION

IX
Abundant Recompense

The full title of Wordsworth and Coleridge's era-defining collection of poems is *Lyrical Ballads, with A Few Other Poems*. By "few other poems," the authors appear to be referring to those poems *not* written in rhyming stanzas that imitate the many variations of medieval ballad rhythm. These poems—most notable of which are Coleridge's "The Nightingale" and Wordsworth's "Tintern Abbey"—are written in blank verse: a form that consists of an unrhymed series of ten-syllable lines in which the even syllables are stressed. Milton chose to use this form for *Paradise Lost*, for he felt it came closest to capturing both the stately grandeur and the rush and power of Homer's epic line. Shakespeare, in contrast, used blank verse for most of his soliloquies because of its ability to mimic the movement of the mind in contemplation. Without any rhymes to impede the flow of thought, the long meditative lines of blank verse allow poets to capture each twist and turn of the ruminating mind as it combines ideas and images in a subtle weave of associations.

Wordsworth and Coleridge, skilled as they were with rhyming stanzas, were masters of blank verse. Indeed, their creative work in that form can be favorably compared with that of Shakespeare and Milton. Wordsworth even chose to write his autobiography (*The Prelude*) in the form of a Miltonic blank verse epic. What the two Romantic poets brought to the form was an even greater subtlety that allowed them to employ it as a sort of surgical tool for mental, emotional, and spiritual introspection. In addition to using the form to weave ideas and images, they used it to effect a temporal layering by which past and present could, through the power of memory, exist simultaneously.

Re-Collecting the Past

Although Wordsworth's Preface is concerned mostly with the poems written in ballad rhythm, he does includes a passage that reads like an autobiographical account of how he came to write what is arguably the greatest and most definitive blank verse lyric of the Romantic Age, "Tintern Abbey":

> I have said that poetry is the spontaneous overflow of powerful feelings: it takes its origin from emotion recollected in tranquillity: the emotion is contemplated till, by a species of reaction, the tranquillity gradually disappears, and an emotion, kindred to that which was before the subject of contemplation, is gradually produced, and does itself actually exist in the mind. In this mood successful composition generally begins, and in a mood similar to this it is carried on; but the emotion, of whatever kind and in whatever degree, from various causes, is qualified by various pleasures, so that in describing any passions whatsoever, which are voluntarily described, the mind will, upon the whole, be in a state of enjoyment. (365)

It is significant that Wordsworth uses the word "recollected" rather than "remembered." For Wordsworth, memory was a far more vital and energetic process than it is for most people; it entailed the actual recalling and re-experiencing of a past event. We already saw in Chapter Five that one of Wordsworth's qualifications for a true Romantic poet was someone who could experience absent things as though they were present. In the quoted passage, Wordsworth effects this by so contemplating and re-collecting the emotion linked to the event that the emotion itself resurfaces and is experienced as though it were a present emotion. Of course, such experiences are not to be had simply for the asking: to call back the previous emotion, the poet must be in a state of tranquility; to sustain it, he must remain in a state of enjoyment.

Happily for Wordsworth and his readers, the poet experienced both tranquility and enjoyment when he returned, after an absence of five years, to a place that had long had great significance in his life. Though commonly referred to as "Tintern Abbey," the full title of the poem memorializes the ideal conditions under which the poem was written: "Lines Composed a Few Miles above Tintern Abbey, on Revisiting the Banks of the Wye during a Tour, July 13, 1798." Please note that Wordsworth's perspective is neither beside nor behind Tintern Abbey, but "a few miles above" it. Like Moses, to whom God gave a bird's-eye view of the Holy Land from the top of Mount Nebo (Deuteronomy 34:1-4), Wordsworth's unique vantage point allows him to survey the entire landscape upon which the ruins of the Abbey are situated. And it allows him to do something else as well, something all Romantic poets yearn to do: find a fixed higher ground from which he can survey the personal landscape of his own inner journey.

Wordsworth begins his multi-layered survey with a statement that identifies him immediately as a Romantic poet: "Five years have past; five summers, with the length / Of five long winters" (1-2). From the standpoint of reason and logic, a year is a year is a year, but not when it is perceived through the eyes of a Romantic. As the past five years have been for Wordsworth years of weariness and isolation (of experience rather than innocence, to use Blake's perceptual distinction), each twelve month period has seemed to stretch on for an eon. But now he has returned, and he spends the next twenty lines describing in exquisite detail the peace and tranquility of the landscape that stretches out beneath him.

"Once again" the poet beholds "these steep and lofty cliffs, / That on a wild secluded scene impress / Thoughts of more deep seclusion; and connect / The landscape with the quiet of the sky (4-8). "Once again" he sees "these hedge-rows, hardly hedge-rows, little lines / Of sportive wood run wild: these pastoral farms, / Green to the very door; and wreaths of smoke / Sent up, in silence, from among the trees! (14-18). In the first passage, Wordsworth celebrates the brooding sublimity of the cliffs that seem to press their own seclusion upon his receptive mind; in the second, he celebrates the delicate beauty of the hedgerows that separate field from field in a mad, playful pattern of crisscrossing lines. All is alive, all is in harmony, and all reverberates with an almost palpable silence. The lonely poet—only twenty eight at the time and yet seemingly far older in his mature insight and nostalgic tone—has come home.

Having introduced both the setting and mood of his poem, Wordsworth next goes on to explain the unique and vital ministry that Tintern Abbey and his memories *of* Tintern Abbey have played in his life over the last five years:

> These beauteous forms,
>
> Through a long absence, have not been to me
> As is a landscape to a blind man's eye:
> But oft, in lonely rooms, and 'mid the din
> Of towns and cities, I have owed to them,

> In hours of weariness, sensations sweet,
> Felt in the blood, and felt along the heart;
> And passing even into my purer mind,
> With tranquil restoration: —feelings too
> Of unremembered pleasure: such, perhaps,
> As have no slight or trivial influence
> On that best portion of a good man's life,
> His little, nameless, unremembered, acts
> Of kindness and of love. (22-35)

Here, in the first movement of the poem, Wordsworth reflects with joy and thanksgiving on how the "beauteous forms" of the Wye Valley sustained him through his long sojourn in the city of London. Stranded amidst the unnatural noise and unhealthy fever of the city, the poet had resorted often to his recollections of Tintern Abbey as an outlet of emotional escape, a sort-of psychic safety valve. Far more than mere pretty pictures in the mind, his recollections carry with them a felt weight and presence: felt not just in or by the heart but "*along* the heart." The experience is a tangible and even visceral one for Wordsworth, one that presses down to his very inner being, bringing in its wake a restoration of his lost peace and tranquility.

It brings as well a restoration of lost feelings, feelings linked to what Wordsworth calls, paradoxically, "unremembered pleasures." For Wordsworth, the power of recollection lies in its ability to fuse past emotion and past event, thus uniting subject and object and drawing a single line of sentience between the poet's past and present selves. In recollecting how he once felt, Wordsworth thus recollects as well both what he once did and who he once was. In Book I of *The Prelude*, Wordsworth compares his recollections to seemingly lifeless seeds that were "doomed to sleep / Until maturer seasons called them forth / to impregnate and to elevate the mind" (lines 594-596; final 1850 version). In the process of marrying a portion of his past consciousness with the fullness of his present, the poet brings forth a new and healing birth of "tranquil restoration." And he can do so, in part, because the recollection is itself already the product of a serendipitous marriage between a specific place (Tintern Abbey, for example) and a specific time (one of innocence, goodness, and simple charity). It is for this reason that Wordsworth, in Book XII of *The Prelude*, refers to his recollections, again paradoxically, as "spots of time" (208).

Emotional safety valves, seeds of restoration, preservers of feelings long thought gone: the spots of time linked to Tintern Abbey perform all these functions . . . and something more. In those moments of urban oppression when the poet redirected his full powers of imagination toward re-experiencing his past encounters with nature, he found that this almost spiritual exercise of concentration helped lift him into a mystical, visionary state:

> Nor less, I trust,
> To them I may have owed another gift,
> Of aspect more sublime; that blessed mood,
> In which the burthen of the mystery,
> In which the heavy and the weary weight
> Of all this unintelligible world,
> Is lightened: —that serene and blessed mood,
> In which the affections gently lead us on,—
> Until, the breath of this corporeal frame
> And even the motion of our human blood
> Almost suspended, we are laid asleep
> In body, and become a living soul:
> While with an eye made quiet by the power
> Of harmony, and the deep power of joy,
> We see into the life of things. (35-49)

While continuing to write in the "language really used by men," and while maintaining a diction and a syntax not far removed from good prose, Wordsworth invites the readers to join him in one of the truly great mystical passages in the language. Hindu priests and Buddhist monks have been known to repeat a certain word or phrase (or mantra) over and over again until they enter into a trance-like state during which they may have an out of body experience, or receive a metaphysical vision, or achieve control over their autonomic functions (breathing, heartbeat, etc.). In what appears to be a similar fashion, Wordsworth's concentrated musings on his recollections grow stronger and more focused until all physical, impermanent things fall away and the poet, his bodily motions laid to rest, is transformed into a "living soul."

While in this "serene and blessed mood," the poet is lifted up into a universal harmony of peace and joy that empowers him "to see into the life of things." Transcending even Coleridge's "vision in a dream," Wordsworth moves into a state in which bodily eye gives way to spiritual eye and the breath of his physical lungs is replaced by a higher life that breathes through all things. In a sense, Wordsworth's vision is a pantheistic one in which man and nature are seen to be animated by the same divine breath. He even uses the pronouns "us," "our," and "we" in lines 31-39 to suggest that we are all capable of participating—and perhaps *have* participated—in such a vision of utter oneness. Still, what holds Wordsworth's mystical encounter within a Judeo-Christian, rather than Hindu-Buddhist, worldview is the poet's desire and determination to retain his own unique individuality rather than lose himself in an amorphous One Soul. At the end of Wordsworth's visionary journey waits not Nirvana—that is, the annihilation of all pleasure and pain and of selfhood itself—but an increased awareness of his own psychic integrity and the preservation of his consciousness through any and all variations in time and place. The poet is never more himself than when he returns from one of his recollection-induced reveries.

Stages of Life

Having reviewed and assessed the vital ministry that the "beauteous forms" of the Wye Valley have played over the last five years, Wordsworth next moves on to the second great movement of the poem. Here in the central lines of the lyric, Wordsworth surveys the past stages of his life. Not merely five years ago, but throughout his life, he has visited and revisited Tintern Abbey. Indeed, Tintern Abbey has been more than a place of joy and refuge; it has served as a yardstick, a touchstone against which the poet can measure his own personal growth and development. With this in mind, Wordsworth looks down a second time on the Valley below and sees the shadow of his former selves moving across the landscape. He is the same person, and yet he has also

> . . . changed, no doubt, from what I was when first
> I came among these hills; when like a roe
> I bounded o'er the mountains, by the sides
> Of the deep rivers, and the lonely streams,
> Wherever nature led: more like a man
> Flying from something that he dreads than one
> Who sought the thing he loved. For nature then
> (The coarser pleasures of my boyish days,
> And their glad animal movements all gone by)
> To me was all in all. —I cannot paint
> What then I was. The sounding cataract
> Haunted me like a passion: the tall rock,
> The mountain, and the deep and gloomy wood,
> Their colours and their forms, were then to me

> An appetite; a feeling and a love,
> That had no need of a remoter charm,
> By thought supplied, nor any interest
> Unborrowed from the eye. (66-83)

Though Wordsworth pauses in his two parenthetical lines to recall the "glad animal movements" of his early childhood, the bulk of the passage focuses on William the grown boy and his fresh, passionate relationship with the natural world. The adult poet has a hard time putting into words the vitality of the boy, who bounds through the landscape like a roe and who devours the sights and sounds and smells of nature as though they were nourishment. It's an odd kind of love, a love that almost borders on a kind of fear, and yet it is one that wholly consumes the boy.

As he recollects those days, Wordsworth experiences again the numinous dread that seized him when he heard the thunderous roar of waterfalls, or felt the ominous presence of the woods, or fixed his gaze on the sublime heights of a mountain spire. For the boy, such feelings were as frequent as they were unspoiled by any form of intellectual analysis or self-conscious musing. The boy merely felt: direct, spontaneous, unmediated. Nature to him was not an object of study to be held at arm's length; it was everything.

At first, Wordsworth's memories of his younger self fill him with a sense of joy, but the very intensity of the joy cuts backward against time, plunging the adult poet into an even stronger sense of loss:

> —That time is past,
> And all its aching joys are now no more,
> And all its dizzy raptures. (83-85)

Grieved that he can no longer return to the "aching joys" and "dizzy raptures" of his youth, the poet suffers an acute emotional and perceptual crisis. Can it be that he will never again feel the all-consuming passions of his youthful intercourse with nature? Has the world of innocence been lost to him forever? Is he to know only the weary over-self-consciousness of the world of experience?

For a brief, terrible moment, it seems that Wordsworth will succumb to despair. But then, in one of the most profound and mature moments in all literature, the poet accepts the loss of the direct intimacy of his youth to embrace a less passionate yet richer and more integral communion with the natural world.

> Not for this
> Faint I, nor mourn nor murmur; other gifts
> Have followed; for such loss, I would believe,
> Abundant recompense. (85-88)

Let me encourage all of my readers, no matter their age or background, to pay close attention to this, the most vital and human section of the poem. For you see, all of us, at one time in our lives, will go through just such a moment of crisis. The thoughtless, carefree days of our youth will rise up in our minds, and we will be tempted to do one of two things: cast off our adult responsibilities and try to recapture that youth; or reject that youth in favor of a self-satisfied stoicism. If we marry, we will face the crisis again after several years of marriage have separated us from the easy and spontaneous passions of our honeymoon. And again, we will be tempted to pursue one of two extremes: either run off and find a new love to "honeymoon" with or resign ourselves to a passionless marriage of duty and convenience. If we are a devout religious believer, especially if we are a Christian who has made a personal commitment to Jesus Christ, we will face the crisis a third time when the early days of religious rapture (a phase that many Christians refer to as the "honeymoon period" of their faith) cool down and lose their spiritual immediacy. The immature believer will face the crisis by rushing from one church to the next seeking an emotional high; the cynical believer will simply dismiss as nonsense all of his youthful enthusiasm for God and settle into a dead legalism or a genteel hypocrisy.

If Wordsworth's poem teaches us anything, it is that *neither* option is a healthy one. The proper response to any of these crises is to be thankful and even a bit nostalgic for our past joys, to accept fully our present stage of life, and then to press forward to find a quieter yet richer joy that combines the wisdom of age with the passion of youth. That is exactly what Wordsworth does, as he discovers in nature something more beautiful and more wonderful than his youthful eyes could have ever perceived:

> For I have learned
> To look on nature, not as in the hour
> Of thoughtless youth; but hearing oftentimes
> The still, sad music of humanity,
> Nor harsh nor grating, though of ample power
> To chasten and subdue. And I have felt
> A presence that disturbs me with the joy
> Of elevated thoughts; a sense sublime

> Of something far more deeply interfused,
> Whose dwelling is the light of setting suns,
> And the round ocean and the living air,
> And the blue sky, and in the mind of man:
> A motion and a spirit, that impels
> All thinking things, all objects of all thought,
> And rolls through all things. (88-102)

The loss of his youthful perceptions of nature have given way to a deeper, more mature insight that allows the poet to commune with a presence that indwells both object and subject, both nature and the mind of man. Yes, he has lost something precious, but for that loss he has been abundantly compensated. Behind the crashing chords of the cataract, he hears now a softer, autumnal music that is not averse to the sterner, more somber chords of sorrow.

Wordsworth the boy was never still enough or aware enough to sense the presence that the adult poet now senses all around him. The presence does not reside in any one tree or mountain or lake, but pervades them all. It is a fluid, plastic force that binds and unites all into a purposeful whole. As before, Wordsworth borders here on pantheism, while never surrendering the real and essential distinction between subject and object, spirit and matter, mind and nature. What Wordsworth yearns for is not an Eastern from of Monism that would collapse all things into a single universal substance, but the more Christian understanding of Incarnation that even Blake, in his most heterodox phase, could not wholly abandon.

The adult finds to his surprise and delight that he is "connected" to nature in a way that the boy never was. And it is this discovery that prevents him from losing heart. Rather, the poet boldly proclaims:

> Therefore am I still
> A lover of the meadows and the woods,
> And mountains; and of all that we behold
> From this green earth; of all the mighty world
> Of eye, and ear, —both what they half create,
> And what perceive; well pleased to recognise
> In nature and the language of the sense
> The anchor of my purest thoughts, the nurse,
> The guide, the guardian of my heart, and soul
> Of all my moral being. (102-11)

In a sense he has given up nothing in his journey from boyhood to manhood. His love for nature has not been lost; it has only deepened and matured. Indeed, only now has he come to realize how formative his youthful interactions with nature have been in his life. Only now does he understand the subtle ways in which nature has helped to build the mental, emotional, and spiritual dimensions of his adult being. And only now does he realize that what he saw in nature was, both then and now, "half create[d]" by his perceptions of it.

In the final movement of the poem, Wordsworth turns to his beloved sister, Dorothy, and perceives in her still-innocent demeanor a vision of the boy he once was:

> . . . in thy voice I catch
> The language of my former heart, and read
> My former pleasures in the shooting lights
> Of thy wild eyes. Oh! yet a little while
> May I behold in thee what I was once,
> My dear, dear Sister! and this prayer I make,
> Knowing that Nature never did betray
> The heart that loved her . . . (116-123)

Nothing, it seems, has really been lost. The line of sentience that connects Wordsworth the boy with Wordsworth the man connects as well brother and sister, even as it connects all people who share in what Wordsworth calls, in his Preface, "the native and naked dignity of man." Modern, more cynical readers of Wordsworth have tended to take the poet to task for his optimistic and even naïve faith "that Nature never did betray / The heart that loved her," but the criticism is not a wholly fair one. Wordsworth was well acquainted with the "still, sad music of humanity": at the tender age of seven, he lost his mother, and was separated for many years from Dorothy; by age thirteen, he had lost his father as well. And he knew, as he documents in his poetry, that nature could be a cruel and harsh mistress to those without hearth or home.

Still, in the face of loss and hardship, Wordsworth retained his faith in the basic goodness of the natural world. The Proverbs promise us that "if we train up a child in the way he should go . . . when he is old, he will not depart from it" (22:6). In the same way, Wordsworth's early interactions with nature had been such as to build up in him a simple but indomitable faith:

> 'tis her [nature's] privilege,
> Through all the years of this our life, to lead

> From joy to joy: for she can so inform
> The mind that is within us, so impress
> With quietness and beauty, and so feed
> With lofty thoughts, that neither evil tongues,
> Rash judgments, nor the sneers of selfish men,
> Nor greetings where no kindness is, nor all
> The dreary intercourse of daily life,
> Shall e'er prevail against us, or disturb
> Our cheerful faith, that all which we behold
> Is full of blessings. (123-134)

It has often been asserted that the Romantics "invented" childhood as a distinct stage of growth. Though this is certainly an exaggeration, it is nevertheless true that poets like Wordsworth helped us to see how our adult consciousness rests upon the experiences of our early childhood as a building rests upon its foundation. Wordsworth performed this task supremely in *The Prelude*, but here in this passage we catch a glimpse of how thankful the poet was for the subtle ways in which nature impressed upon his youthful mind peace, patience, and a love for beauty. There are many things that stunt or even kill the adult soul: the contrivances of cruel and envious men; the cutting words that poison and wound; the lack of human warmth and sincere concern. Worst of all there is the daily, dreary grind of life—what we today call the rat race—with its petty concerns, its skewed values, and its monumental apathy. Against these soul-killers, Wordsworth holds up the richer lore that nature instilled in him from his cradle.

For Wordsworth, first impressions are everything. If once he knew peace and joy in the core of his being, then surely he can know it again. If once he was strong, then he can be strong again. "So feeling come in aid / Of feeling, and diversity of strength / Attends us, if but once we have been strong" (*The Prelude*, XII.269-271). Wordsworth was a poet who delighted in paradox, but he never wrote a paradox greater or truer than this: "the Child is father of the Man" ("My Heart Leaps Up," line 7). In poems like "Tintern Abbey" and *The Prelude*, Wordsworth proves the truth of this paradox in the only laboratory where it can be proved: that of memory.

The Things Which I Have Seen

"Tintern Abbey" embodies perfectly all of the conventions of what is perhaps the definitive sub-genre of Romanticism: the crisis poem. In such poems, a still-young speaker suffers an internal crisis that disconnects him from the natural and human world. Whether the crisis be a mental, emotional, or spiritual one, it always manifests itself in terms of a loss of perceptual freshness and a mood of dejection and despair that intensifies the very crisis that initiated it. Trapped within his own isolated self-consciousness, the poet yearns for a resolution that will allow him once again to interact with nature, to transcend his fears for the future, and to feel, *really* feel joy.

Although Wordsworth and Coleridge wrote several crisis poems in blank verse—with the latter half of *The Prelude* offering an epic version of the same basic crisis-resolution structure as "Tintern Abbey"—each poet also composed a major crisis poem in the demanding form of the irregular ode. Tracing its roots back to the Greek poet Pindar, odes are marked by a lofty style and tone, a serious, meditative subject matter, and a complex stanzaic structure. Odes take their reader on a journey through shifting images, ideas, and moods, often ending where they began but, like *The Rime of the Ancient Mariner*, on a higher level. Technically speaking, the units that make up the ode are referred to not as stanzas but as strophes and antistrophes (Greek for "turn" and "counterturn"), a convention which, historically speaking, points back to the dramatic origins of Pindar's odes but which, aesthetically speaking, captures precisely the unexpected shifts in thought and emotion that mark the ode.

Whereas regular odes are composed in a fixed stanza form, the stanzas (or strophes) that make up the irregular ode vary wildly in their rhyme scheme, in their total number of lines, and in the length of each individual line. These variations allow the poet to carefully modulate the rise and fall of emotion and to embody something of the "shape" of his mood at any given point in the poem. In 1802, Wordsworth experimented successfully with a crisis poem in the form of a regular ode ("Resolution and Independence"); however, when, in the same year, he began work on a second ode ("Ode: Intimations of Immortality from Recollections of Early Childhood"), he discovered that the subject demanded the greater complexity and unexpected shifts of the irregular ode. The story of crisis and resolution that he felt compelled to tell could not be expressed in any other way.

#

Unlike "Tintern Abbey" and "Resolution and Independence," both of which move at a leisurely pace before stating their central crisis, the

"Intimations Ode" begins swiftly and decisively. The use of past tense in the first line signals immediately that all is not as it should be; by the end of the first stanza we learn why:

> There was a time when meadow, grove, and stream,
> The earth, and every common sight,
> To me did seem
> Apparelled in celestial light,
> The glory and the freshness of a dream.
> It is not now as it hath been of yore;—
> Turn wheresoe'er I may,
> By night or day,
> The things which I have seen I now can see no more. (1-9)

Before the onset of his crisis, the poet had looked out through the windows of his senses onto a world of perpetual wonder and freshness. Wherever he turned his gaze, he seemed to perceive a heavenly glow emanating from earth and field, forest and stream. All was ordinary, and yet all was extraordinary. No veil of familiarity prevented him from seeing the celestial radiance that hung around the common objects of nature as a corona does around the sun.

But now, when he looks upon the same objects of nature, he no longer perceives the glory. Something is missing; something has been lost that once filled his watchful eye with glimpses of the divine. Hungry to regain that vision, the poet shifts his eye from earth to field to forest to stream, but the glory which he seeks is gone. In order to capture rhythmically the pain of his lost vision, Wordsworth stretches the last line of the stanza from the expected pentameter (ten-syllable, five-stress line) to an unexpected hexameter (twelve syllables with six beats). The longer line, each of whose twelve syllables constitutes a single word, mimics the sadness and melancholy felt by the poet and brings the first stanza to a heavy, ominous close.

In the second stanza, Wordsworth, hoping perhaps to "jump start" his senses and thus regain his initial vision, celebrates the beauty of the rainbow, the rose, and the moon. But it availeth not. The last two lines of the second stanza echo the somber close of the first, even to the use of a second hexameter line (or alexandrine):

> But yet I know, where'er I go,
> That there hath past away a glory from the earth. (17-18)

At this point, the reader, if he is familiar with either "Tintern Abbey" or "Resolution and Independence," will expect Wordsworth to begin the slow build up to his resolution. And indeed, for the next thirty lines, he seems to do just that. Here is how he begins stanza three:

> Now, while the birds thus sing a joyous song,
> And while the young lambs bound
> As to the tabor's sound,
> To me alone there came a thought of grief:
> A timely utterance gave that thought relief,
>
> And I again am strong: (19-24)

Though no one can say for sure what Wordsworth meant by a "timely utterance" (the critical "best guess" is that he is referring to the earlier "Resolution and Independence"), the clear implication is that something has "clicked" within the poet's psyche that has enabled him once again to perceive traces of glory and freshness in the natural world.

The crisis, it appears, has been solved by a strange and sudden (perhaps divine) intervention, and Wordsworth responds by singing a joyful paean to the May morning that leaps to life around him. The celebration spills over into the fourth stanza as Wordsworth, who seems to be situated in some kind of park or communal field, focuses his attention on a group of shepherd boys who gather flowers and gambol on the grass. As he watches the children at play, the newly revived adult exclaims:

> The fulness of your bliss, I feel—I feel it all.
> Oh evil day! if I were sullen
> While the Earth herself is adorning,
> This sweet May-morning,
> And the Children are culling
> On every side,
> In a thousand valleys far and wide,
> Fresh flowers; while the sun shines warm,
> And the Babe leaps up on his Mother's arm:—
> I hear, I hear, with joy I hear! (41-50)

Yes, for a Romantic poet like Wordsworth, it would be a true tragedy if he could witness such joy and yet not be able join in it himself. But the poet brushes away such fears, choosing instead to luxuriate in the life and joy that he both feels and hears.

And it is at that moment, while Wordsworth is rejoicing in his victory over his earlier loss of vision, that the crisis returns with a force and an urgency that almost paralyze him:

> —But there's a Tree, of many, one,
> A single Field which I have looked upon,
> Both of them speak of something that is gone:
> The Pansy at my feet
> Doth the same tale repeat:
> Whither is fled the visionary gleam?
> Where is it now, the glory and the dream? (51-57)

Even here, amidst the frolicking shepherd boys and the colorful flowers of May, dark, hollow spaces open before the poet. A palpable emptiness and absence that devour the palpable silence that Wordsworth discerns in the opening section of "Tintern Abbey" yawn like an abyss as the disenchanted poet turns his eye to gaze on a single tree or field or flower. It is gone after all, that glory and freshness that the younger Wordsworth had seen lurking behind every twig and blade of grass. No longer can he perceive the supernatural shining in and through the natural. It is just nature now; the vision is fled.

Many who go through the grieving process will find that their second bout of grief is more acute than their first. So Wordsworth finds to his despair as his crisis resurfaces with a greater strength and intensity than before. So intense, in fact, is this second bout that it constrains the poet to put down his poem for two full years until he can find both an emotional and aesthetic resolution to his perceptual crisis.

Not in Utter Nakedness

When Wordsworth takes up his pen again in 1804, he does so armed with a metaphysical metaphor that empowers him to deal emotionally and poetically with his visionary loss:

> Our birth is but a sleep and a forgetting:
> The Soul that rises with us, our life's Star,
> Hath had elsewhere its setting,
> And cometh from afar:
> Not in entire forgetfulness,
> And not in utter nakedness,
> But trailing clouds of glory do we come
> From God, who is our home:
> Heaven lies about us in our infancy!
> Shades of the prison-house begin to close

> Upon the growing Boy,
> But He beholds the light, and whence it flows,
> He sees it in his joy;
> The Youth, who daily farther from the east
> Must travel, still is Nature's Priest,
> And by the vision splendid
> Is on his way attended;
> At length the Man perceives it die away,
> And fade into the light of common day. (58-76)

Playing off of various elements from Platonic and neo-Platonic philosophy, Wordsworth suggests that our soul, rather than being "born" at the same moment as our body, pre-existed for an indefinite period in heaven. In keeping with this philosophy, Wordsworth reasons, in his characteristically paradoxical manner, that our birth is not so much a waking as it is a sleeping, a forgetting of the glories that we once knew when our soul dwelt in heaven. That is why, in our early childhood, we still catch glimpses of the heavenly glory we saw in our pre-existence, but then gradually lose those glimpses as we move farther away from our ante-natal life in heaven. In keeping with a universal archetype based on the rising and setting of the sun, Wordsworth charts this journey as a movement from east to west.

In his 70's, Wordsworth, in an interview with Isabella Fenwick, insisted that he did not mean actually to teach the pre-existence of the soul as a doctrine of faith, but merely to make poetic use of it.[11] That is no doubt true, and yet, the Platonic doctrine of the pre-existence of the soul accords well with the Romantic privileging of imagination over reason and intuition over logic. When Wordsworth writes that our soul comes into this world "Not in entire forgetfulness / And not in utter nakedness," he both lays the foundation for the resolution of his personal crisis and offers a Romantic critique of John Locke's famous argument that we are all born as a tabula rasa (or "blank slate"). Under the Lockean dispensation, we can only gain knowledge through the exercise of our senses; it is the accumulation of objective data recorded via our senses on to our mind that creates our subjective self-consciousness. Not so for the Romantics, who not only yearn for the mystical, revelatory wisdom that comes via inspiration but who shape nature itself by projecting their own subjectivity on to the objective world.

---

11   Noyes includes the full Fenwick Note to the "Intimations Ode" on page 327.

In "Tintern Abbey," we saw how a Man can find tranquil restoration by recollecting the feelings of the Boy; here we discover that the feelings of the Boy are themselves a product, at least in part, of the Boy's recollections of his pre-existent state in heaven. That unmediated freshness that all the Romantics accepted as one of the supreme gifts of childhood, and that all mourned the loss of, may have, it seems, a decidedly mystical origin. Perhaps the veil of familiarity that Wordsworth sought to tear down in his poetry was simply the result of the slow fading of our youthful recollections of heaven. In that sense, it is not the darkness of pain or cynicism or apathy that blots out the glory but, paradoxically, the "light of common day."

In stanzas six and seven, Wordsworth identifies two natural processes that coalesce to accelerate the fading of the glory. First, nature, like a "homely nurse [or kindly governess]

> doth all she can
> To make her Foster-child, her Inmate Man,
> Forget the glories he hath known,
> And that imperial palace whence he came. (81-84)

Nature does not do this out of envy or cruelty, but because she knows that until we forget our heavenly origins and accept the earth as our (temporary) home, we will be unable to find our place in the world. Meanwhile, as nature presses on us her immediacy and fullness, the child assists in his own movement away from the pre-existence by mimicking the actions and behaviors of those around him. With each round of imitation, he dulls further his ante-natal memories and grows more a part of the physical world. In the end, the child becomes an adult, and all traces of glory fade away.

Yes, the process is a natural one, and yet, how sad that it should be so. In the eighth stanza, Wordsworth sounds the depth of a great irony that frustrates both child and adult

> Thou, whose exterior semblance doth belie
> Thy Soul's immensity;
> Thou best Philosopher, who yet dost keep
> Thy heritage, thou Eye among the blind,
> That, deaf and silent, read'st the eternal deep,
> Haunted for ever by the eternal mind,—
> Mighty Prophet! Seer blest!
> On whom those truths do rest,
> Which we are toiling all our lives to find,
> In darkness lost, the darkness of the grave;

> Thou, over whom thy Immortality
> Broods like the Day, a Master o'er a Slave,
> A Presence which is not to be put by;
> Thou little Child, yet glorious in the might
> Of heaven-born freedom on thy being's height,
> Why with such earnest pains dost thou provoke
> The years to bring the inevitable yoke,
> Thus blindly with thy blessedness at strife?
> Full soon thy Soul shall have her earthly freight,
> And custom lie upon thee with a weight,
> Heavy as frost, and deep almost as life! (108-128)

Just as Wordsworth was lampooned for the hyperbolic language of "The Tables Turned," so here too his critics ridiculed him for seemingly advocating the absurd. Does Wordsworth, having claimed that birds can teach us more about ourselves and our world than preachers, now wish us to believe that a Child (the somewhat unclear antecedent of the word "Thou" with which the stanza begins) is both the "best Philosopher" and a "Mighty Prophet"? Of course, as before, Wordsworth no more desires that we should take philosophy classes from infants than that we should learn our theology from linnets and throstles. Rather, he means to suggest that young children, on account of their nearness to heaven, are more in touch with the metaphysical realties on which all true philosophy and prophecy rest.

And therein lies the melancholy irony. The child, who cannot communicate what he knows, apprehends directly those very mystical truths that the adult, who possesses the ability to enshrine what he knows in language, seeks vainly to acquire. The child, though he lacks the mental and critical capacity to think in philosophical or theological terms, lives in daily communion with a divine mind whose Presence haunts the child, brooding over his unformed intellect as the Spirit of God brooded over the primal waters of creation (Genesis 1:2). Those things which the adult toils all his life to learn, the child knows intuitively, and yet, ignorant that he will one day join the ranks of these toiling adults, the child does all he can to cast off his "heaven-born freedom" and take upon himself the heavy burdens and cares that come with age.

Once again, the tragedy of it all threatens to catapult Wordsworth back into his crisis, but a joyous thought steps boldly in to intercede between the poet and his grief:

> O joy! that in our embers

> Is something that doth live,
> That nature yet remembers
> What was so fugitive! (129-132)

Though he has traveled far along his westerly path, not every trace of glory has been irrevocably lost. As it often chances that live embers remain, buried beneath the ashes and smoke of a dying fire, so there is a part of us that remembers the glory, even when the visionary gleam itself has faded from before our eyes. The poet can still receive "intimations of immortality," not from direct apprehension of the celestial radiance but from his "recollections of early childhood." In fact, Wordsworth goes on to assert, our ability to see anything beyond brute physicality can be traced back to our early metaphysical encounters.

In the Fenwick note to the poem, Wordsworth explains that when he was a child, he often found it hard to accept the existence of a fixed, material world separate from himself. Although it is doubtful that all small children have shared exactly that feeling, it is likely that most have experienced a sense of estrangement from the world, a sense that there is something both behind nature and within themselves that is more real and vivid than the bare shapes of the physical world. It is these "obstinate questionings / Of sense and outward things" (141-142) that Wordsworth hails as being "the fountain-light of all our day . . . a master-light of all our seeing" (151-152). Wordsworth's recollections of his early encounters are like lights shining in the darkness: he both *sees* them and sees *by* them. Whatever insight he possesses as an adult is but an extension of that visionary gleam that shines out to him over the bridge of memory.

It is precisely those precious visionary gleams from the dawn of our childhood that

> Uphold us, cherish, and have power to make
> Our noisy years seem moments in the being
> Of the eternal Silence: truths that wake,
> To perish never:
> Which neither listlessness, nor mad endeavor,
> Nor Man nor Boy,
> Nor all that is at enmity with joy,
> Can utterly abolish or destroy! (153-160)

As we saw in our analysis of "Tintern Abbey," good beginnings are everything. If once the poet has been strong, if once he has touched the imperishable heart of peace and of truth, then, to paraphrase St. Paul (Romans 8:38-39), neither apathy nor frenzy, neither the past nor the present, nor any joy-denying power can ever separate him from the tranquil restoration that is his rightful inheritance. Though all should grow dark, the embers will burn on:

> Hence in a season of calm weather
> Though inland far we be,
> Our Souls have sight of that immortal sea
> Which brought us hither,
> Can in a moment travel thither,
> And see the Children sport upon the shore,
> And hear the mighty waters rolling evermore. (161-167)

Our lifelong journey from east to west is also a journey from the mystic shore of eternity to the land-locked country of time and decay. Still, there are moments when the dry and weary traveler casts a backward glance toward that faint, distant shore that gave him birth. And, for a moment, his eyes see again the Child he once was, and his ears hear again the sound of many waters. Like the final lines of stanzas 1 and 2, the final line of stanza 9 is an alexandrine, but oh, how different the texture and resonance of that line. Freed from the heaviness and weariness of the previous two lines, the third seems to stretch on and on to infinity.

#

By the end of stanza nine, Wordsworth has resolved the central crisis of the poem, but he presses on for two more stanzas that he might make clear, as he does in "Tintern Abbey," that what he has gained has not only made up for but exceeded what he has lost along the way:

> What though the radiance which was once so bright
> Be now for ever taken from my sight,
> Though nothing can bring back the hour
> Of splendour in the grass, of glory in the flower;
> We will grieve not, rather find
> Strength in what remains behind;
> In the primal sympathy
> Which having been must ever be;
> In the soothing thoughts that spring
> Out of human suffering;
> In the faith that looks through death,
> In years that bring the philosophic mind. (175-186)

Not all the beautiful words of all the great poets can restore to him the splendor and radiance he once saw in field and flower. That is gone, as childhood itself is gone, but for this the poet will not grieve. Instead, he will seek the "abundant recompense" of "Tintern Abbey": a deeper and more mature wisdom that can find truth and joy even in the midst of suffering and death. Indeed, in the closing lines of the poem, Wordsworth can claim with triumph that because of the insight he has gained both into nature and the human heart, "the meanest [most ordinary] flower that blows can give / Thoughts that do often lie too deep for tears" (202-203).

X
Solipsism with a Vengeance

After writing the first four stanzas of the "Intimations Ode," Wordsworth, as was his custom, read them aloud to Coleridge. So moved was Coleridge by the form and content of his friend's crisis poem that he was inspired to compose his own crisis poem along similar lines and in the same demanding form of the irregular ode. The final poem, which went through many drafts and alterations, was titled "Dejection: An Ode"; like Wordsworth's "Intimations Ode," it documents a perceptual crisis that disconnects the poet from the natural world and plunges him into despair. Coleridge's dejection, however, proves to be far deeper and darker than that of his fellow poet.

The Correspondent Breeze

As befitting a poet who wrote the greatest medieval-style ballad of the Romantic Age (*The Rime of the Ancient Mariner*), Coleridge begins his poem with an epigraph taken from an actual medieval ballad, "The Ballad of Sir Patrick Spence":

> Late, late yestreen I saw the new Moon,
> With the old Moon in her arms:
> And I fear, I fear, my Master dear!
> We shall have a deadly storm.

It is significant that Coleridge should select a stanza in which a sympathetic relationship is felt to exist between the objective heavens above and the subjective fears and anxieties within. Though Coleridge, like all the Romantic poets, would intensify the psychological aspects of the old medieval romances and internalize their quest narratives, he nevertheless remained true to an element that appears often in both medieval and renaissance poetry: the interplay between macrocosm and microcosm. That the movements of the heavens could and did affect our physical and emotional well being was a concept well understood in pre-Enlightenment Europe; it was also understood, though to a far lesser degree, that our moods could exert their own influence on the cosmos. The Romantics, while retaining the former concept, increased several fold the force and influence of the latter. On one thing the Romantics were clear: the road that links external nature to internal mind is a two-way street.

As though attempting, by the power of poetry, to break down the boundaries of time and space, Coleridge employs a literary device for which I can find no clear precedent. He uses his epigraph not merely to highlight a theme he plans to pursue in his own poem, but as the actual starting point *for* his poem:

> Well! If the Bard was weather-wise, who made
> The grand old ballad of Sir Patrick Spence,
> This night, so tranquil now, will not go hence
> Unroused by winds, that ply a busier trade
> Than those which mould yon cloud in lazy flakes,
> Or the dull sobbing draft, that moans and rakes
> Upon the strings of this Æolian lute
> Which better far were mute. (1-8)

Though the poet lives in a different century and is situated in a different location than the speaker of his epigraph, he begins his poem in direct dialogue with the anonymous author of "Patrick Spence." He shares the fears of the speaker of the old ballad that the seeming tranquility of the evening is but the prelude to a furious squall, a deceptive calm before the storm. Most of Coleridge's poem hovers in this frozen moment of anticipation.

As he waits with baited breath for the winds to come and shake the heavens, he listens to the music that rises up from a nearby Aeolian lute. More commonly known as an Aeolian (or wind) harp—Aeolus was the Greek god of the wind—this simple but unique instrument consists of a rectangular wooden sounding board over which are stretched a number of strings. As the wind blows over the strings, the instrument trembles into life and song. Coleridge describes accurately the strange music that emanates from the harp, almost more a hum than a melody, like the buzz of a hundred cicadas on a lazy evening; but he humanizes the sound. The poet's words transform the wind into a lover and the harp into his beloved, though the phrase "moans and rakes" leaves it unclear as to whether this is a romance, a forceful seduction, or a rape. Whichever way we interpret it, however, a strong sense remains that the harp has no choice but to offer up its/her music to the provocation of the wind.

Aeolian harps make frequent appearances in the work of the Romantic poets for they embody in a vivid, concrete manner the Romantic understanding of how creativity works. Just as the wind blows over the passive harp stirring it into song, so inspiration blows over the passive poet stirring him into poetry. In the absence of a strong wind or breath of inspiration, both harp and poet remain mute. Of course, as I argued in my analysis of Wordsworth's "Expostulation and Reply," Romantic passivity is in reality an active thing, a "wise passiveness" that vigorously receives and discerns the inspiration of nature. In the opening paragraph of his "Defense of Poetry," Shelley explains this paradox of active passivity:

> Man is an instrument over which a series of external and internal impressions are driven, like the alternations of an ever-changing wind over an Æolian lyre, which move it by their motion to ever-changing melody. But there is a principle within the human being, and perhaps within all sentient beings, which acts otherwise than in the lyre, and produces not melody alone, but harmony, by an internal adjustment of the sounds or motions thus excited to the impressions which excite them. It is as if the lyre could accommodate its chords to the motions of that which strikes them, in a determined proportion of sound; even as the musician can accommodate his voice to the sound of the lyre. (1097)

Like the link between external nature and internal mind, the relationship between the breath of inspiration (melody) and the "internal adjustment" made by the poet (harmony) is a two-way street. Romantic poetry necessitates a creative give and take between the impressions that flood over the poet and his own efforts to so accommodate his art as to incarnate those impressions in a body of poetry. Unless the external breeze of inspiration be met by what Wordsworth calls a "correspondent breeze" from within (*The Prelude*, I.35), both poet and poetry will stagnate.

Such a stagnation afflicts the poet of "Dejection: An Ode"; in the closing lines of the first stanza, we learn that his correspondent breeze has ceased to respond to the beautiful sounds of nature. If only, he laments:

> Those sounds which oft have raised me, whilst they awed,
> And sent my soul abroad,
> Might now perhaps their wonted impulse give,
> Might startle this dull pain, and make it move and live! (17-20)

But they cannot. There is a dullness and deadness within the poet that cannot accommodate itself to the melody of nature. In "Tintern Abbey," Wordsworth tells us that his recollections of the Wye Valley would often put him into a state during which he would be "laid asleep / In body, and become a living soul." This form of escape is denied to the speaker of "Dejection: An Ode," who is too firmly imprisoned within his own melancholy self-consciousness to be able to move out of himself. He desperately needs to be shaken out of his mental, emotional, and aesthetic stupor, but the external breeze alone cannot accomplish this. In an effort to express the weight of his stupor, Coleridge, like Wordsworth, ends the first stanza of his irregular ode with a long, heavy alexandrine.

He then goes on to describe the exact nature of his dejection in words that exceed in anguish and despair anything in the Wordsworth cannon:

> A grief without a pang, void, dark, and drear,
> A stifled, drowsy, unimpassioned grief,
> Which finds no natural outlet, no relief,
> In word, or sigh, or tear— (21-24)

Remarkably, these four lines, written over two centuries ago, read like a textbook description of what psychologists today call clinical depression. Far worse than mere depression, clinical depression defines a state of internal deadness, an almost total lack of feeling. Even anger itself is swallowed up by the black pit of emptiness that slowly devours the sufferer. Patients today who are diagnosed with clinical depression are invariably prescribed medication, for one of the symptoms of this condition is precisely that the patient cannot "get out" of the depression on his own. As Coleridge describes it, the grief which crushes him has left him stifled and drowsy, drained of all passion; he can neither speak nor groan nor weep.

Wordsworth, as far as we can tell, never experienced this level of depression. Though the crisis that Wordsworth suffers in the "Intimations Ode" leaves him temporarily unable to see and respond to the glory of nature, Coleridge's crisis robs him of his ability to feel at all. Whereas Wordsworth is cut off from the mystical visions of his early childhood,

Coleridge is cut off from nature itself. Thus, after spending the next dozen lines gazing at the wonders of the night sky in a vain attempt to "jump start" his dead psyche, he concludes despairingly with these two lines:

> I see them all so excellently fair,
> I see, not feel, how beautiful they are! (37-38)

In stanza 4 of the "Intimations Ode," Wordsworth celebrates his ability to "feel" the fullness of the children's bliss and declares that it would be an "evil day" if he were ever "sullen / While the Earth herself is adorning" (41-43). Even during the height of his crisis, when he despairs of ever seeing again the visionary gleam of his childhood, Wordsworth does not lose this ability to feel and participate in nature's essential beauty. Not so Coleridge, who discovers that nothing in the natural world can lift him out of his passionless lethargy.

The Loss of Original Participation

Having stated the problem in emotional and psychological terms in stanza 2, Coleridge proceeds in stanza 3 to restate it in perceptual and aesthetic terms:

> My genial spirits fail;
> And what can these avail
> To lift the smothering weight from off my breast?
> It were a vain endeavour,
> Though I should gaze for ever
> On that green light that lingers in the west:
> I may not hope from outward forms to win
> The passion and the life, whose fountains are within. (39-46)

In Chapter One, I used the phrase externalization of the internal to describe the perceptual process by which Romantic poets project their internal mood on to the external world. In this dark and somber stanza, Coleridge experiences what might best be termed the externalization of the internal *with a vengeance*. When a poet's inner state is one of joy, peace, and love, the externalization of the internal enables him to project that joy, peace, and love on to the world around him. But such a process carries with it a danger: if the poet is dead inside, his psyche shrouded in darkness and despair, then he risks infecting all of nature.

In philosophy, the word solipsism is used to refer to the belief that the self is all there is. Formed from two Latin words that mean "alone" and "self," solipsism can range from the belief that the self, or ego, is the only thing we can know for certain ("I think, therefore I am"), to the more radical belief that the external world only exists as a function of my perceptions of it. All the Romantics toyed with solipsism both in their lives and their poetry, but in "Dejection: An Ode," we get to see the full dark side of a solipsism that would confine the poet to his own cramped and isolated ego. Once we make the self the only fountain of life and hope and passion, we necessarily cut ourselves off from any form of external inspiration or restoration. Of course, as long as our internal state is healthy and joyous, we can get by fine on our own inner resources and strength. But once let that internal state sicken and stagnate, and we are stuck. If we are dead inside, then no amount of "outward forms," be they ever so beautiful and inspiring, will avail to pull us out of our sickness and stagnation.

Readers of *The Great Gatsby* have often wondered why it is that the title character spends so much time gazing on a green light on an island west of his mansion. He does so because Fitzgerald's enigmatic hero suffers from exactly the same affliction described in stanza 3. Both Coleridge and Gatsby are dead inside—the former because he has lost his ability to feel the beauty of nature; the latter because he has lost Daisy—and no manner of external excitation—whether from the wonders of the night sky or from the lavish parties that Gatsby throws—can stir them back to life. Indeed, it "were a vain endeavour, / Though [they] should gaze for ever / On that green light that lingers in the west." Their restoration can only come from within.

Trapped within his own solipsistic nightmare, Coleridge tries to explain his predicament to an unnamed lady whom earlier drafts of the poem identify as Sara Hutchinson. Although he remained faithful to his wife, Coleridge's marriage was an unhappy one; to make matters worse, shortly after Wordsworth introduced him to Sara Hutchinson (whose sister would eventually become Mrs. Wordsworth) he came to love and pine after her with something of the intensity and hopelessness with which Gatsby loved Daisy. It is therefore appropriate that he addresses his emotional and perceptual entrapment to her:

> O Lady! we receive but what we give,
> And in our life alone does Nature live:
> Ours is her wedding garment, ours her shroud!
> And would we aught behold, of higher worth,
>
> Than that inanimate cold world allowed

> To the poor loveless ever-anxious crowd,
> Ah! from the soul itself must issue forth
> A light, a glory, a fair luminous cloud
> Enveloping the Earth—
> And from the soul itself must there be sent
> A sweet and potent voice, of its own birth,
> Of all sweet sounds the life and element! (47-58)

In an extreme expression of solipsism, Coleridge here claims that nature not only is affected by our perceptions of her, but that she actually lives inside of us. Whether our relationship with nature be that of a marriage or a funeral lies fully in the light and glory which proceeds from our soul. If we recall that Coleridge's ode was written in response to Wordsworth's, then we can theorize that Coleridge means in part to suggest that the "glory . . .Enveloping the Earth" that the young Wordsworth saw emanating from nature was itself a projection from his glory-filled soul.

As a poet possessed of a lively inner life, Coleridge had always perceived in nature something quite invisible to that mass of men who, to borrow Thoreau's pregnant phrase, live lives of quiet desperation. To the "poor loveless ever-anxious crowd," nature is nothing but a cold and lifeless object, for they fail to project on to it their own animated (and animating) subjectivity. Much of Coleridge's dejection stems from the sad fact that he has sunk to the level of the crowd; since the onset of his crisis, he too can see only "that inanimate cold world."

In his still timely book, *Saving the Appearances* (1957), British philosopher Owen Barfield argues that whereas modern man holds an objective view of nature, those who lived in the classical and medieval period saw their world in subjective terms. We post-Enlightenment moderns look upon things that lie outside of us as existing apart from us, as removed objects, things to be studied from a distance. The Medievals, from whom the Romantics learned so much, did not see it the same way. They and the objects around them were linked in what Barfield terms "original participation." The universe did not exist as an object apart from them, but existed in—and together with—their perceptions of it. Still retaining traces of the pagan classical world, they looked out upon a cosmos animated with divine presence and filled with a plenitude of intermediary spiritual beings: the very world, in fact, that Coleridge dramatizes in *The Rime of the Ancient Mariner*. Alas, somewhere along the road to the modern, scientific world, we cut the universe loose from our perceptions of it and, in the process, "un-godded" nature of its wonder and mystery. Romanticism, inasmuch as it marked a counter-movement to the Enlightenment, sought to reconnect man and nature, even if they knew deep down that they could not simply return to a semi-pagan original participation. Indeed, Barfield argues that Wordsworth's occasional flirtations with pantheism betrayed his "nostalgic hankering after *original* participation."[12]

Romanticism instead sought to press forward to a new, and ultimately higher, relationship between man and nature. Romantic theory, explains Barfield, tells us

> that we must no longer look for the nature-spirits—for the Goddess Natura—on the farther side of the appearances; we must look for them *within ourselves*. . . . Pan has shut up shop. But he has not retired from business; he has merely gone indoors. Or, in the well-known words of Coleridge:
>
> > *We receive but what we give*
> > *And in our life alone does Nature live.*[13]

Pan was a Greek god of the countryside who appeared in the form of a satyr (half man/half goat) and whose presence would often bring awe, fear, and "pan-ic" to villagers. That sacred and numinous awe has long since fled from the natural world; however, in the work of the Romantic poets, it returns to take up residence within. Although Coleridge's perceptual crisis had rendered him temporarily unable to access his inner resources, he does pause in stanza 5 to assure Sara that *if* he could regain and hold on permanently to that inner glory he has lost, he would be able to effect a marriage between the mind of man and the natural world that would surpass the pagan and even the medieval paradigm to usher in what Barfield terms "final participation."

The Esemplastic Power

True, the music of Coleridge's soul has been stilled by his crisis, but that does not mean that the poet is therefore unaware of what that music is and what it is capable of doing:

> *O pure of heart! thou need'st not ask of me*
> *What this strong music in the soul may be!*

---

12 Owen Barfield, *Saving the Appearances*, Second Edition (Hanover, NH: Wesleyan University Press, 1988), 130.
13 *Ibid*, 129-130.

> What, and wherein it doth exist,
> This light, this glory, this fair luminous mist,
> This beautiful and beauty-making power.
> Joy, virtuous Lady! Joy that ne'er was given,
> Save to the pure, and in their purest hour,
> Life, and Life's effluence, cloud at once and shower,
> Joy, Lady! is the spirit and the power,
> Which wedding Nature to us gives in dower
> A new Earth and new Heaven,
> Undreamt of by the sensual and the proud—
>
> Joy is the sweet voice, Joy the luminous cloud—
> We in ourselves rejoice!
> And thence flows all that charms or ear or sight,
> All melodies the echoes of that voice,
> All colours a suffusion from that light. (59-75)

The music, the passion, the glory that can only spring upward from the soul is here revealed, somewhat unexpectedly, to be joy. Seasoned readers of Romantic poetry might have expected Coleridge to identify that music as love or imagination, but he chooses instead to call it joy. His reason for doing so becomes quite clear when we realize that, for the Romantic, love, joy, and imagination partake of the same essential nature. All three possess that most coveted of Romantic powers: the ability to unite, to fuse, to synthesize. All three have the ability first to discern similitude in the midst of dissimilitude and then to bring about that similitude through an incarnation of the two into one.

Joy, says Coleridge, is not only beautiful in itself but has the power to make others things beautiful. Likewise, as a cloud both contains and showers forth life-giving water, so joy both has life within itself and the power to scatter that life abroad. The same can be said, and often is said by Coleridge and the Romantics, about love (which is both the goal that lovers seek and the process by which they are made one) and imagination (which is both a skill necessary to poets and a creative process that births a new nature out of the old). In describing joy in such high and mystical terms, Coleridge secularizes the Christian understanding of the Incarnate Christ, who is both God and the Revelation of God, both the Giver of the Gift and the Gift itself, both the Eternal Word (or Logos) and the Word made Flesh. To say that Coleridge here secularizes the Incarnation is not to say that he in any way disrespects or parodies it. Rather he, like Blake in "The Lamb," extends a central Christian doctrine so that it incorporates not only the healing of the division between God and man but the healing of the division between man and nature.

Indeed, in the second half of stanza 5, Coleridge goes on to secularize one of the most powerful teachings of Christianity—that our present age will be ushered out and the new age ushered in by the Marriage Feast of the Lamb. As I explained in my analysis of "The Lamb," this Great Marriage—described with prophetic and aesthetic sublimity in the closing chapters of Revelation—will bring about the eternal union of Christ (the Lamb or Bridegroom) and his Church (the Bride). Without in anyway debunking or demythologizing this glorious doctrine, Coleridge prophesies a parallel marriage that will take place here and now, not in heaven but on this earth that is our present home. Through the incarnational power of joy (and love and imagination), a wedding will be celebrated and consummated between Nature and the Mind of Man, a wedding that, like the coming Great Marriage of Christ and the Church, will usher in "a new Heaven and a new Earth." Furthermore, as the Bible warns that sinners (those guilty of what 1 John 2:16 identifies as "the lust of the flesh, and the lust of the eyes, and the pride of life") will not inherit that new and glorious Kingdom, so Coleridge warns that "the sensual and the proud" will be unable to conceive—or, better, *perceive*—the glory that will be revealed when Barfield's "final participation" unites man and nature in a higher synthesis of subject and object.

Although Coleridge's vision of "a new Earth and a new Heaven" (one which he shared with Wordsworth) is what ultimately provides the resolution to his crisis, at the time he describes it, he is as yet unable to participate in it. His dejection is still too strong. As a result, Coleridge returns, in stanza 6, to describing his crisis, this time offering a narrative account of his slow but inexorable fall from inner joy into inner darkness:

> There was a time when, though my path was rough,
> This joy within me dallied with distress,
> And all misfortunes were but as the stuff
> Whence Fancy made me dreams of happiness:
> For hope grew round me, like the twining vine,
>
> And fruits, and foliage, not my own, seemed mine.
> But now afflictions bow me down to earth;
> Nor care I that they rob me of my mirth;
> But oh! each visitation
> Suspends what nature gave me at my birth,

> My shaping spirit of Imagination.
> For not to think of what I needs must feel,
> But to be still and patient, all I can;
> And haply by abstruse research to steal
> From my own nature all the natural man—
>
> This was my sole resource, my only plan:
> Till that which suits a part infects the whole,
> And now is almost grown the habit of my soul. (76-93)

Attentive readers will, I hope, note that the first four words of this stanza are identical to those with which Wordsworth begins his "Intimations Ode," and that the last line of the stanza—like the last line of Wordsworth's stanza—is an alexandrine. There *was* a time, Coleridge recalls, when the joy within him was so strong that it was undisturbed by any and all misfortune. Depression and grief would strike him now and then, but they would not drag him down, for he knew that his joy would return and restore him. But now, his inner joy has fled, leaving him prey to each new visitation of grief.

Something within him has been suspended, something which he identifies in stanza 5 and the first part of stanza 6 as "joy," but which he abruptly and somewhat confusingly identifies in line 86 as his "shaping spirit of Imagination." Of course, this sudden shift in terminology should not surprise us, as we have already seen how intimately related the powers of love, joy, and imagination were in the mind of Coleridge and his fellow Romantics. In his *Biographia Literaria*, published 15 years after "Dejection: An Ode," Coleridge, perhaps reflecting back on his "shaping spirit of Imagination," would coin a new word ("esemplastic") to describe what he considered to be the imagination's supreme quality. Formed from the Greek words for "into," "one," and "to shape," the word esemplastic means, literally, "to shape into one"; as such, the word highlights that very incarnational quality shared by love, joy, and imagination.

At the core of Coleridge's crisis is not just the loss of joy/love/imagination per se, but the loss of his ability to shape, to synthesize, and to fuse. Robbed of his ability to effect, physically, emotionally, aesthetically, or otherwise, the marriage of mind and nature, Coleridge is left stranded in a dead world. For a while, Coleridge preserves himself from a total breakdown by feeding parasitically on his own diminishing stores of joy. But this negative method soon catches up with him. Like a foolish retiree who, having squandered the interest generated by his savings goes on to squander his principal as well, Coleridge eventually eats up all his emotional and perceptual reserves. Infected by what modern motivational speakers call the "paralysis of analysis," Coleridge's "meddling intellect"—if I may paraphrase Wordsworth's "The Tables Turned"—both misshapes the beauteous forms of nature and dissects his own inner being. Ironically and tragically, Coleridge has himself become the vampire-like Spectre-Woman who curses the Ancient Mariner with the horror and despair of Life-in-Death.

#

In the final two stanzas of his Ode, Coleridge attempts to move toward a final resolution, but that resolution sadly lacks the clarity and authority of the one we encounter in Wordsworth's Ode. First, over the course of his lengthy and meandering seventh stanza, Coleridge turns his thoughts away from his grief and dejection and listens to the storm which has finally come and which rips out of the Aeolian harp a mad and frenzied song. Then, in the shorter eighth, he turns his attention back to Sara and wishes her well:

> 'Tis midnight, but small thoughts have I of sleep:
> Full seldom may my friend such vigils keep!
> Visit her, gentle Sleep! with wings of healing,
> And may this storm be but a mountain-birth,
> May all the stars hang bright above her dwelling,
> Silent as though they watched the sleeping Earth!
> With light heart may she rise,
> Gay fancy, cheerful eyes,
> Joy lift her spirit, joy attune her voice;
> To her may all things live, from pole to pole,
> Their life the eddying of her living soul!
> O simple spirit, guided from above,
> Dear Lady! friend devoutest of my choice,
> Thus mayest thou ever, evermore rejoice. (126-139)

Clearly, by the end of the poem, Coleridge has found some degree of rest and peace, but by what means? Though Coleridge does not, to my mind at least, make the means of his restoration clear, I would suggest that his peace is restored to him when he does two things that have been known to bring relief to modern sufferers of clinical depression. First, in stanza 7, he turns his attention away from himself and his own over-self-consciousness. By thus forgetting himself and the crushing weight of his grief for a space, he gains perspective on his depression and is able to see it for what it is. Second, in stanza 8, he actively helps someone else, showing an eagerness to prevent her from ever suffering the grief he suffers and to assist her in preserving her inner joy. If, as I suggested in my analysis of Blake's "The Little Black Boy," love is most accurately defined as the movement out of narcissism, then the tender and heartfelt generosity that Coleridge lavishes upon Sara—a generosity similar to that which Wordsworth lavishes on Dorothy in the final movement of "Tintern Abbey"—unlocks his latent stores of love.

Still, though I believe this twofold "therapy" plays a decisive role in mitigating the weight of Coleridge's crisis, the real resolution of "Dejection: An Ode" is to be found, not in the final two stanzas, but in the vision the poet conjures for us in stanza 5 of "a new Heaven and a new Earth." Only by effecting this higher synthesis of mind and nature, subject and object, internal and external can the poet hope to move out of his dejection toward a final participation that will unite him with nature in a manner that transcends both the pantheistic paganism of the past and the scientific rationalism of the present.

What Coleridge's Ode both yearns for and foresees is a secularization of one of the strangest and most exhilarating passages in the epistles of St. Paul:

> I consider that our present sufferings are not worth comparing with the glory that will be revealed in us. The creation [nature] waits in eager expectation for the sons of God to be revealed. For the creation was subjected to frustration, not by its own choice, but by the will of the one who subjected it, in hope that the creation itself will be liberated from its bondage to decay and brought into the glorious freedom of the children of God.
>
> We know that the whole creation has been groaning as in the pains of childbirth right up to the present time. Not only so, but we ourselves, who have the firstfruits of the Spirit, groan inwardly as we wait eagerly for our adoption as sons, the redemption of our bodies. (Romans 8:18-23; NIV)

In *Saving the Appearances*, Barfield quotes the second sentence of this passage and then follows it with this gloss from the German Romantic poet Novalis: "Man is the Messiah of nature."[14] Just as the Bible teaches that, through Christ's Incarnation, Crucifixion, and Resurrection, the human race was freed from its subjection to sin, so does this passage suggest that it will be through the mediation of a redeemed humanity that nature will be freed from her bondage to futility, corruption, and

---

14   *Ibid*, 160.

decay. Or, to put it another way, it is only after man has been glorified from within that his inner radiance will be reflected in a new and glorified nature.

According to the gnostic and solipsistic vision of Blake's *Marriage of Heaven and Hell*, "If the doors of perception were cleansed every thing would appear to man as it is, infinite." According to the redemptive solipsism of Coleridge's vision, when man finally learns to perceive the world through the esemplastic powers of love, joy, and imagination, he will initiate the marriage, not of heaven and hell, but of nature and the mind of man. And when that happens, Wordsworth's goal of rendering the natural supernatural and Coleridge's goal of rendering the supernatural natural will become the same goal.

Then, and only then, will Blake's "Tyger" truly be able to lay down with his "Lamb."

XI
Trumpet of a Prophecy

Though we often speak of the British Romantics as if they were all exact contemporaries, the major poets actually fall into two distinct generations. The first generation—Blake (1757-1827), Wordsworth (1770-1850), and Coleridge (1772-1834)—were already of age when the French Revolution began If we put aside for a moment the highly idiosyncratic and fiercely independent Blake and consider only Wordsworth and Coleridge, both of whom were—together with their friend Robert Southey (1774-1843)—far more representative of their generation, we will discern a recognizable pattern of post-Bastille youthful enthusiasm and political liberalism giving way, after the horrors of the Terror and the tyrannies of Napoleon, to a more conservative and even reactionary outlook. In the face of revolutionary ideals gone sour and profound internal crises, they ultimately find solace in the beauty of the English countryside (especially the Lake District) and the less complicated, more authentic life of those who dwell there. Though they never fully lose their focus on the centrality of perception, they learn to balance it with a deep and even patriotic love both for nature and for their homeland.

The second generation—Lord Byron (1788-1824), Percy Bysshe Shelley (1792-1822), and John Keats (1795-1821)—were born too late to have experienced either the hopeful heights of the Storming of the Bastille or the despairing depths of the Reign of Terror. They did come of age in the shadow of Napoleon, but without having lived through the prelude to Napoleon, they were more apt to view him as a highly romanticized and even misunderstood figure: in short, as a Byronic hero to be admired and pitied rather than reviled and feared. Since all three poets died young, we cannot say for sure that they would not themselves have grown more conservative with age, but such a scenario seems unlikely. Their romanticism tended to be more extreme than that of their predecessors, and not only in terms of behavior—though Byron and Shelley were notorious for their frequent and usually scandalous amours, and both were active in political and revolutionary causes (Byron actually died, of illness, while fighting for Greek Independence against the Turks). The second generation of Romantic poets pressed even further inward, expressing through their poetry an increased personal angst and an increased desire to escape the confines of our world. Like all Romantics, they write about nature, yet they are unable to find ultimate satisfaction in nature. Rather, they yearn to transcend it: through the magic of poetry, through aesthetic or prophetic inspiration, through tapping the power that runs behind nature, through imitating the pure song of the bird, or through entering the timeless time of great art. As for finding solace in love of their homeland, this was denied them. All three died outside of England—Byron in Greece, Shelly and Keats in Italy—in a partly self-imposed exile. And all three suffered, in varying degrees, from a persecution complex, from a sense of their own martyrdom to physical, social, and/or emotional forces outside their control.

Byron, as we saw in Chapter Eight, channeled much of his own persecution complex into creating the semi-autobiographical figure of the Byronic hero. Shelley and Keats would also write some excellent long works featuring tormented, angst-ridden characters onto whom they would project their own struggles and desires. They did, however, also fashion some of the finest lyrics of the Romantic Age, crisis poems that rival those of Wordsworth and Coleridge. Interestingly, though the crisis poems of the former two poets generally present us with more extreme and conflicting emotions than those of the latter two, Shelley and Keats consciously chose to compose their crisis poems in the form of a regular, as opposed to irregular, ode. Indeed, it may be precisely *because* the emotional level of their odes is so intense that Shelley and Keats chose to contain that intensity within the strict confines of a regular stanza.

Too Soon Grown Old

When he sat down, in December of 1818, to compose "Stanzas Written in Dejection, Near Naples," Shelley had much reason to be depressed: two years earlier, his first wife Harriet had drowned herself; one year earlier, he had been refused custody of his and Harriet's children and had begun to have serious financial difficulties; three months earlier,

Clara, his daughter with his wife Mary (author of *Frankenstein*), had died, and the poet himself was overcome with debilitating physical pain. Though the magnificent landscapes of Naples spoke to Shelley's sensitive nature, they could neither shield him from his personal pain nor rescue him from his deep melancholy and his feelings of personal failure.

Following the example of Wordsworth and Coleridge, Shelley begins his crisis poem by describing for us in exquisite detail the beauty of his natural setting:

> The sun is warm, the sky is clear,
> The waves are dancing fast and bright;
> Blue isles and snowy mountains wear
> The purple noon's transparent might;
> The breath of the moist air is light,
> Around its unexpanded buds;
> Like many a voice of one delight,
> The winds, the birds, the ocean floods,
> The City's voice itself, is soft like Solitude's. (1-9)

All of nature is at peace; all exists, from earth to sky to sea, in a universal harmony. Influenced by the Romantic flirtation with pantheism, Shelley presents his reader with waves that dance, air that breathes, and mountains that array themselves in splendid garments. A critic of Shelley—and Shelley has had more than his fair share of critics—might complain that the poet's descriptions of nature are derivative, and even hackneyed; but Shelley saves himself from such a charge in the last line of the stanza. In a surprising, and non-Romantic, move, Shelley assimilates the voice of the city into that of wind and bird and flood. The peace and harmony of nature are so strong that they include within their hushed solitude—a solitude that shimmers with potential energy—the unnatural stillness of the sleeping city.

And the power and magic of that last line is itself made more powerful and magical by the unique form that Shelley adopts for his poem. Shelley employs a modified version of the Spenserian stanza that Edmund Spenser invented for his epic *Faerie Queene*. Built upon a challenging, interwoven rhyme scheme of ABABBCBCC, the Spenserian stanza consists of eight iambic pentameter lines followed by a closing alexandrine. Though Shelley wrote one of his major long poems, *Adonais*, in Spenserian stanzas of remarkable precision and beauty, he chooses here to make a slight alteration: he retains the alexandrine, but shrinks lines 1-8 from iambic pentameter to iambic tetrameter (8 syllables, with accents on the even syllables). This change causes the closing alexandrine to feel stretched and unnaturally drawn out. In line 9 that drawn out feeling harmonizes perfectly with the unexpected stillness of Naples a stillness that contrasts sharply with what Wordsworth calls (in "Tintern Abbey") the "din of towns and cities."

Having carefully created this feeling of breathlessness in the last line of his first stanza, Shelley moves on, in stanza 2, to describe his crisis. Once he does so, the mood and feel of his closing alexandrines also shift to capture, not the hushed stillness of the setting, but the inner grief and weariness of the poet. We already discussed in the previous two chapters how both Wordsworth and Coleridge used alexandrines in their irregular odes to convey their own grief and weariness. Because of the greater metrical gap that he places between his shortened lines (1-8) and his long alexandrines (9), Shelley intensifies the effect achieved in the "Intimations Ode" and "Dejection: An Ode." Indeed, he intensifies it even further by establishing the alexandrine as a fixed part of his stanza. Since the regular nature of Shelley's ode decrees that the alexandrine *will* return at the end of each stanza, the poet effectively traps himself within a melancholy refrain from which he cannot escape.

Thus, after spending the next eight lines describing the rich and strange beauty of the sea floor, Shelley ends stanza 2 with the following alexandrine: "How sweet! did any heart now share in my emotion" (18). As heavy and weary as line 9 is light and mystical, Shelley's second alexandrine capture perfectly the feeling of isolation that overwhelms the dejected poet. What good can all this beauty do if the poet lacks a kindred spirit to share it with him? He develops the thought and the feeling in stanza 3:

> Alas! I have nor hope nor health,
>
> Nor peace within nor calm around,
>   Nor that content surpassing wealth
>
> The sage in meditation found,
>
> And walked with inward glory crowned—
>   Nor fame, nor power, nor love, nor leisure.
>
> Others I see whom these surround—
>   Smiling they live, and call life pleasure;—
>   To me that cup has been dealt in another measure. (19-27)

Like the Ancient Mariner, Shelley here feels cut off from the rest of society; he is a border figure doomed to live his life in the margins. Though he is as secluded and solitary as a sage in meditation, he does not share the sage's hope or peace or contentment. On the faces of others he sees life and joy, but in his own he sees only the grief and anguish of the One who, at Gethsemane, prayed to his Father that he might take away from him the "cup" of suffering he would soon endure on the Cross (Matthew 26:39). Without intending either blasphemy or parody, the poet uses his biblical allusion to suggest how wide and deep are his feelings of physical and emotional martyrdom.

When I teach this poem, and others by Shelley, to my female college students, I find that some react by wanting to hold the weeping poet to their breast, while others (generally the majority!) want to shake him by the lapels, give him a smack, and tell him to "get a life." Though I am more sensitive than most to Shelley's complaints, it must be admitted that Shelly does betray a strong tendency to feel sorry for himself. His weepiness and over-emotionalism have, in fact, garnered him much critical attack over the last two centuries. In his defense, I can only say that Shelley himself felt keenly the emotions he conveys in his poetry. As a poet and as a man, he knew both the joys and the dark side of living in close companionship with his deeper feelings and allowing his internal perceptions to color the world around him.

Shelly was the type of person who takes everything to heart, and he spent most of his life feeling like a scapegoat:

> Yet now despair itself is mild,
>
> Even as the winds and waters are;
>   I could lie down like a tired child,
>
> And weep away the life of care
>
> Which I have borne and yet must bear,
>   Till death like sleep might steal on me,
>
> And I might feel in the warm air
>   My cheek grow cold, and hear the sea
> Breathe o'er my dying brain its last monotony. (28-36)

There is in Shelley's poetry a constant sense of the pain and suffering that he *"must* bear." Even in moments of rest when "despair itself is mild," he feels the need for tears to bathe and soothe his "life of care." He lives each day haunted by an ultimately suicidal desire to pass away into non-existence. Like Shakespeare's great proto-Romantic hero, Shelley's deepest wish is for oblivion: "O that this too too sullied flesh would melt, / Thaw and resolve itself into a dew!" (*Hamlet*, I.ii.129-130).

Hamlet and his Romantic heirs seek not just death, but annihilation, an end to the weary weight of ceaseless introspection and burdensome over-self-consciousness. The closing lines of the stanza record Shelley's wish (fear? prophecy?) to feel the undulating waters pass over him and slowly obliterate the feverish workings of his brain. In a sad and eerie irony, Shelley's death came to him in that exact manner, in a boating accident that left him, like his first wife Harriet, to drown in the arms of the sea.

And when the waters have closed over him, the poet wonders, will anyone care:

>Some might lament that I were cold,
>
>As I, when this sweet day is gone,
> Which my lost heart, too soon grown old,
>
>Insults with this untimely moan;
>
>They might lament—for I am one
> Whom men love not,—and yet regret,
>
>Unlike this day, which, when the sun
> Shall on its stainless glory set,
>Will linger, though enjoyed, like joy in memory yet. (37-45)

Shelley's martyr complex again emerges in his firmly held belief that he is "one / Whom men love not," a belief that deepens his isolation and increases his dejection. Like the Byronic heroes I described in Chapter Eight, Shelley is what might be called an "old young man": young in years but old in experience and in thought. He lacks a kindred spirit, but that is because he is himself of a different order than the people who dwell around him. He hopes that some will lament his passing as he does the passing of the day; yet he knows that even those who do lament his passing will not remember him with joy as he with joy will remember this day when it passes into darkness, never to return.

I Fall upon the Thorns of Life

Just as Shelley invented a modified Spenserian stanza to incarnate the grief and isolation of "Stanzas Written in Dejection," so did he invent a modified version of Dante's terza rima to help him work through the emotional crisis of "Ode to the West Wind." Terza rima, a form that Dante invented for his epic *Divine Comedy*, consists of a succession of three-line stanzas (known as tercets) interlocked by rhyme: ABA, BCB, CDC, etc. Whereas each canto of Dante's *Comedy* is built around an unbroken series of tercets, Shelley divides his poem into five distinct 14-line sections, each composed of four tercets and a rhyming couplet: ABA, BCB, CDC, DED, EE. As fourteen lines is the standard length for sonnets, Shelley's ode can be interpreted simultaneously as a canto in the manner of Dante or a short sonnet sequence in the manner of Shakespeare.

To add to the complexity of the ode, Shelley does something that is uncharacteristic of Romantic odes and even more so of Shelley's own practice in his lyrics: he holds off the first-person pronoun, the "I," until the fourth section of the poem. Generally considered the most egocentric and solipsistic of the Romantic poets, Shelley shows remarkable restraint in allowing the natural world, rather than his perceptions of it, to dominate the first three sections. His ability to do so rests, I believe, on the fact that his poem, "Ode to the West Wind," might more accurately be titled, "Hymn to the West Wind." The dejected and anguished poet praises the West Wind as though it were almost a deity:

> O, wild West Wind, thou breath of Autumn's being,
> Thou, from whose unseen presence the leaves dead
> Are driven, like ghosts from an enchanter fleeing,
>
> Yellow, and black, and pale, and hectic red,
> Pestilence-stricken multitudes: O, thou,
> Who chariotest to their dark wintry bed
>
> The wingèd seeds, where they lie cold and low,
> Each like a corpse within its grave, until
> Thine azure sister of the spring shall blow
>
> Her clarion o'er the dreaming earth, and fill
> (Driving sweet buds like flocks to feed in air)
> With living hues and odours plain and hill:
>
> Wild Spirit, which art moving everywhere;
> Destroyer and preserver; hear, oh, hear! (1-14)

Shelley's description of the West Wind apotheosizes it from a mere natural phenomenon into a pantheistic power that propels and interpenetrates all things. Its true counterpart is not to be found in that "presence that disturbs [Wordsworth] with the joy / Of elevated thoughts" in "Tintern Abbey," but in the Orcic energy that Blake celebrates in his prophetic poetry.

For the West Wind, like the Tyger, is neither good nor evil; rather, it is a force, a power that transcends good and evil When Shelley hails the West Wind as being both a "Destroyer and preserver," he conjures a vision that is far more Eastern than Western. Although Hinduism identifies three main gods, the Hindu triad (or Trimurti) of Brahma, Vishnu, and Shiva is very different from the Christian Trinity of Father, Son, and Holy Spirit. Aside from the obvious fact that only the Christian Trinity represents a single God in three Persons, the functions of the three betray a worldview difference between West and East. Whereas both the Father and Brahma are Creators and both Christ and Vishnu are Saviors, the role of the Spirit contrasts sharply with that of Shiva. The Holy Spirit preserves and empowers; Shiva destroys. This distinction in divine function overlaps with two radically different conceptions of time. Christianity is founded upon a linear view of history, one that has a beginning (the Fall), a middle (the Life, Death, and Resurrection of Christ), and an end (the Second Coming). Hinduism, in contrast, is cyclical, marked by a potentially endless cycle of creation, destruction, and recreation.

Although the motif of life-death-rebirth is central to Christianity, and although Shelley's "clarion" (10) seems to allude to the horn that the archangel Gabriel will blow to usher in the Second Coming, the West Wind, as described in the poem, is too impersonal and arbitrary to qualify as an embodiment of any part of the Christian Trinity. Like the "sacred river" that bursts out of the volcano in Coleridge's "Kubla Khan," the West Wind is an apocalyptic, revolutionary force that destroys indiscriminately all in its path. In its fury, however, it paves the way for new life. Carl Jung, who was himself more Eastern/Romantic than Western/Rationalistic in his worldview, distinguished between a man's conscious masculine outer self (his animus) and his unconscious feminine inner self (or anima). Writing a century before Jung, Shelley gives the destructive masculine animus of his West Wind a gentler, nurturing feminine anima. Whereas the West Wind blows the autumn leaves in a mad dance of death, its "azure sister" (its feminine anima) blows in the spring and recalls the leaves from their sleep of death.

Still, the promise of the "azure sister" places no limits on the uncontrollable West Wind. Just as its shakes the trees, causing the leaves to scatter and fall, so does it shake the heavens:

> Thou on whose stream, 'mid the steep sky's commotion,
> Loose clouds like Earth's decaying leaves are shed,
> Shook from the tangled boughs of Heaven and Ocean,
>
> Angels of rain and lightning: there are spread
> On the blue surface of thine aëry surge,

> Like the bright hair uplifted from the head
>
> Of some fierce Mænad, even from the dim verge
> Of the horizon to the zenith's height,
> The locks of the approaching storm. Thou dirge
>
> Of the dying year, to which this closing night
> Will be the dome of a vast sepulcher,
> Vaulted with all thy congregated might
>
> Of vapors, from whose solid atmosphere
> Black rain, and fire, and hail will burst: oh, hear! (13-24)

In one of his most sublime images, Shelley transforms the sky into a vast tree from whose "tangled boughs" the West Wind tears out clouds as though they were so many "decaying leaves." Nothing in the heavens or on the earth can resist its fierce energy.

In search of just the right metaphor to embody the West Wind's violent frenzy, Shelley settles on a Greek figure whose origin is itself Eastern. The Maenads (line 21), as I explained in my analysis of "Kubla Khan," were wild women who fled from the polis to follow in the train of Bacchus, and who abandoned order and rationality in favor of intoxication and emotional excess. Like the Maenads, the West Wind cares little for the concerns of the polis—the concerns, that is, of civilization; it obeys instead its own primal, revolutionary instinct to purge from the world all that is old or worn or decayed. In the closing lines of section two, Shelley imagines the West Wind forming a "vast sepulchre" in the sky from whose (paradoxical) womb-tomb "black rain and fire and hail . . . burst." Again, we cannot help but recall the "deep romantic chasm" of "Kubla Khan" that gives birth, in "fast thick pants," to a "mighty fountain" and to "huge fragments" which rush down to the ocean, bringing to Kubla dark intimations of a coming war.

And still the West Wind blows on. In sections 1 and 2, Shelley's almost demonic Wind rips leaves from trees and clouds from the sky; in section 3, it rips out even the waves as its mighty breath cleaves the ocean in twain. The very abyss trembles with fear, and the foliage that clings to the bottom of the sea changes its color in sympathy with the dying leaves.

In the midst of this threefold display of power we encounter a poet in crisis who desperately needs the kind of hectic and frenzied inspiration that only the West Wind can give:

> If I were a dead leaf thou mightest bear;
> If I were a swift cloud to fly with thee;
> A wave to pant beneath thy power, and share
>
> The impulse of thy strength, only less free
> Than thou, O, uncontrollable! If even
> I were as in my boyhood, and could be
>
> The comrade of thy wanderings over heaven,
> As then, when to outstrip thy skiey speed
> Scarce seemed a vision; I would ne'er have striven
>
> As thus with thee in prayer in my sore need,.
> Oh! lift me as a wave, a leaf, a cloud!
> I fall upon the thorns of life! I bleed!
>
> A heavy weight of hours has chained and bowed
> One too like thee: tameless, and swift, and proud. (43-56)

Throughout the first three sections of the poem, we now realize, Shelley has been envying the leaves and the clouds and the waves. It is he, the conscious poet, who desires to be lifted up like the leaves, carried along like the clouds, and seduced like the waves. I do not use the word "seduced" facetiously. In line 45, Shelley clearly places himself in the feminine position of a swooning maiden swept off her feet by a fiercely masculine suitor. Shelley's wish is to be passively taken up by the Wind that he might share in its active, uncontrollable strength, that he might feel its wild impulses course through his languid veins.

Like the poets of "Tintern Abbey," the "Intimations Ode," and "Dejection: An Ode," Shelley yearns for both restoration and rejuvenation. The adult poet has lost the power and spontaneity that he once knew in his youth. As the young Wordsworth and Coleridge lived in direct, joyous communion with the beauty and majesty of nature, so the young Shelley rejoiced in his close proximity to the West Wind. Indeed, in his boyhood, he often imagined that, with the West Wind blowing on his back, he could "outstrip [its] skiey speed." But the years have taken their toll on the indomitable spirit of the boy, weighing him down with grief and care and beating out of him his enthusiasm and hope. In place of his early visions of limitless speed and power, a stifling persecution complex has taken root in his tormented psyche. As a result, the poet of "Stanzas Written in Dejection," who had fancied himself sharing the emotional agony of the "cup" of Gethsemane, now complains that he shares as well the physical pain of Golgotha: "I fall upon the thorns of life! I bleed!" Combining the torments of Christ's crucifixion with the pain and humiliation of the crown of thorns, Shelley casts himself in the role of a suffering scapegoat who is rejected and forsaken by society.

And yet, deep down, he knows that he is not a sinless scapegoat. His use of the word "too" in line 56 is telling. On the one hand, it suggests that he is *also*, like the West Wind, "tameless, and swift, and proud." On the other, it suggests that in his tamelessness, his swiftness, and his pride, he is *too much* like the West Wind. Like the heroes of Greek tragedy, it is partly his own hubris, his own excessive arrogance, that has led to his downfall. In fact, his use of the word "chained" in line 55 suggests that he is less like Christ than he is like Prometheus, the proud Titan and proto-Byronic hero whose love for mankind mingled with his rebellious nature led to his chaining by the vengeful Zeus.

What then does the adult Shelley wish to receive from the West Wind? What can it give him that will help him to resolve his crisis? In the final section, Shelley makes his desires clear:

> Make me thy lyre, even as the forest is:
> What if my leaves are falling like its own!
> The tumult of thy mighty harmonies
>
> Will take from both a deep, autumnal tone,
> Sweet though in sadness. Be thou, Spirit fierce,
> My spirit! Be thou me, impetuous one!
>
> Drive my dead thoughts over the universe
> Like withered leaves to quicken a new birth!
> And, by the incantation of this verse,
>
> Scatter, as from an unextinguished hearth
> Ashes and sparks, my words among mankind!
> Be through my lips to unawakened Earth
>
> The trumpet of a prophecy! O, Wind,
> If Winter comes, can Spring be far behind? (57-70)

The lyre referred to in line 57 is, of course, our old friend the Aeolian harp, but Shelley adds to this common Romantic metaphor his own brilliant touch. Like all Romantic poets, Shelley yearns to be a living, conscious harp, to be played on by inspiration as the harp is by the wind, but Shelley extends the analogy to encompass the full power of the West Wind. Just as the earthly wind caresses the strings of the harp to produce music, so the cosmic West Wind bends the tall pines of the forest causing them to tremble and quiver into song. It is that kind of power that the poet will need if he is to pull himself out of his crisis and remain true to his poetic calling. Though Shelley was not yet thirty when he wrote the poem, he felt already as though he were old, as though his life had fallen into the sear. Perhaps if the West Wind can draw an autumnal music from the yellow, withered leaves of a November forest, it can do the same for the poet.

If only Shelley can both merge with the fierce spirit of the West Wind and allow it to flow unimpeded through him, then he need not fear the crushing weight of his melancholy thoughts. To the contrary, those very thoughts, lifted up by the West Wind, can be renewed and reborn. Better yet, those renewed thoughts, carried and scattered abroad by the Wind, can reach the minds and hearts of all those who have ears to hear. And when that happens, Shelley will be transfigured into what he most desires to be: a Romantic poet-prophet. He will speak to the dreaming earth, asleep beneath its wintry blanket, and, by the incantatory power of his verse, call it back to a new and more glorious spring. He will be the angelic trumpet through which the apocalyptic strains will be sounded. He will be the herald and the harbinger of a new dawn.

Unpremeditated Art

Though Shelley's longing to channel the music and inspiration of the wind is not unheard of among Romantic poets, Shelley and his fellow Romantics were far more likely to seek such music and inspiration in the joyous song of birds. The reason for this becomes evident when we recall how highly the Romantics privileged direct, unmediated freshness and spontaneity. What could be more pure, more emphatic, more free from the burden of over-self-consciousness than the sweet, undiluted melody of the skylark? So Shelley felt, and he incarnated this feeling in one of the most beautiful lyrics to come out of the Romantic Age.

As with "Stanzas Written in Dejection" and "Ode to the West Wind," Shelley carefully fashioned a new poetic form to help capture the exact mood he wished to express in his poem. This time, Shelley invented a tight five-line stanza composed of four lines of trochaic trimeter (five or six syllables with accents on the odd syllables) followed by an alexandrine. The effect of this unique stanza is to generate a tension and expectation in the four short lines that is then released in the long closing line. Unlike the alexandrines of "Stanzas Written in Dejection," which feel both heavy and weary, the alexandrines of "To a Skylark" provoke a sense of freedom and flight as they stretch outward to the horizon.

From the very first stanza, Shelley makes it clear why the song of the skylark speaks to him with such power:

> Hail to thee, blithe Spirit!
> Bird thou never wert,
>   That from heaven, or near it,
> Pourest thy full heart
> In profuse strains of unpremeditated art. (1-5)

Less a physical bird than a spirit of pure song, the skylark inspires both pleasure and awe in the listening poet, who wonders to himself if the skylark is not, in fact, an angelic being. The bird's song does not merely issue from its throat; it cascades forth in a flood of melody that overwhelms the poet. Neither planning nor forethought has gone into the bird's song; it sings with total abandon, pouring every ounce of its being into its music.

Though some birds only sing while they are motionless, perched on the ground or on the branch of a tree, the skylark possesses the skill to sing and fly simultaneously:

> Higher still and higher
> From the earth thou springest
>   Like a cloud of fire;
> The blue deep thou wingest,
> And singing still dost soar, and soaring ever singest. (6-10)

Like the mythical phoenix that is born anew out of its own funereal ashes, the skylark springs upward into the sky. In a rush of motion and of sound, the unconquerable spirit of the bird leaves behind the sullen earth with its mundane weight of cares to embrace the heavens. In the closing alexandrines of the next three stanzas, Shelley explains why the dizzying flight of the skylark increases its appeal:

> Like an unbodied joy whose race is just begun. (15)
> Thou art unseen, but yet I hear thy shrill delight. (20)
> Until we hardly see, we feel that it is there. (25)

For the second generation of Romantic poets, the sought-after ideal is a joy that transcends both the physical world and their own bodily existence. While Wordsworth and Coleridge yearned to fix and incarnate their ideal in a real, concrete setting (hence their longing to effect a marriage of mind and nature), Byron, Shelley, and Keats longed to escape altogether from the confines of the physical. Hence, Shelley's enjoyment of the bird is enhanced by the fact that, though he hears its song, he cannot actually see the skylark. It remains forever an "unbodied joy," a pure song untrammeled by the weight and pain of matter.

Shelley's fascination with the skylark's unseen melody is carried into the second movement of the poem (stanzas 7-11), during which the poet seeks to find an appropriate simile to describe the bird and its song. Whether he compares the bird to a "Poet hidden" (36), a "high-born maiden / In a palace tower" (41-42), a "glow-worm golden" (46), or a "rose embowered" (51), Shelley makes it clear that one of the chief qualities of the skylark is its invisibility. Though poet, maiden, glow-worm, and rose remain sequestered from the eyes of their fellow creatures, the music or color or scent that flows out from them brings love and joy and beauty to the world. The first of these similes is perhaps the most vital, for it expresses most clearly the kind of poet Shelley wishes he could be:

> Like a Poet hidden
>
> In the light of thought,
>   Singing hymns unbidden,
>
> Till the world is wrought
> To sympathy with hopes and fears it heeded not— (36-40)

As we saw in the closing lines of "Ode to the West Wind," Shelley desperately wants to be heard, to be the "trumpet of a prophecy" that will awaken the world from its slumber. So here, the poet would sing an unpremeditated ("unbidden") song that will nevertheless move and change all those who (over) hear it.

Having explored through simile the nature of the skylark and its song, the poet presses on to pose a question which burns within him:

> Teach us, Sprite or Bird,
> What sweet thoughts are thine:
>   I have never heard
> Praise of love or wine
> That panted forth a flood of rapture so divine:
>
> Chorus Hymenæal,
> Or triumphal chaunt,
>   Match`d with thine, would be all
> But an empty vaunt,
> A thing wherein we feel there is some hidden want.
>
>   What objects are the fountains
> Of thy happy strain?
>   What fields, or waves, or mountains?
> What shapes of sky or plain?
> What love of thine own kind? what ignorance of pain? (61-75)

What, the poet wonders, can possibly be the source of the bird's song? What could have inspired this passionate "flood of rapture so divine."? Shelley has heard songs before that celebrated the pleasures of love and of wine, or the joys of the wedding day, or the triumphs of military victory, but none of them came close to capturing the higher bliss and ecstasy of the skylark's song. Could it be the beauties of nature that have inspired the bird? Or a sense of avian pride and patriotism? Perhaps the skylark lives free of physical pain and thus sings out of its own unblemished health and well being?

The poet is bewildered, and his bewilderment increases his awareness of his own inability either to sing a song of such joy or to know within himself the kind of joy that could inspire such a song. As in "Ode to the West Wind," Shelley, whose awe-struck focus remains firmly on the object of his near worship, holds off all first-person pronouns (I, me, we, us) until the poem is well underway. That does not mean, however, that the poem is merely descriptive. It is Shelley's intense concentration on the bird and its song that both provokes his internal crisis and offers the possibility of resolution.

Confronted by the song of the skylark, Shelley becomes painfully aware of what he lacks:

> With thy clear keen joyance
> Langour cannot be—
>   Shadow of annoyance
> Never came near thee:
> Thou lovest—but ne'er knew love's sad satiety.
>
>   Waking or asleep,
> Thou of death must deem
>   Things more true and deep
> Than we mortals dream,
> Or how could thy notes flow in such a crystal stream? (76-85)

The skylark exists in a higher mode of being shut off from the poet, a realm in which one's joys can increase and expand without ever becoming lethargic or satiated. Imagine, if you can, a perpetual honeymoon in which the passion of the two lovers grows stronger every day while yet remaining as fresh and unspoiled as it did on their first night of love. No, the poet insists, the bird must possess some type of wisdom that we lack, some knowledge of death denied to us; else it could not sustain the beauty of its song.

For we mortals who grunt and sweat under the weary burden of over-self-consciousness, the bird's joy seems as unattainable as it is inexplicable:

> We look before and after
> And pine for what is not:
>   Our sincerest laughter
> With some pain is fraught;
> Our sweetest songs are those that tell of saddest thought.
>
>   Yet if we could scorn
> Hate, and pride, and fear;
>   If we were things born
> Not to shed a tear,
> I know not how thy joy we ever should come near. (86-95)

Like the melancholy Bard of Blake's *Songs of Experience* who "Present, Past, & Future, sees," we are unable to live emphatically in the present moment. Casting our eye now backward with sorrow and regret, now forward with fear and apprehension, we live timid, trembling lives of remorse. Even when we laugh, our laughter is tainted by pain; our sweetest songs, those that we might hold up as embodiments of pure joy, are themselves founded upon sadness and loss. Even if we could put aside our hate, humble our pride, and overcome our fear, even then, the poet laments, we could not approach the purity of the skylark's joy.

Still, though Shelley the man feels incapable of living his life in the midst of such undiluted joy, Shelley the poet yet reaches for inspiration:

>   Better than all measures
> Of delightful sound—
>   Better than all treasures
> That in books are found—
> Thy skill to poet were, thou scorner of the ground!
>
>   Teach me half the gladness
> That thy brain must know,
>   Such harmonious madness
> From my lips would flow
> The world should listen then—as I am listening now! (96-105)

One can hear lurking behind Shelley's second-to-last stanza the strains of St. Paul's famous love chapter (1 Corinthians 13). Though the poet should speak with the tongues of men and of angels, though he should be in possession of all mysteries and all knowledge, if he has not the skill of the bird, he is but a sounding brass and a tinkling cymbal. But if he could learn, like the bird, to scorn all that is petty and mundane, if he could channel but half the Bacchic joy that burns like a fire in the lark's brain, then would he sing such a song of beauty and power that the whole world would be compelled to listen.

Then would he truly become the Romantic poet-prophet.

XII
Process in Stasis

In the space of a single year, John Keats created a handful of the finest lyrics ever written in English . . . and then died of tuberculosis at the age of 25. The finely-honed genius of his poetry, combined with his early death, has led many to theorize that had Keats lived another 25 years, he could have matured into a poet as great as Shakespeare or Milton. But that is not necessarily the case. Keats's greatest poems were born out of the crucible of his own inner grief and angst. Even more so than Wordsworth and Coleridge, Keats worked out his struggles *through* his poetry; it is that, I believe, which gives his crisis poems their unique quality of immediacy and nakedness. Though never as "weepie" as those of Shelley, Keats's deeply personal lyrics carry the reader to the very core of the poet's anguished soul. Or, to put it another way, the same students (and English professors!) who ridicule Shelley for his protestations of martyrdom ("I fall upon the thorns of life! I bleed!"), will, in nearly all cases, extend both their sympathy and their respect to Keats and his work.

Though Keats left us three narrative poems of exquisite beauty, power, and insight (*Hyperion*, *The Eve of St. Agnes*, and *Lamia*) and six or seven sonnets that rank among the best ever written, he is today most remembered for his great odes: "Ode to Psyche," "Ode on Indolence," "Ode to a Nightingale," "Ode on a Grecian Urn," "Ode on Melancholy," and "To Autumn." In the best of these, those to the Nightingale and the Grecian Urn, Keats invites us to join him as he wrestles with death and life, illusion and reality, sorrow and joy, the mortality of flesh and the immortality of art—wrestles, and takes the prize. The reason I believe that a 30 or 40 year old Keats would not have been a greater artist than the 23 year old poet of the odes is that the 23 year old proved so successful in resolving, *through his odes*, his major emotional, spiritual, and aesthetic crises. Though "doctor's orders" forbad Keats from writing during his last year of life, I think there may have been a second reason that the miraculous creativity of 1819 did not carry over into 1820. Like few poets before or since, Keats had fully realized his struggles through the mediation of his art, and, by so doing, had achieved both catharsis and clarification.

Though Keats suffered greatly during his final year, and though he certainly had little inkling of the exalted status his works would one day enjoy, I believe that the peace and wisdom he achieved through his poetry sustained him until the end. Indeed, when I meditate on the death of John Keats, I think often of the bitter sweet words with which the dying Aragorn consoles Arwen in one of the appendices to Tolkien's *Lord of the Rings*: "In sorrow we must go, but not in despair."[15]

Full-Throated Ease

The opening stanza of "Ode to a Nightingale" leaves little doubt in my mind that Keats, like Coleridge, suffered from clinical depression:

> My heart aches, and a drowsy numbness pains
> My sense, as though of hemlock I had drunk,
> Or emptied some dull opiate to the drains
> One minute past, and Lethe-wards had sunk:
> 'Tis not through envy of thy happy lot,
> But being too happy in thine happiness,—
> That thou, light-winged Dryad of the trees,
> In some melodious plot
> Of beechen green, and shadows numberless,
> Singest of summer in full-throated ease. (1-10)

In "Dejection: An Ode," Coleridge describes his depression as a "grief without a pang, void, dark, and drear, / A stifled, drowsy, unimpassioned grief." So here, Keats highlights not the ferocity but the deadness of his emotions; he has been not so much overwhelmed by as drained of all feeling and desire. Though Keats did not share Coleridge's addiction to opium, his reference to having "emptied some dull opiate to the drains" calls up an image of an unconscious man stretched out on the floor of an opium den, whose addiction has left him devoid not only of purpose but of selfhood. This sense of lost identity is strengthened by Keats's reference to Lethe, a river in hades whose waters brought forgetfulness to all who drank of them.

---

15 J. R. R. Tolkien, *The Lord of the Rings* (New York: Houghton Mifflin, 2005), 1063.

A third reference to the drinking of hemlock fixes the exact mood that Keats so skillfully constructs in his opening four lines. Hemlock was the poison that the Athenian judges decreed Socrates must drink. In the Platonic dialogue that details the death of Socrates (*Phaedo*), we are given this description of what followed after the condemned philosopher drank the hemlock:

> Socrates walked about, and presently, saying that his legs were heavy, lay down on his back—that was what the man recommended. The man (he was the same one who had administered the poison) kept his hand upon Socrates, and after a little while examined his feet and legs; then pinched his foot hard and asked if he felt it. Socrates said no. Then he did the same to his legs; and moving gradually upwards in this way let us see that he was getting cold and numb. Presently he felt him again and said that when it reached the heart, Socrates would be gone.[16]

Plato's haunting account of how Socrates' body slowly grows cold and numb parallels precisely Keats's own fear that his depression will continue to creep through his veins until it freezes his blood and turns his heart to stone. Just as the poison of the hemlock drives Socrates on to his back before taking his life, so the weight of Keats's depression drags down his spirit and plunges him into suicidal despair.

It is not until the end of the first stanza that the poet reveals the cause of his depression. Keats, we learn, has been catapulted into his state of "drowsy numbness" by the song of a nightingale. Like Shelley's skylark, Keats's nightingale remains unseen throughout the poem; indeed, as Shelley wonders if the unbodied joy he hears does not belong rather to a spirit than a bird, so Keats wonders if the pure melody of the nightingale does not issue in truth from a dryad (or wood nymph). The unpremeditated freshness and spontaneity of the skylark's song is what speaks most powerfully to Shelley. For Keats, it is the utter abandonment with which the nightingale sings ("full-throated ease") that captivates him. Though Keats does not envy the bird its joyous, pain-free existence, the bird's song nevertheless causes the poet to experience grief and anguish. Lifted up for a moment into the higher mode of existence in which the nightingale lives, Keats quickly realizes that his mortal frame cannot sustain

---

16 Plato, *Phaedo*, in *The Last Days of Socrates*, translated by Hugh Tredennick (London: Penguin, 1969), 182-183. It may or may not be a coincidence that Shakespeare (in *Henry V*, Act 2, Scene 3) describes the death of Falstaff in a manner that closely parallels this passage from the *Phaedo*.

such a state of undiluted bliss. For a brief moment, Keats is pierced by the delight and ecstasy of the nightingale's song, but that piercing brings on a surfeit of pleasure that overwhelms the poet's capacity for joy. As a result, he is thrown backward into the state of dejection he describes in the first four lines.

No, if he is to follow the nightingale upward into that higher mode of being which is its natural element, Keats will need to partake of an anti-hemlock that will equip and strengthen him for the journey:

> O, for a draught of vintage! that hath been
>   Cool'd a long age in the deep-delved earth,
> Tasting of Flora and the country green,
>   Dance, and Provençal song, and sunburnt mirth!
> O for a beaker full of the warm South,
>   Full of the true, the blushful Hippocrene,
> With beaded bubbles winking at the brim,
>   And purple-stained mouth;
> That I might drink, and leave the world unseen,
>   And with thee fade away into the forest dim: (11-20)

In Washington Irving's beloved tale, Rip Van Winkle drinks a cold, frothy brew given him by the dwarfs and falls into a twenty-year slumber. Keats yearns to partake himself of such a vintage, one that "hath been / Cool'd a long age in the deep-delved earth." The poet craves something that he cannot quite define, something that is at once a taste, a temperature, and a texture. Something that blends the sights and sounds and tastes and smells of the countryside.

I have often wished myself that I could, by some mystical, alchemical process, filter out the essence of a glorious spring day and suspend it, with all its rare and fragrant beauty intact, in an elixir. Then, if ever the cold grew too bitter or the heat too oppressive, if ever I felt disconnected from the life and fecundity of nature, I could take a sip from the elixir and be filled again with the unremembered pleasures of that day. When Keats asks for "a beaker full of the warm South," he means, literally, a goblet filled with wine from Provence (a region in the south of France), but the line contains a second meaning. What the poet wants to take into himself is not just the wine from Provence, but Provence itself, replete with the songs and dances of the medieval troubadours who hailed from the region and whose spirits still hover there. He would not merely drink the wine, but press it against his palate until mouth and tongue and lips were died with its deep purple hue.

In his finest sermon, "The Weight of Glory," C. S. Lewis explains what it is that we *really* desire when we speak of the heavenly beauty that awaits us:

> We do not want merely to see beauty, though, God knows, even that is bounty enough. We want something else which can hardly be put into words—to be united with the beauty we see, to pass into it, to receive it into ourselves, to bathe in it, to become part of it. That is why we have peopled air and earth and water with gods and goddesses and nymphs and elves—that, though we cannot, yet these projections can enjoy in themselves that beauty, grace, and power of which Nature is the image.[17]

Lewis was an orthodox Christian, yet he uses here the same pantheistic language that we encounter so often in the poetry of the Romantics. Our true longing, as Lewis and the Romantics both understood, is not just to admire from without the beauty of nature, but to participate in it: in a word, to heal the division between subject and object. For Wordsworth and Coleridge, who, like Lewis, gradually matured into belief, the healing of that division was to be accomplished by the marriage of mind and nature (itself, as we have seen, a secularization of the Great Marriage of Christ and the Church). For Blake, the Gnostic mythmaker, the division was to be healed by the apocalyptic cleansing of our senses. Byron and Shelley, both of whom defined themselves in opposition to traditional religious belief, pursued that healing in one of two (contradictory) ways: either through the revolutionary restructuring of society or through the abandonment of society. But for Keats, who led the most intensely interior life of all the Romantics, that healing had little to do with religion per se.

Neither an adherent nor a critic of Christianity, Keats seems to have channeled whatever religious impulses he had into art; if he worshipped a God at all it was Apollo, the Greek god of music and of poetry. I do not say this to ridicule or parody Keats; indeed, I sometimes think of Keats more as a pre-Christian pagan poet from ancient Greece than an inhabitant of either Christian or post-Christian Europe. For Keats, art, especially poetry, was everything—both the classic, timeless poetry of Homer, Dante, Shakespeare, and Milton and his own attempts to create poems that could someday take their place in the aesthetic pantheon. It is no coincidence that the drink which Keats craves in stanza 2 comes not

---

17   C. S. Lewis, *The Weight of Glory and Other Addresses* (New York: Macmillan, 1980), 16.

only from the deep-delved earth and the warm fields of France but from Hippocrene, a fountain on Mt. Helicon that was sacred to the Muses and which the ancients sought as a source of poetic inspiration.

Unlike the "milk of paradise," the consumption of which turns the poet of "Kubla Khan" into an outcast and a contagion, the vintage Keats seeks will, if drunk, enable him to fade away into the forest alongside the nightingale and its song. Keats is far less concerned than Coleridge, Byron, or Shelley with becoming a Romantic poet-prophet. He merely wishes, as Shelley does in "Stanzas Written in Dejection," to imitate the opening lines of Hamlet's first soliloquy: "O that this too too sullied flesh would melt, / Thaw and resolve itself into a dew!" The alexandrine with which Keats ends his second stanza captures something of his desire simply to fade away into nothingness. The stanza that follows helps us to understand why it is that Keats longs so strongly to fade away:

> Fade far away, dissolve, and quite forget
>   What thou among the leaves hast never known,
> The weariness, the fever, and the fret
>   Here, where men sit and hear each other groan;
> Where palsy shakes a few, sad, last gray hairs,
>   Where youth grows pale, and spectre-thin, and dies;
> Where but to think is to be full of sorrow
>   And leaden-eyed despairs,
> Where Beauty cannot keep her lustrous eyes,
>   Or new Love pine at them beyond to-morrow. (21-30)

Less than six months before writing this stanza, Keats had lost his brother, Tom, to tuberculosis, the same slow, agonizing disease that would soon rob the poet of his own life. During the long and grueling months of Tom's illness, Keats stood by his bedside and watched him waste away. The horror of those terrible months engraved themselves in the poet's mind, leaving him with this image of the world as a vast tubercular ward. When set over against this grim image, Keats's desire for oblivion becomes easier to understand and to sympathize with.

Though both Byron and Shelley suffered throughout their lives from bouts of physical pain, they at least lived vigorous lives with plenty of fresh air and exercise. Keats's life was far more sheltered and stifling; he alone knew what protracted illness, weakness, and stagnation could do to the human spirit. Here and throughout Keats's poetry we are met by images of feverish brows, pale cheeks, and wasted visages; on every side we are greeted by the sad and weary groans of men from whom life is being drained. And yet, even as the body wastes away, the mind continues to be active, burdened by over-self-consciousness and silent despair. In such a world, beauty is fragile and fleeting and love cannot last beyond the day. In contrast, the life of the nightingale transcends all pain and weariness and despair. The bird and the song of the bird live in a world of process in stasis, a world where there exists, paradoxically, both growth and change (process) and eternal perfection (stasis).

The Viewless Wings of Poesy

As the fourth stanza begins, the poet renews his determination to reach the nightingale's world of process in stasis, but, in a move typical of Keats, he abruptly announces a shift in his modus operandi:

> Away! away! for I will fly to thee,
>   Not charioted by Bacchus and his pards,
>   But on the viewless wings of Poesy (31-33)

For the last two stanzas, Keats has been attempting to pursue the nightingale through the intoxicating power of Bacchus, who was often depicted in a chariot pulled by leopards. Now, he realizes that the "vintage" of stanza 2 is too earthy, too bodily to sustain his journey into the nightingale's higher mode of existence. Rejecting the Bacchic revelry of Coleridge's "Kubla Khan" and Shelley's "Ode to the West Wind," Keats chooses instead the way of Apollo. It will be on the "viewless [invisible; unbodily] wings of Poesy" that he will ascend to the nightingale and not through the consumption of wine. As he does so often in his poetry, Keats ultimately chooses the sensuous over the sensual, the aesthetic over the physical.

Having built himself up to a high pitch of emotional intensity, Keats provides himself and his reader with a brief respite. Stanza 5 turns its focus away from the feelings and struggles of the poet to describe the natural setting (or bower) in which the poet stands as he recites his ode to the nightingale. Once this pastoral interlude is ended, however, Keats returns to his crisis with a renewed sense of urgency:

> Darkling I listen; and, for many a time
>   I have been half in love with easeful Death,
> Call'd him soft names in many a mused rhyme,
>   To take into the air my quiet breath;
> Now more than ever seems it rich to die,
>   To cease upon the midnight with no pain,

> While thou art pouring forth thy soul abroad
>   In such an ecstasy!
> Still wouldst thou sing, and I have ears in vain—
>   To thy high requiem become a sod. (51-60)

The poetry of the second generation of Romantic poets abounds with suicidal imagery, but none is more powerful or poignant than this stanza from "Ode to a Nightingale." The poet here confesses his often morbid fascination with death, though, as with Shelley, the death he yearns for is a passive one. In fact, Keats highlights the passive nature of the death he seeks by pointedly referring to death with a masculine pronoun ("call'd *him* soft names"), as if to suggest that death were a male suitor courting and being courted by the feminized poet.

Whereas men who commit suicide tend to use a gun or some other violent means to end their lives, women more often resort to an overdose of pills, a far more passive method than that employed by their male counterparts. The death that Keats imagines for himself closely mimics the effects of an overdose of barbiturates, with the poet's pain slowly ebbing away as he slips peacefully into unconsciousness. In true Romantic fashion, Keats even attempts to orchestrate his final moments: as he slides toward oblivion, he desires that the nightingale would pour out its soul in an ecstatic requiem. Keats's death wish is a powerful and haunting one that gives voice to the dark and dangerous side of his generation's flirtation with suicide, but it is not the last word of the poem, and it does not serve as the final resolution to Keats's crisis.

As is the nature of odes, whether regular or irregular, Keats surprises us with an unexpected shift in mood and tone that lifts him temporarily out of his despair and gives him a sense of perspective on his own grief:

> Thou wast not born for death, immortal Bird!
>   No hungry generations tread thee down;
> The voice I hear this passing night was heard
>   In ancient days by emperor and clown:
> Perhaps the self-same song that found a path
>   Through the sad heart of Ruth, when, sick for home,
> She stood in tears amid the alien corn;
>   The same that oft-times hath
> Charm'd magic casements, opening on the foam
>   Of perilous seas, in faery lands forlorn. (61-70)

Having aestheticized his own death and set it to the tune of the nightingale, Keats now meditates on the tune itself. Though the poet feels isolated and disconnected, the song of the nightingale provides him with a portal looking out on to a boundless vista. As the poet listens, the song of the bird swells into an eternal voice linking generation to generation with its timeless melody. Like love, like joy, like imagination, the song of the bird is an esemplastic power that draws together past and present, rich (emperor) and poor (clown), the "real" world and the world of faerie. Perhaps, Keats fancies, the same song he now hears was heard by the poor, widowed Ruth as she gleaned grain in a wheat field far from her homeland. Though Ruth felt stranded then as the poet does now in an alien world, the immortal song of the nightingale brings hope to both. And with hope it brings the promise of magic, wonder, and beauty, the promise of escape from the confines of this narrow room we call the world. Those who wish to experience visually the faerie power of the last three lines of the stanza need only view Magritte's many paintings of a blue sky spied through doors and windows of every conceivable shape and size.

But alas, in Keats's world of sorrow and pain the magic of the song cannot be sustained. The willing suspension of disbelief is lost and what was for a moment illusion becomes delusion. Since line 33, when Keats declared that he would fly to the nightingale not on the chariot of Bacchus but on the "viewless wings of Poesy," his flight has been powered by words. Now, at the very moment of consummation, the words betray him and send him crashing back to earth:

> Forlorn! the very word is like a bell
>   To toll me back from thee to my sole self!
> Adieu! the fancy cannot cheat so well
>   As she is fam'd to do, deceiving elf.
> Adieu! adieu! thy plaintive anthem fades
>   Past the near meadows, over the still stream,
> Up the hill-side; and now 'tis buried deep
>   In the next valley-glades:
> Was it a vision, or a waking dream?
>   Fled is that music:—Do I wake or sleep? (71-80)

"In the fairy tale," writes G. K. Chesterton, "an incomprehensible happiness rests upon an incomprehensible condition. A box is opened, and all evils fly out. A word is forgotten, and cities perish. A lamp is lit, and love flies away. A flower is plucked, and human lives are forfeited. An apple is eaten, and the hope of God is gone."[18] None of the Romantics

---

18 G. K. Chesterton, *Orthodoxy* (New York: Image Books, 1990), 56.

understood this fragility better than Keats, for none sought with such fervor to leave the mundane world behind and enter the realms of faerie. Though not an "escapist" in the negative sense of the word, Keats nevertheless yearned for escape. In his odes, sonnets, and narrative poems alike, both he and the characters he creates attempt at some point to transcend the limits of space and time to enter a world where one can love and grow in love without experiencing what Shelley, in "To a Skylark" calls "love's sad satiety." What Keats desires is a world not of suspended animation but of animated suspension. A world, that is, of process in stasis.

And yet, though Keats sought that world more fiercely than his fellow Romantics, he knew far better than they how little it took to shatter it. In the closing stanza of the poem, the chiming of the word "forlorn" is all it takes to pull Keats out of his reverie and back to his "sole self." Even the imagination ("fancy") as expressed through poetry cannot hold Keats forever in the world of the nightingale. Indeed, as Keats slowly comes back to himself and hears the song of the bird retreating from him into the next valley, he finds, like the author of "Kubla Khan," that he cannot define for himself or for us the exact state in which the song of the bird has held him. Has he been sleeping or awake? Has he witnessed a vision or a dream? The poet cannot say, and yet, through the mediation of his waking trance, he has found resolution. True, he cannot remain in the faerie world of dreams and poesy and nightingale songs, but his glimpse of that world has drawn him out of his clinical depression and his thoughts of suicide. Through the "magic casement" of imagination, he has caught sight of "perilous seas" that have brought him, perhaps paradoxically, internal peace and stability.

Frozen Ecstasy

If "Ode to a Nightingale" ends with a sense of uncertainty as to the state of the poet (awake, asleep, or in a trance), then "Ode on a Grecian Urn" begins with a similar type of uncertainty as to the state of the urn: "Thou still unravish'd bride of quietness" (1). Keats frequently used the word "still" in his poetry, for it is a word that, as paradoxical as it may sound, means both itself and its opposite. Just as the word "cleave" can mean both "to separate" (cleave a piece of meat in half) and "to join together" (cleave unto his wife), so the word still can suggest both continual motion (I'm still waiting) and motionlessness (still as a statue).

In the first line of the poem, Keats may be saying that the urn is an "as yet unravish'd bride" or an "unmoving unravish'd bride." The reason I highlight Keats's pun (a pun he repeats in line 26) is that the word "still" holds within its own dual/contradictory nature the very essence of that world of process (as yet) in stasis (motionlessness) which Keats yearns to enter.

Of course the urn itself, as an object of art, exists in just such a world of process in stasis. As I so often try to explain, with varying success, to my students, when we write or speak about the arts we always do so in present tense. If I write about an event that happened to me when I was 12, I will use past tense, for the event took place at a specific moment in the past and no longer exists, *as* an event, in the present. But art, whether it be poetry, painting, sculpture, music, or film, exists in a perpetual present; unlike the artist's creation of his work, which occurred at a specific moment in time, the work of art itself is always "happening" now. The Church fathers, particularly Augustine, understood God and heaven to exist in just such a perpetual present; in fact, they were wont to say that the closest intimation we have of eternity is the present moment. For to enter heaven means to enter a state, not where time goes on forever, but where time itself no longer exists: a state where all is stasis but where process yet continues. Great art dwells forever in that timeless time of process in stasis—in the "artifice of eternity" to borrow an apt phrase from Yeats—and it is thus not surprising that Keats's poetry looks often to the arts—especially the enduring arts of the Golden Age of Athens—for traces of animated suspension.

In "Ode on a Grecian Urn," Keats's finest and most complete meditation on the nature of art, we are invited to contemplate the urn in all its paradoxical beauty and truth:

> Thou still unravish'd bride of quietness,
>   Thou foster-child of silence and slow time,
> Sylvan historian, who canst thus express
>   A flowery tale more sweetly than our rhyme:
> What leaf-fring'd legend haunts about thy shape
>   Of deities or mortals, or of both,
>   In Tempe or the dales of Arcady?
>   What men or gods are these? What maidens loth?
> What mad pursuit? What struggle to escape?
>   What pipes and timbrels? What wild ecstasy? (1-10)

As Keats the word-wielding poet gazes on the urn, he comes face to face with the truth of the Chinese proverb: a picture's worth a thousand words. The urn, with its painted scenes of men and gods in various poses, actions, and states of feeling, captures and preserves human passion at its height, untainted and unspoiled by what Keats, in his sonnet "On Seeing the Elgin Marbles," calls "the rude / Wasting of old time" (12-13). As he contemplates the urn, the poet participates in a frenzied, Bacchic activity that neither wearies nor exhausts itself. The frozen ecstasy of the urn perseveres even in the midst of our world of decay.

The poet next sharpens his gaze to focus on those details that best express the aesthetic magic of the urn:

> Heard melodies are sweet, but those unheard
>   Are sweeter: therefore, ye soft pipes, play on;
> Not to the sensual ear, but, more endear'd,
>   Pipe to the spirit ditties of no tone:
> Fair youth, beneath the trees, thou canst not leave
>   Thy song, nor ever can those trees be bare;
>   Bold Lover, never, never canst thou kiss,
> Though winning near the goal—yet, do not grieve;
>   She cannot fade, though thou hast not thy bliss,
> For ever wilt thou love, and she be fair! (11-20)

Just as Keats, in "Ode to a Nightingale," forsakes the sensual vehicle of wine for the sensuous vehicle of poesy, so here he privileges the unheard (sensuous) melody of the flutes painted on the urn over the heard (sensual) music of physical flutes. In doing so, I believe that Keats provides the answer to a debate that has been raging for many years in the world of classical music. When playing a symphony by Mozart, the debate goes, should we use our own modern versions of the flute or violin or should we use contemporary instruments (that is, facsimiles of the kinds of flutes and violins that existed in Mozart's day)? Were Keats alive today, I believe he would favor using our own modern instruments, which are technically superior to those on which Mozart's contemporaries would have played. Keats, as the above stanza shows, understood that an artist like Mozart does not compose his music for this or that violin but for the perfect violin that only exists in the imagination and which can only be heard by the "mind's ear." (On that score, Beethoven, who was deaf when he wrote his famous ninth symphony, would surely have concurred!) Therefore, the music of Mozart *should* be played on the best instruments available, in order that the performance might approach as closely as possible the sound of that perfect violin which can never be made by the hand of man or heard by the "sensual ear."

And, just as the music of the unheard pipes is, for Keats, sweeter and more endearing than the "real" music of physical pipes, so is the painted lover's courtship of his beloved all the more precious for remaining unconsummated. To the purely sensual-minded viewer, the predicament of the lover on the urn, who stands poised ready to kiss—but never kissing—his fair beloved, would seem one of torment and frustration. But not to Keats. To the sick and weary poet who feels stranded in, yet also disconnected from, this melancholy world in which "youth grows pale, and spectre-thin, and dies," the image of the lovers on the urn promises a freshness and an eagerness that will never fade or grow old. They hang suspended in a word of process in stasis, a world of perpetual spring, everlasting song, and endless, breathless anticipation.

The image so thrills Keats that he spills over with an excess of emotion that totters perilously on the edge of melodrama:

> Ah, happy, happy boughs! that cannot shed
>   Your leaves, nor ever bid the Spring adieu;
> And, happy melodist, unwearied,
>   For ever piping songs for ever new;
> More happy love! more happy, happy love!
>   For ever warm and still to be enjoy'd,
>   For ever panting, and for ever young;
> All breathing human passion far above,
>   That leaves a heart high-sorrowful and cloy'd,
> A burning forehead, and a parching tongue. (21-30)

In the closing stanza of "Ode to a Nightingale," the poet is forced to bid adieu to the nightingale as it (or, to be more precise, its song) passes away into the next valley. That is something the leaf-covered boughs on the urn will never have to do. Indeed, it is something they "cannot" do for the spring *will* remain and the pipes *will* continue to play, no matter what passes in the world outside the urn. And the songs that issue from those pipes, though they will be repeated again and again, will be forever new, as if they had been heard only then for the first time. On the urn everything is motionless ("warm and still"), and yet everything pants with the expectation of some greater love and beauty to come ("still to be enjoyed"). In the midst of this perpetual honeymoon, this frozen rapture, the tubercular Keats feels flushed and parched. The wild ecstasy of the urn is too much for him to contemplate, too much for him to bear. How can anything mortal exist in the presence of such high passion!

As if to shield himself from the intensity of the passion, Keats retreats for a moment from the "bold lover" and the "happy boughs" to gaze upon a quieter, more somber scene:

> Who are these coming to the sacrifice?
>   To what green altar, O mysterious priest,
> Lead'st thou that heifer lowing at the skies,
>   And all her silken flanks with garlands drest?
> What little town by river or sea shore,
>   Or mountain-built with peaceful citadel,
>   Is emptied of this folk, this pious morn?
> And, little town, thy streets for evermore
>   Will silent be; and not a soul to tell
> Why thou art desolate, can e'er return. (31-40)

I have commented many times before in this book that all that is most strange and wonderful in Romanticism carries within itself a dark side. In stanza 4 of Keats's ode we catch, even on the urn, a glimpse of that dark side. If eternal fullness is possible, then its contrary, eternal emptiness, must also be possible. The lovers who stand poised on the threshold of their kiss will forever remain so. The participants in the religious ceremony described in stanza 4 have left their town to perform a sacrifice to their god. Like the lovers, their corporate longing for consummation will also persist in its original purity. But if the people of the town remain forever in transit to the altar, then shall their town remain forever "emptied of [its] folk." Its streets will linger on in silence, barren of life and motion with "not a soul to tell / Why [it is] desolate." Process in stasis, we might say, with a vengeance.

Keats, however, does not choose to dwell on this dark side. For him, the urn is a wholly positive symbol of what he most desires:

> O Attic shape! Fair attitude! with brede
>   Of marble men and maidens overwrought,
> With forest branches and the trodden weed;
>   Thou, silent form, dost tease us out of thought
> As doth eternity: Cold Pastoral!
>   When old age shall this generation waste,
>   Thou shalt remain, in midst of other woe
> Than ours, a friend to man, to whom thou say'st,
>   "Beauty is truth, truth beauty,"—that is all
>   Ye know on earth, and all ye need to know. (41-50)

"Brede" is an archaic word (related to our modern word "braid") that signifies an embroidered, interwoven edge. Keats describes the brede as being "overwrought" (ornamented) with images of men and women, but he is also making a pun. The maidens depicted on the urn are themselves "overwrought" with an excess of frenzied emotion that the urn can barely contain. In one of his more felicitous oxymorons, Keats refers to the urn as a "Cold Pastoral," thus highlighting the urn's ability to contain within its still and "silent form" the full physical and emotional vitality of that pastoral world that Blake celebrates in his *Songs of Innocence*.

The urn, as "a friend to man," preserves that lost world for us in all its innocence and beauty, but that is not the primary service for which the poet lifts his thankful praise. The urn, by its very nature, stands as a testimony to the existence of a higher mode of being (process in stasis). Through contemplating that existence, we who dwell in the world of change and corruption can be lifted out of our spatiotemporal prison to contemplate eternity. In a sense, the urn performs the same function as those Zen Buddhist riddles (What is the sound of one hand clapping? If a tree falls in a forest and no one is there to hear it, does it make any noise?) that Americans, misunderstanding their purpose, love to parody. Zen riddles are not meant to be solved but to be used as vehicles to "tease us out of thought"—to clear our mind of rationalistic, overly-logical thinking so that we might be freed to contemplate the greater mysteries that transcend human reason and logic.

Though Keats never wrote any formal literary criticism to compare with Wordsworth's Preface or Coleridge's *Biographia Literaria* or Shelley's "Defense of Poetry," he was a skilled and prolific letter writer. When taken together, Keats's letters provide us with insight not only into Keats's poetic theory and practice but into the very essence of poetry. In a letter to his brothers that Keats wrote in December of 1817, he coined a phrase that testifies to Keats's (unconscious) awareness of the nature of Zen riddles and that provides us with a (perhaps conscious) foreshadowing of the final stanza of "Ode on a Grecian Urn." In search of that elusive quality that made Shakespeare such a great poet, Keats settles on a quality that he calls "negative capability" and which he defines thus: "when a man is capable of being in uncertainties, mysteries, doubts, without any irritable reaching after fact and reason" (1211).

I have noted several times before that Romanticism embodies a vision of the world that is not only more Eastern than Western, but more feminine than masculine. Anyone who has studied the different ways by which men and women perceive and interact with the world will recognize immediately that the quality that Keats calls "negative capability" is one possessed more often by women than men. Whereas most men are driven by an inner urge to solve problems and to establish clear parameters of cause and effect (in a word, to "figure things out"), most women are willing to accept things as they are without having to calculate or dissect them. This is particularly true when it comes to feelings and emotions. Men will interrogate their wives until they can determine the exact cause of their wife's mood of joy or sorrow, but the wife feels no such compulsion to assess the origin of her present mood. But it is also true with regard to the deeper riddles of our existence. Women, like Romantic poets, are better able to hold in creative tension the paradoxes of their lives, to rest peacefully in the midst of uncertainties, to embrace mystery *as* mystery without needing to convert it into a logical proposition or a rational proof.

And it may be true as well that women, with their finer and more carefully honed intuitive skills, understand better than their male counterparts the one clear message that the urn sends out like a beacon: "Beauty is truth, truth beauty." Perhaps no phrase from the Romantic Age has caused more controversy than this, a controversy that continues to reverberate in our own day, when both beauty and truth have been unceremoniously booted out of many of our leading academies, and ugliness and relativism invited in to take their place. Rather than engage directly in this controversy, I would end my study of Romantic perception by considering briefly a passage from one of Keats's letters that both offers a key to interpreting his beauty-is-truth riddle and that may serve as a final statement of the themes of this book.

Writing in November of 1817, Keats, in the same letter that contains his comment about Adam's dream that I quoted in my analysis of *The Rime of the Ancient Mariner*, makes the following bold statement about the nature of beauty, truth, and the imagination:

> I am certain of nothing but of the holiness of the Heart's affections and the truth of Imagination. —What the imagination seizes as Beauty must be truth—whether it existed before or not—for I have the same Idea of all our Passions, as of Love; they are all in their sublime, creative of essential Beauty. . . . I have never yet been able to perceive how anything can be known for truth by consequetive reasoning—and yet it must be. Can it be that even the greatest Philosopher ever arrived at his goal without putting aside numerous objections. However it may be, O for a Life of Sensations rather than of Thoughts! (1210)

Without attacking or wholly dismissing the importance of reason and logic, Keats affirms that there are other, better ways to arrive at beauty and truth. I have said before that the Romantics often treat love, joy, and imagination as almost interchangeable; here, Keats adds beauty and truth to the list of those esemplastic forces that have the power to discern similitude in the midst of similitude and effect an incarnational union of the two into one. At the core of love, joy, imagination, beauty, and truth is a kind of harmony or balance that is essentially creative and that builds a bridge between our perceptions of the world and the world itself. Though more aesthetic than religious in his sensibilities, Keats recognizes something deeply sacred in the affections of the heart (the fountain of love and joy) and in the imagination's ability to seize a moment of beauty and, transcending all narrow objections and apparent contradictions, lift it up into the eternal realm of truth.

Many Americans, whose true creed is empirical science, common sense, and pragmatism, look askance at the Romantics for their privileging of subjective feeling over objective observation, of emotion over reason, of a "Life of Sensations" over one of "Thoughts," but in so criticizing Blake, Wordsworth, Coleridge, Byron, Shelley, and Keats they merely highlight their most enduring legacy. In the face both of modernism and postmodernism, the Romantics stand as a living witness that we can seek and even locate beauty and truth in our perceptions of them without therefore falling into relativism and nihilism. We can boldly assert that the heart has reasons that reason knows nothing about, that beauty lies often in the eye of the beholder, and that there are times when the truth of a thing is to be found not in what it is but in how it is perceived without sacrificing in the process absolute moral, philosophical, or aesthetic standards.

Perhaps the final and greatest of Romantic paradoxes is simply this: that the Good, the True, and the Beautiful, while remaining Platonic forms that exist outside and above our world of change, are also, in part, the products of our deepest yearnings, our most refined perceptions, and our loveliest dreams.

EPILOGUE
The Darkness Within

I have attempted in this book to explore a central theme of Romanticism that manifests itself in a variety of different ways in the major lyrical poetry of the Romantics. That theme, stated simply, is this: things are not as they are but as they are perceived. Built itself upon the Romantic privileging of subject over object, epistemology over ontology, this foundational tenet of Romanticism undergirds Blake's distinction between innocence and experience, Wordsworth and Coleridge's plan for *Lyrical Ballads*, and the need felt by all Romantic poets to seek resolution for crises that are more internal than external, emotional than rational, perceptual than physical. It is precisely because the Romantic poets believed that beauty often resides in the eye of the beholder and practiced in their own lives and art the externalization of the internal that we feel when reading their lyric poetry that we are eavesdropping.

The Victorian economist and political writer John Stuart Mill, whose reading of Wordsworth and Coleridge helped pull him out of a nervous breakdown, famously suggested that true (lyric Romantic) poetry is not heard but overheard. I think there is much truth in Mill's comment, but that truth does not rest on the misleading belief that Romantics write only about themselves or that we need to study their biographies if we are to understand the meaning of their poems. The reason their poetry is so intensely personal, the reason it makes us feel like voyeurs when we read it, is that the makers of the poetry have staked all they have and all they are on the quality of their internal feelings and perceptions. The Romantic poets rarely leave themselves an emotional exit strategy; if they cannot achieve resolution, they risk a kind of inner bondage—either to an immobilizing over-self-consciousness or to the misery of Blake's mind forged manacles.

Perhaps no Romantic lyric captures so succinctly and so powerfully the dangers inherent in living through one's perceptions than John Keats's non-autobiographical internalized medieval romance in miniature, "La Belle Dame Sans Merci." In the first three stanzas of the poem, the speaker, who may or may not be Keats himself, addresses a knight on whose face he reads great depths of anguish and despair. In the remaining nine stanzas, the knight—who is *not* Keats but who nevertheless embodies fully the Romantic over-reliance on internal perception—recounts his tragic tale:

> Oh what can ail thee, Knight at arms,
>   Alone and palely loitering?
> The sedge has withered from the Lake,
>   And no birds sing!
>
> Oh what can ail thee, Knight at arms,
>   So haggard and so woe-begone?
> The Squirrel's granary is full,
>   And the harvest's done.
>
> I see a lily on thy brow,
>   With anguish moist and fever-dew;
> And on thy cheeks a fading rose
>   Fast withereth too.
>
> I met a Lady in the Meads,
>   Full beautiful, a faery's child,
> Her hair was long, her foot was light,
>   And her eyes were wild.
>
> I made a Garland for her head,
>   And bracelets too, and fragrant zone;
> She looked at me as she did love,
>   And made sweet moan.
>
> I set her on my pacing steed,
>   And nothing else saw, all day long;
> For sidelong would she bend, and sing
>   A faery's song.
>
> She found me roots of relish sweet,
>   And honey wild, and manna dew;
> And sure in language strange she said,
>   "I love thee true."
>
> She took me to her elfin grot,
>   And there she wept and sigh'd full sore;
> And there I shut her wild, wild eyes
>   With kisses four.

> And there she lulled me asleep
>   And there I dreamed, ah woe betide!
> The latest dream I ever dreamt,
>   On the cold hill side.
>
> I saw pale Kings, and Princes too,
>   Pale warriors, death-pale were they all;
> They cried, "La belle dame sans merci
>   Hath thee in thrall!"
>
> I saw their starv'd lips in the gloam
>   With horrid warning gaped wide—
> And I awoke, and found me here,
>   On the cold hill's side.
>
> And this is why I sojourn here,
>   Alone and palely loitering;
> Though the sedge is withered from the Lake,
>   And no birds sing.

The poem begins and ends in a season that we might call late autumn. For the knight, it is a late autumn that will soon give way to winter, but that will never give way to spring. Worse yet, the knight, unlike the squirrel and the harvester of stanza 2, has no stores to support him through the long winter ahead.

At first, it seems that the knight's tale will be one of high adventure and romance. His quest takes him to magical lands and brings him together with a fairy woman whose love, we think, will draw the knight upward into a higher mode of existence. The knight's senses are seduced by a sensual and sensuous beauty that ravishes not only his eye and ear but his organs of taste, smell, and touch. At the height of passion, the lovely lady ("la belle dame") lulls him to sleep, and we are allowed for the briefest of moments to hope that the lovers will remain forever in their dream of romance.

But it is not to be. The lovely lady proves to be without mercy ("sans merci"), and she abandons her knight at the very moment when he has invested in her the fullness of his inner being. The dream becomes a nightmare, and the knight is met by the ghastly faces of countless brave others who have also fallen prey to the seduction of la belle dame sans merci. In the end, the knight wakes from his soul-crushing nightmare to find himself alone on the cold hill's side.

The poem is a strange and disturbing one. Why can't the knight simply go back to his former life? After all, the lady has not really *done* anything to him. But then that is the whole point of the poem. The lady *hasn't* injured the knight physically. His destruction proceeds from within; it is not the lady but his own surrender to utter despair that brings his doom upon him. The late autumn setting of the poem, I would argue, does not ultimately define an external season of the year. The nearly identical first and last stanzas—the former spoken by the speaker, the latter by the knight—describe an inner landscape of desolation that the knight has projected, via the externalization of the internal, on to the world around him. Together these dark and hopeless stanzas form a closed loop, an existential No Exit that would cause Jean Paul Sartre himself to tremble. In one sense, the knight should remind us of the ancient Mariner, for both end up exactly where they started. But there, I'm afraid, the similarity ends. Whereas the Mariner's circular journey leaves him on a higher level, the knight's failed quest leaves him trapped in a cycle of futility from which he is powerless to escape. Like the truncated last line of each stanza (four syllables/two stresses each instead of the expected eight/four), the knight's fall into perceptual darkness amputates his will and emasculates any hope of future growth or fruition.

Few Romantic poems are quite as dark as "La Belle Dame Sans Merci," and yet, beneath all the lyrics of Blake, Wordsworth, Coleridge, Byron, Shelley, and Keats there ever lurks the danger of the dark side. Though it is certainly true that all those who live by the sword shall die by the sword, it is also frequently the case that those who live by perception alone shall suffer the most when perception darkens and the inner light threatens to go out. Perhaps the last and greatest Romantic angst is the perpetual struggle to keep that inner light aglow.

Timeline

1756	1st edition of Burke's *Inquiry of the Sublime and the Beautiful*
1757	Birth of William Blake
1762	Rousseau publishes *The Social Contract*
1789	French Revolution begins
1770	Birth of William Wordsworth
1772	Birth of Samuel Taylor Coleridge
1788	Birth of George Gordon, Lord Byron
1789	French Revolution begins
1789	Blake engraves *Songs of Innocence*
1790	Kant publishes his *Critique of Judgment*
1790	Blake engraves *The Marriage of Heaven and Hell*
1792	Birth of Percy Bysshe Shelley
1793-4	The Reign of Terror
1794	Blake engraves *Songs of Experience*
1795	Birth of John Keats
1797	Friendship and collaboration of Wordsworth & Coleridge begins
1797	Coleridge writes "Kubla Khan" and *Rime of the Ancient Mariner*
1797-1807	Wordsworth's Great Decade
1798	Wordsworth and Coleridge publish *Lyrical Ballads*
1800	2nd edition of *Lyrical Ballads* includes Wordsworth's "Preface"
1802	Wordsworth begins "Intimations Ode"; reads stanzas to Coleridge
1802	Coleridge writes "Dejection: An Ode"
1804	Wordsworth finishes "Intimations Ode"
1805	Wordsworth completes *Prelude*; spends next 45 years editing it

1812-1816 Byron's oriental tales make him famous at home and in Europe
1816   Personal scandal causes Bryon to leave England for self exile
1816   Bryon writes "Prometheus"
1817   Byron publishes his finest treatment of the Byronic hero: *Manfred*
1817   Coleridge publishes his *Biographia Literaria*
1817   Keats writes his "negative capability" letter
1818   Bryon begins *Don Juan*, a mock epic that satirizes Byronic hero
1818   Shelley writes "Stanza Written in Dejection"
1819   Keats writes "La Belle Dame Sans Merci"
1819   Keats writes *Hyperion*, *The Eve of St. Agnes*, and *Lamia*
1819   Keats writes "Ode to a Nightingale" and "Ode on a Grecian Urn"
1820   Shelley's "Ode to the West Wind" and "To a Skylark" published
1820   *Prometheus Unbound*, Shelley's version of the myth appears
1821   Keats dies in Italy at age 25
1821   Shelley publishes an elegy on the death of Keats: *Adonais*
1821   Shelley writes "A Defense of Poetry"
1822   Shelley dies in Italy in a boating accident
1824   Byron in Greece to aid Greek War for Independence; dies of fever
1827   Death of Blake
1834   Death of Coleridge
1837   Victoria becomes Queen
1843   Wordsworth appointed poet laureate
1843   Wordsworth interview with Isabella Fenwick
1850   Death of Wordsworth

Bibliographic Essay

I have chosen in this bibliography to adopt a paragraph format that I think will be more helpful to the general reader; the authors and titles of books will be indicated in bold face. After a lengthy section on general works, I will devote six briefer sections to each of the poets covered in this book. I will suggest an accessible biography, some standard editions of their work, and a few critical assessments of their poetry and their legacy. In all cases, I will be suggesting works that are meant for the lay reader rather than for specialists in the field. I will focus especially on slightly older works that have stood the test of time and have proven their value for opening up the Romantics and their poetry to the general reader. I will also be guided in my selections by works that have exerted a strong influence on my own reading of British Romantic Poetry.

You will note that throughout this bibliography I will be strongly encouraging you to purchase books from a series known as **The Norton Critical Editions**. In these excellent editions, the editors devote the first half of the book to an authoritative, well-annotated edition either of a single classic work or a selection of poems from a single poet, and the second half to a dozen or so essays written by various critics from various time periods and various schools. Each book in the series also offers an extensive bibliography. These books are often the best single resource for a given book or author. (Note: in this bibliography, I have included the Norton Critical Editions that I have used myself; the reader should be aware, however, that most of these have since gone into a revised or second edition.) It should also be mentioned here that reliable, inexpensive paperback anthologies of each poet have been published through the **Modern Library College Editions** (from Random House) and the **Oxford Poetry Library** (from Oxford UP). The Modern Library has put out a particularly helpful combined edition of the **Complete Poems of Keats and Shelley**.

I. General Works

I strongly suggest that all readers of this book purchase **English Romantic Poetry and Prose**, selected and edited by **Russell Noyes** (Oxford UP, 1956). This is the textbook that I use when I teach the Romantic Age, and I have made sure that, with the exception of two minor poems by Blake, all the works analyzed in this book can be found in Noyes's magisterial anthology. That is to say, if you have this single book in hand, it will give you access to all the poetry (and prose) discussed in this book. Noyes's anthology is also helpful for several other reasons: 1) Noyes provides samples from a wealth of Romantic writers not generally included in anthologies; 2) his introductions to the Romantic Age and to each author are excellent and are geared to the layman; 3) he offers well-detailed mini-biographies for each of the poets covered in this book together with timelines of their lives and works. After reading these biographies, you will be in a good position to decide whether you wish to read a full biography of the poet.

Another excellent textbook is the standard, well-respected **Norton Anthology of English Literature, Volume II** (available in a number of different editions, any of which is acceptable), which covers all English literature from 1800 to the present. Although the Romantic Age represents only a section of this book, it is a large and well-represented section that is prefaced by an excellent introduction. If you are serious about English literature, you should really own a copy of this book. It also includes bibliographical information in the back.

I still think that the best two collections of essays about the Romantics remain **English Romantic Poets: Modern Essays in Criticism**, edited by **M. H. Abrams** (Oxford UP, 1975), and including Abrams's seminal essay on Romantic inspiration ("The Correspondent Breeze") together with four or five solid essays on each of the six major poets, and **Romanticism and Consciousness: Essays in Criticism**, edited by **Harold Bloom** (Norton, 1970). Among the many fine essays in this anthology—which includes general studies of Romanticism along with specific studies of each of the six major Romantic poets—make sure at least to read "English Romanticism: The Spirit of the Age" and "Structure and Style in the Greater Romantic Lyric" by M. H. Abrams, "The Internalization of the

Quest-Romance" by Bloom, "The Romance of Nature and the Negative Way" and "Romanticism and 'Anti-Self-Consciousness'" by Geoffrey Hartman, and "The Road of Excess" by Northrop Frye.

If I had to choose one Romantic critic as my favorite it would have to be M. H. Abrams. In addition to the essays mentioned above, I strongly encourage the reader to get a hold of **Abrams's Natural Supernaturalism: Tradition and Revolution in Romantic Literature** (Norton, 1971). I consider this the single best book on Romanticism, one that offers, among other things, two helpful perspectives from which to view the work of the Romantic poets: 1) that their work often provides a secularization of key biblical beliefs and terminology; 2) that Romantics tend to make circular journeys which bring them back to where they started but on a higher level. **Abrams's The Mirror and the Lamp: Romantic Theory and the Critical Tradition** (Oxford UP, 1953) provides one of the best overviews of Romantic critical theory—in particular, how poet-critics like Wordsworth and Coleridge saw a direct correlation between the questions "what is a poet?" and "what is a poem?". Abrams's book explains in rich detail the sources, assumptions, and legacies of the romantic theorists, both English and German, both major and minor. In a 24-lecture audio/video series I produced with **The Teaching Company** (www.teach12.com), **Plato to Postmodernism: Understanding the Essence of Literature and the Role of the Author,** I devote three lectures to the German Romantic theories of Kant, Hegel, and Schiller, and two lectures to *Lyrical Ballads* and Wordsworth's "Preface." I also offer partial lectures on Plato's *Ion* and Horace's *Art of Poetry*.

If you are interested in the German theoretical background to Romanticism, then your single best source is **James Engell's The Creative Imagination: Enlightenment to Romanticism** (Harvard UP, 1981). This book offers the best and most lucid study of German romantic theory. **Engell** has also (together with **Walter Jackson Bate**) edited an absolutely brilliant edition of **Coleridge's** own seminal study of German and British romantic theory in the form of an autobiography, **Biographia Literaria** (Volume 7 of the Collected Works of Samuel Taylor Coleridge; Princeton UP, 1983). Reading Coleridge's work together with Engell and Bates's notes will provide you with a rich and full understanding of Romanic literary theory. **Romanticism: Points of View,** edited by **Robert Gleckner** and **Gerald Enscoe** (Wayne State UP, 1975) is a classic collection of essays that offers contrasting views of romantic theory. To read these often acerbic essays, which span a century of writing, is to leap into the critical fray.

Walter Jackson Bates's From Classic to Romantic: Premises of Taste in Eighteenth Century England (Harper Torchbook, 1961) builds a helpful bridge from the Enlightenment to Romantic thought.

C. M. Bowra's The Romantic Imagination (Oxford UP, 1969) offers a very helpful study of the vital role played by the imagination; it includes analyses of Blake's *Songs*, "The Rime of the Ancient Mariner," "The Intimations Ode," and "Ode on a Grecian Urn." **Cleanth Brooks's The Well-Wrought Urn** (Harcourt, Brace and Company, 1947), though not specifically about Romantic Poetry, offers famous close readings of Wordsworth's "Intimations Ode" and Keats's "Ode on a Grecian Urn." **Harold Bloom's The Visionary Company: A Reading of English Romantic Poetry** (Doubleday, 1961) offers a good critical overview of the major works of all six poets; this is a good place to start.

Two academic studies of the Romantic poets that I have found helpful and that are fairly accessible are **Edward Bostetter's The Romantic Ventriloquists: Wordsworth, Coleridge, Keats, Shelley, Byron** (U of Washington P, 1963) and **David Perkins's The Quest for Permanence: The Symbolism of Wordsworth, Shelley and Keats** (Harvard UP, 1959). Those interested in the pastoral imagery that dominates much of Romantic poetry beginning with Blake's *Songs of Innocence* might enjoy **Lore Metzger's One Foot in Eden: Modes of Pastoral in Romantic Poetry** (U of North Carolina P, 1986). I have avoided (like the plague) politicized studies of the Romantic poets that have issued, and continue to issue, from the New Historicist School of criticism. The book that started this trend is **Jerome McGann's The Romantic Ideology: A Critical Investigation** (U of Chicago P, 1983). You may wish to consult this book if you'd like to see the beginning of a trend that is still with us.

For a famous critique of Romanticism that takes the Romantic poets to task for their over-emotionalism and eccentricity, their privileging of self-expression over self-control, and their lack of a moral/ethical center, see **Rousseau and Romanticism** by **Irving Babbitt** (World Publishing Company, 1919).

II. William Blake

A well-written biography of Blake can be found in **Peter Ackroyd's Blake: A Biography** (Ballantine Books, 1995). **The Norton Critical Edition** of **Blake's Poetry and Design**, edited by **Mary Lynn Johnson and John E. Grant** (Norton, 1979) is particularly good with a generous number of illustrations in color and black and white. Lovers of the **Songs of Innocence and Experience**, however, should also purchase the **Oxford University Press Edition** (1967). This edition includes facsimiles of all of Blake's original plates with the text of the poems printed on the back of each plate and with brief but incisive commentary on the relationship between Blake's images and words by **Geoffrey Keynes**. **Dover Publications**, in addition to offering its own inexpensive facsimile editions of the *Songs*, also offers a $5 facsimile edition of **The Marriage of Heaven and Hell** (1994). A classic complete text is **The Poetry and Prose of William Blake**, edited by one of the great Blake critics, **David Erdman** (Doubleday, 1965) and including commentary by Harold Bloom. For a shorter version, see **David Erdman's The Selected Poetry of Blake** (New American Library, 1976).

For an excellent, accessible, and richly illustrated study of Blake's art, see **Kathleen Raine's William Blake** (Thames and Hudson, 1970; part of the World of Art series). For a classic study that gets to the heart of Blake's powerful archetypes, consult **Northrop Frye's Fearful Symmetry: A Study of William Blake** (Princeton UP, 1947). For another classic study that surveys all of Blake's major works and delves to the heart of Orc, consult **Harold Bloom's Blake's Apocalypse: A Study in Poetic Argument** (Cornell UP, 1963). For an interesting study of Blake's link to Jung, see **June Singer's The Unholy Bible: Blake, Jung and the Collective Unconscious** (Sigo Press, 1986).

It should be admitted here that in portraying the later Blake as a Gnostic, I am swimming against the stream of modern Romantic criticism: although the still prolific Harold Bloom would certainly be more open to seeing gnostic elements in Blake and A.D. Nuttall argues for Blake's Gnosticism in *The Alternative Trinity: The Gnostic Heresy in Marlow, Milton, and Blake* (Oxford UP: 1998; reissued in paperback in 2007). For a more detailed study of Blake's Gnosticism, see Peter J. Sorensen's William *Blake's Recreation of Gnostic Myth: Resolving the Apparent Incongruities* (Edwin Mellen Press, 1995).

III. William Wordsworth

A brief, accessible biography of Wordsworth can be found in **Carl Woodring's Wordsworth** (Houghton Mifflin Company, 1965). **W. J. B. Owen** has edited (Oxford UP, 1969) a fine and affordable facsimile edition of Wordsworth and Coleridge's **Lyrical Ballads: 1798**. It includes a helpful introduction, and, in an appendix, the full text of the 1800 Preface collated with the later 1802 version. Although I confined myself in this book to Wordsworth's short poetry, all lovers of the poet must attempt at some point to tackle his poetic autobiography, the *Prelude*, a work that exists in three versions: his initial mini-*Prelude* in two books, the full *Prelude* which he completed in 1805, and the edition that was published shortly after his death in 1850 and that contained 45 years of editing by the poet. **The Prelude: 1799, 1805, 1850**, edited by **Jonathan Wordsworth, M. H. Abrams, and Stephen Gill** (Norton, 1979) is arguably the finest **Norton Critical Edition** of them all. All lovers of Wordsworth must have it on their shelf. For the full Wordsworth corpus, see **The Complete Poetical Works of William Wordsworth** (Houghton Mifflin, 1904).

A good overview of Wordsworth's work can be found in **Helen Darbishire's The Poet Wordsworth** (Clarendon Press, 1966). **Russell Noyes's William Wordsworth** (Twayne Publishers, 1971) is particularly accessible. One of the finest studies of Wordsworth remains **Geoffrey Hartman's Wordsworth's Poetry: 1787-1814** (Yale UP 1964), which offers a close and subtle assessment of Wordsworth's poetic craft. Another classic study, written by a descendant of the poet, is **Jonathan Wordsworth's William Wordsworth: The Borders of Vision** (Clarendon Press, 1982).

Helpful overviews of Wordsworth's thought can be found in **Alan Grob's The Philosophic Mind: A Study of Wordsworth's Poetry and Thought 1797-1805** (Ohio State UP, 1973), **R. D. Havens's The Mind of a Poet: A Study of Wordsworth's Thought with Particular Reference to the Prelude** (Johns Hopkins Press, 1941), and **Arthur Beatty's William Wordsworth: His Doctrine and Art in their Historical Relation** (U of Wisconsin P, 1962).

IV. Samuel Taylor Coleridge

A fine biography of Coleridge written by one of the great Romantic scholars is **Walter Jackson Bate's Coleridge** (Macmillan, 1968). A handy anthology of all of Coleridge's poetry can be found in **Samuel Taylor Coleridge: The Complete Poems**, edited by **William Keach** (Penguin Classics, 1997). An accessible overview of Coleridge's life and writings can be found in **Virginia R. Radley's Samuel Taylor Coleridge** (Twayne Publishers, 1966). **John Livingston Lowes's The Road to Xanadu: A Study in the Ways of the Imagination** (Houghton Mifflin, 1927) offers a famous, exhaustive analysis of "The Ancient Mariner." A study that is worth reading in conjunction with my own is the slightly academic but still very readable **The Hamlet Vocation of Coleridge and Wordsworth** by **Martin Greenberg** (U of Iowa P, 1986).

V. Lord Byron

Leslie Marchand's Byron: A Biography (Knopf, 1957) is a good standard life of the poet that avoids the endless sexual muckraking that mars so many biographies of the poet. My favorite anthology of Byron is **George Gordon, Lord Byron: Selected Works**, edited by **Edward Bostetter** (Holt, Reinhart and Winston, 1972), though I also strongly recommend the Norton Critical Edition of **Byron's Poetry**, edited by **Frank D. McConnell** (Norton, 1978). Those who want to tackle Byron's ultimately anti-Romantic masterwork are encouraged to consult **Don Juan by Lord Byron**, edited by **Marchand** (Houghton Mifflin, 1958; one of the fine Riverside Editions). Marchand has also written a good introduction to Byron's work, **Byron's Poetry: A Critical Introduction** (Houghton Mifflin, 1965).

VI. Percy Bysshe Shelley

Edmund Blunden's Shelley: A Life Story (Oxford UP, 1965) offers a good standard biography. **Percy Bysshe Shelley: Selected Poetry and Prose**, edited by **Kenneth Neill Cameron** (Holt, Reinhart and Winston, 1951) offers a good selection and is one of the fine Rinehart Editions. The Norton Critical Edition of **Shelley's Poetry and Prose,** edited by **Donald Reiman and Sharon Powers** (Norton, 1977) is also excellent. **Shelley: A Collection of Critical Essays**, edited by **George M. Ridenour** (Prentice-Hall, 1965; part of the Twentieth Century Views series), offers a series of helpful essays on different aspects of Shelley's work, as does **Shelley: Modern Critical Views**, edited by **Harold Bloom** (Chelsea House, 1984).

VII. John Keats

For a solid, accessible biography of Keats, I would suggest **Douglas Bush's John Keats: His Life and Writings** (Weidenfeld and Nicolson, 1966). The best one-volume collection of Keats's poetry is **John Keats: Complete Poems**, edited by **Jack Stillinger** (Belknap Press, 1978). **Keats: A Collection of Critical Essays**, edited by **Walter Jackson Bate** (Prentice-Hall, 1964; part of the Twentieth Century Views series), offers a series of very accessible essays that give both general overviews of the poet and close analyses of his major poems (including separate essays on his Nightingale and Grecian Urn Odes). See especially Bate's essay on "Negative Capability"; readers who enjoy this essay may wish to read **Bate's** book-length study of this topic, **Negative Capability: The Intuitive Approach in Keats** (Harvard UP, 1939).

Index

NOTE: This index does not include entries from the bibliography or footnotes.

Authors and their Works

Aeschylus 103
   Oresteia. 103
Barfield, Owen 159, 160
   Saving the Appearances 159, 160, 165
Blake, William 3, 6, 28, 30, 43, 50, 64, 97, 206, 212, 213
   "Auguries of Innocence" 48, 60
   "The Mental Traveller" 48
   Ah! Sun-Flower [ah, sun-flower] 38, 40
   America: A Prophecy 48
   Angel, The 39, 40
   Book of Thel, The 48
   Book of Urizen, The 48
   Chimney Sweeper of Experience, The 41, 44
   Chimney Sweeper of Innocence, The 30, 31, 81
   Clod and the Pebble, The 8, 9, 22, 27, 32, 59
   Earth's Answer 34, 35, 36, 37
   Europe: A Prophecy 48
   Four Zoas, The 47
   Garden of Love 41, 42, 43
   Introduction to Experience 33, 34
   Introduction to Innocence 33
   Jerusalem 47, 48
   Lamb, The 17, 18, 19, 20, 26, 28, 30, 39, 81, 107, 165
   Little Black Boy 20, 21, 24, 25, 26, 28, 30, 39, 81, 107, 165
   London 43, 44, 56
   Marriage of Heaven and Hell, The 16, 24, 38, 48, 53, 56, 57, 61, 112, 114, 206, 213
   Milton 47, 48, 57
   Nurse's Song of Experience, The 30
   Nurse's Song of Innocence, The 30
   Sick Rose, The 30, 37, 40, 51
   Songs of Experience 3, 8, 10, 16, 30, 32, 36, 39, 48, 50, 114, 182, 206
   Songs of Innocence 21, 22, 24, 26, 28, 30, 32, 34, 39, 42, 53, 64, 106, 198, 206, 212, 213
   Songs of Innocence and Experience 3, 7, 8, 30, 34, 213
   Tyger, The 50, 51, 52, 53, 56, 82, 126, 173
Bunyan, John 108
   Pilgrim's Progress 108
Burke, Edmund 5
   Philosophical Inquiry into the Origin of Our Ideas of the Sublime and the Beautiful 5
Byron, George Gordon, Lord 206, 215
   Bride of Abydos, The 125
   Childe Harold's Pilgrimage 126, 130
   Corsair, The 125
   Don Juan 126, 130, 207
   Giaour, The 125
   Lara 125
   Manfred 126, 130, 207
   Prisoner of Chillon, The 125
   Prometheus 51, 52, 56, 57, 126, 127, 128, 129, 130, 177, 207
   Siege of Corinth, The 125
Chesterton, G. K. 67, 68, 192
   Orthodoxy 67, 68, 192
Coleridge, Samuel Taylor 64, 96, 206, 211, 214

Biographia Literaria 65, 71, 73, 76, 163, 198, 207, 211
Dejection: An Ode 153, 155, 156, 158, 163, 165, 170, 176, 185, 206
Kubla Khan 114, 116, 117, 118, 119, 121, 125, 127, 174, 175, 189, 190, 193, 206
Nightingale, The 132, 184
Rime of the Ancient Mariner 67, 69, 96, 97, 98, 124, 143, 153, 159, 199, 206, 212
Dante 23, 172, 173, 188
Divine Comedy 23, 48, 97, 172
Eliot, T. S. 109
Four Quartets 109
Little Gidding 109
Euripides 124
The Bacchae 124
Fitzgerald, F. Scott 64, 158
The Great Gatsby 158
Hawthorne, Nathaniel 42
The Scarlet Letter 42
Hesiod 15
Theogeny 15
Homer 33, 98, 132, 188
Odyssey 101
Horace 123, 124, 125, 211
Art of Poetry 124, 211
Irving, Washington 187
Rip Van Winkle 187
Joyce, James 47
Ulysses 47
Kant 5, 206, 211
Critique of Judgment 5, 206
Critique of Practical Reason 5
Critique of Pure Reason 5
Keats, John 108, 167, 184, 185, 202, 206, 215
Defense of Poetry 121, 155, 198, 207
Eve of St. Agnes, The 184, 207
Hyperion 184, 207

La Belle Dame Sans Merci 202, 203, 204, 207
Lamia 184, 207
Ode on a Grecian Urn 184, 193, 194, 198, 207, 212
Ode on Indolence 184
Ode on Melancholy 184
Ode to a Nightingale 184, 185, 191, 193, 195, 196, 207
Ode to Psyche 184
Ode to the West Wind 172, 173, 178, 180, 181, 190, 207
On Seeing the Elgin Marbles 195
Prometheus Unbound 207
Stanzas Written in Dejection 168, 172, 176, 178, 189
To a Sky-Lark 178, 193, 207
*To Autumn.*184
Lewis, C. S. 61, 64, 97, 188
A Preface to Paradise Lost 61
Great Divorce, The 61
Weight of Glory, The 188
Lucas, George 50
Star Wars 50, 70
Marlowe, Christopher 12
Doctor Faustus 12
Milton, John 7, 9, 21, 36, 49, 52, 53, 54, 56, 57, 61, 93, 101, 108, 132, 184, 188
Paradise Lost 7, 9, 21, 32, 36, 48, 49, 53, 56, 57, 59, 61, 101, 108, 132
Munch, Edvard 43
The Scream 43, 44
Plato 123, 124, 186, 211
Ion 123
Phaedo 186
Republic 123
Rousseau, Jean Jacques 2
Social Contract 2, 206
Sartre, Jean Paul 204
No Exit 204

Shakespeare, William 7, 21, 33, 76, 93, 106, 132, 171, 173, 184, 186, 188, 198
    Hamlet 7, 33, 44, 106, 171, 172, 189, 214
    Il Penseroso 7
    L'Allegro 7
Shelley, Mary 105, 125, 169
    Frankenstein 105, 125, 169
Shelley, Percy Bysshe 121, 167, 206, 215
    Adonais 169, 207
Spenser, Edmund 73, 169
    The Faerie Queene 73
Tolkien, J. R. R. 50, 64, 94
    The Lord of the Rings 50, 94, 185
Virgil 28, 98, 132, 188
    Aeneid 101, 119
Wordsworth, William 1, 64, 117, 206, 213, 214
    Essays Upon Epitaphs 117, 118
    Expostulation and Reply 89, 92, 100, 114, 155
    Goody Blake 67
    Idiot Boy, The 67
    Intimations Ode, The 212
    Lines Written in Early Spring 87, 93
    Lyrical Ballads 64, 65, 66, 67, 70, 71, 72, 80, 81, 96, 132, 201, 206, 211, 213
    My Heart Leaps Up 142
    Preface to *Lyrical Ballads*
    Prelude, The 1, 72, 77, 132, 135, 142, 143, 155, 213, 214
    Resolution and Independence 143, 145
    Simon Lee 67, 80
    Tables Turned, The 92, 114, 149, 164
    Tintern Abbey 132, 133, 134, 135, 136, 137, 142, 143, 145, 146, 147, 150, 151, 156, 165, 170, 173, 176
    We Are Seven 81, 82, 84, 86, 89, 100, 110, 114

Person Index

Abraham 110
Adam 33, 48, 102, 108, 109, 126, 199
Alexander the Great 101
Aquinas 5
Aristotle 4, 5, 60
Augustine 5, 194
Beethoven 195
Buñuel, Luis 64
Burns, Robert ii
Caiaphas 32
Cain 110, 126
Campbell, Joseph 50
Catullus i
Charlemagne 101
Chatterton, Thomas ii
Chaucer 33
Chrétien de Troyes 101
Cowper, William ii
Dali, Salvador 64
David 35
Diaghilev, Sergei 64
Donne, John i
Elijah 46, 120
Emerson, Ralph Waldo 64, 73
Epimenides 76
Eve 48, 102, 108
Fenwick, Isabella 147, 150, 207
Freud 28, 97, 119
Gauguin, Paul 64
God {161}
Gray, Thomas ii
Hemingway, Ernest 64
Herod 32
Hitler 13
Holy Spirit 174

Hutchinson, Sara 133
Jehovah 36, 39, 49, 54, 56, 57
Jesus Christ 47, 139
John the Baptist 18
Johnson, Samuel 42, 76, 86
Jonah 35
Jung, Carl 28, 50, 174, 213
King Arthur 101
Leary, Timothy 128
Locke, John 147
Louis XVI 3
Luther 16, 46
MacDonald, George 61
Magritte, René 192
Mao 13
Marie Antoinette 3
Mill, John Stuart 201
Mozart 195
Napoleon. 3, 167
Nebuchadnezzar 125
Nietzsche 53, 55, 56, 59
Novalis 165
Paine, Thomas 2
Paul 76, 150, 165, 182
Peter 85
Petrarch i
Pindar 143
Pontius Pilate 32
Pope, Alexander 42, 76, 86
Pythagoras 60
Rahab 35
Robespierre 3, 13
Ruth 35
Sappho
Satan 32, 36, 49, 52, 54, 56, 57, 59, 125, 126, 127
Schiller, Friedrich 19, 211
Shelley, Harriet 168, 172
Socrates 123, 186
Southey, Robert 167
Stalin 13
Stravinsky, Igor 64

Swift, Jonathan 76
Thomson, James ii
Thoreau, Henry David 64, 159
Twain, Mark 73
Van Gogh, Vincent 64, 69
Virgin Mary 23, 108
Wordsworth, Dorothy 65, 141, 165
Yahweh 35, 36
Yeats, William Butler 194
Young, Edward ii

Scripture Index

1 Corinthians; 24, 182
1 Kings 120
2 Corinthians 23
Acts 76, 110
Bible 16, 35, 39, 46, 47, 54, 76, 86, 93, 115, 119, 162, 165
Daniel 35, 119, 125
Deuteronomy 134
Ecclesiastes 53, 127
Ezekiel 110, 115
Genesis 19, 33, 108, 149
Isaiah 69, 76, 115, 116
Jeremiah 125
Job 56
John 16, 24, 162
Leviticus 18
Luke 9, 32
Mark 69
Matthew 27, 68, 171
New Testament 35, 86
Old Testament 35, 36, 54, 103
Proverbs 141
Psalms 24
Revelation 19, 35, 109, 116, 119, 162
Romans 150, 165

General Index

"The Ballad of Sir Patrick Spence" 153
Abundant Recompense 132, 139, 151
Aeolian Harp 164, 177
Aeolus 154
Aesthetics 4, 65
Agamemnon 103
Agape 10, 14, 22, 27, 31, 40
Age of Aquarius 1, 3
Age of Reason
Ahab 126
Albatross 102, 103, 104, 105, 107, 108, 112, 126
Alexandrine 144, 151, 156, 163, 169, 170, 178, 179, 189
Allegory 28, 59, 100, 101, 110
American Revolution 2, 49
Angst 3, 6, 7, 43, 108, 122, 168, 184, 204
Animated suspension 193-194
Apocalyptic 47-49, 53, 70, 98, 114, 120, 174, 178, 188
Apollo 119, 121, 188, 190
Aragorn 185
Arcadia 2
Archetype 29, 147
Arians 47
Arwen 185
Assyria 35
Atonement 58
Bacchae 124
Ballad 64, 65, 66, 67, 70, 71, 72, 80, 81, 96, 132, 153, 154, 201, 206, 211, 213
Ballad Rhythm 101, 132, 133
Baptist 85, 85, 90
Bastille 1, 2, 6, 12, 53, 71, 120, 167
Beatitudes 27, 68
Beatrice 23
Blank verse 101, 132, 133, 142, 150, 172
Bower 86, 87, 88, 89, 93, 190

Brahma 174
Bride of Christ 19
Buddhist 91, 136, 137, 198
Byronic Hero 125, 126, 128, 130, 167, 168, 172, 177, 207
Cambridge. 1
Camelot 109
Captain Nemo 125
Caritas 10, 27
Catholic Church 46
Charismatic 85
Childhood 31, 45, 67, 81, 82, 138, 142, 143, 147, 148, 150, 151, 156, 157
China 2, 13
Chinese Revolution 4
Christ the Bridegroom 19
Christianity 35, 47, 162, 174, 188
Christmas 15
Church 13,19,23,30,31,32,38,40,44,46,58,82,138,162,188,194,
Claudius 106
Clinical depression 156, 164, 185, 193
Clytemnestra 103
Correspondent breeze 153, 155, 210
Creator 18, 52, 67, 88, 129
Crisis Poem 142, 143, 153, 169
Cross 126, 171
Crucifixion. 26, 32, 165, 176
Darth Vader 50, 52, 126
Defamiliarization 69
Dejection 143, 153, 155, 156, 158, 159, 162-165, 168, 170, 172, 176, 178, 185, 187, 189, 206, 207
Dionysus 119, 123, 124
Dorian Gray 126
Dr. Frankenstein 125
Dr. Jekyll 125
Dracula 105, 126
Eastern 22, 50, 88, 91, 140, 174, 175, 198
Eden. 1, 3, 13, 20, 24, 33, 39, 41, 43, 109, 212

El Dorado 1
England 2, 64, 69, 75, 168, 207, 212
Enlightenment 1, 19, 42, 46, 53, 67, 85, 89, 94, 119, 129, 154, 159, 160, 211, 212
Epicureans 76
Epistemology 4, 5, 7, 58, 65, 201
Esemplastic 160, 163, 166, 192, 200
Eucharist 85
Evil Emperor 50
Externalization of the Internal 1, 6, 74, 107, 109, 157, 201, 204
Eye of the beholder 5, 48, 58, 200
Fading coal 122
Faith 16, 18, 22, 27, 41, 47, 58, 59, 66, 70, 82, 84, 87, 90, 94, 96, 114, 139, 141, 142, 147, 151
Fall 20, 174
Father 9, 18, 22, 26, 27, 28, 30, 34, 35, 36, 39, 44, 68, 72, 111, 112, 141, 142, 171, 174
Fearful symmetry 50, 51, 52, 82, 213
Feminine 27, 40, 85, 88, 90, 91, 174, 176, 198
Femme fatale 105
Film noir 105
Fragment 42, 53, 114, 115, 116, 118, 119, 121, 175
France 1, 2, 13, 75, 187, 189
Frankenstein 105, 125, 169
Freedom 2, 4, 29, 55, 42, 47, 49, 52, 57, 81, 149, 165, 178
French Revolution 1-7, 49, 64, 125, 167, 206
Gaia 36
Gentile 76
Germany 13, 70
Gethsemane 171, 176
Gnostic 14, 46, 47, 48, 53, 55, 60, 62, 69, 166, 188
Golden Age 3, 194
Golem 105

Golgotha 176
Good Friday 15
Gospel of Philip 48
Great Marriage 19, 162, 188
Greco-Roman 3, 56, 103, 110
Greece 80, 103, 123, 168, 188, 207
Greek Independence 168
Guest/host relationship 103, 104
Hades 49, 185
Hamlet. 7, 33, 44, 106, 171, 172, 214
Heathcliff 126
Helen 103, 214
Hemlock 185-187
Heroic stanzas 21
Heterodox 14, 60, 97, 129, 140
Highlander 126
Hindu 136, 137, 174
Hippocrene 187, 189
Holistic 85, 88
Hyperboreans. 3
Iambic pentameter 21, 169
Impressionism
in medias res 98
Incarnation 14, 15, 16, 18, 19, 22, 24, 26, 47, 48, 55, 58, 85, 117, 118, 140, 161, 165
Industrial Revolution 78
Intuition 74, 85, 86, 100, 119, 124, 147
Isolation 3, 32, 76, 88, 97, 103, 127, 134, 170, 172
Israel 35, 39
Italy 168, 207
Jew 76
Judeo-Christian 3, 13, 50, 103, 110, 137
Judgment 5, 105, 142, 206
Jupiter 56
Kingdom 162
Lake District 167
Language of real men 71
Lethe 185
Liturgy 85

Living soul 136, 156, 164
Logic 19, 71, 75, 83, 84, 85, 87, 101, 121, 135, 147, 198, 201
Logos 161
London 25, 42, 43, 44, 56, 78, 135, 186
Los Angeles 78
Love {125}
LSD 128
Luke Skywalker 50
Macbeth 126
Maenads 124, 175
Magna Charta 43
Manhattan 78
Mary Poppins 25
Masculine 37, 40, 85, 88, 90, 174, 176, 191, 198
Mass 85
Medieval 4, 13, 28, 46, 100, 101, 132, 153, 154, 159, 160, 187, 202
Memory 33, 132, 133, 142, 150, 172
Menelaus 103
Mephastophilis 12, 29
Messiah 35, 56, 165
Middle Ages 13, 80, 86, 101
Mind-forg'd manacles 41, 43, 44, 57
Monism 47, 140
Mount Olympus 52
Mt. Helicon 189
MTV 78
Mummy 126
Muses 121, 189
Narcissism 10, 20, 25, 40, 107, 108, 165
Negative capability 198, 207, 215
Neo-Platonism 16, 24
New Jerusalem 109
Nursery rhymes. 14
Obi Wan Kenobi 50
Ode 143, 144, 147, 153, 155-159, 163-165, 168, 170, 172, 173, 176, 178, 180, 181, 184, 185, 190, 191, 193-198, 206, 207, 212, 215
Oedipus 126
One Soul 137
Ontology 4, 58, 65, 201
Opium 115, 116, 120, 123, 185
Oracle of Delphi 116
Orc 49-57, 120, 128, 213
Orcic energy 49, 50, 52, 54, 55, 56, 82, 119, 125, 173
Original participation 157, 159, 160
Original sin 13, 14, 102, 108
Orthodox 14, 16, 24, 35, 46, 47, 52, 53, 54, 60, 67, 68, 85, 97, 129, 188, 192
Ouranos 36
Over-self-consciousness 7, 108, 138, 164, 172, 178, 182, 190, 201
Pantheism 88, 91, 93, 140, 160, 169
Paris 1, 3, 12, 42, 103
Paris 1, 3, 12, 42, 103
Pentecost 85, 86, 111
Pentecostal 85, 86
Pentheus 124
Pharisees 35, 69
Philosophy 4, 5, 48, 53, 56, 65, 70, 147, 149, 157
Phoenix 179
Pluto 49
Poet-Prophet 34, 49, 58, 111, 116, 123, 125, 127, 178, 183, 189
Polytheism 88
Postmodern 18, 48, 126
Pragmatism 101, 200
Pre-existence of the soul 147
Presbyterian 85
Process in Stasis 184, 190, 193, 194, 196, 197, 198
Prometheus 36, 57, 126-129, 177, 207
Protestant Reformation 16
Protestantism 46
Provence 187
Purgatory 2, 3, 61, 97
Recollection 65, 80, 115, 135, 136,

137, 143, 148, 150, 156
Reign of Terror 3, 6, 12-14, 120, 167, 206
Resurrection 28, 39, 47, 48, 58, 104, 165, 174
Revelation 19, 35, 109, 116, 119, 161, 162
Romance 100, 101, 120, 155, 202, 203, 211
Romanticism 64, 65, 71, 114, 126, 129, 142, 160, 197, 198, 201, 210, 211, 212
Rome 80, 103, 123
Russia 2, 13
Russian Revolutions
Sacraments 85
Sadducees 69
Saints 85, 86
Salvation 16, 28, 29, 47, 59, 61, 108
Savage torpor 78
Savior 18, 47, 174
Science 76, 77, 94, 200
Scribes 69
Second Coming 174
Shangri-La 3
Shiva 174
Sibyl 119
Solipsism 62, 153, 157, 159, 166
Spenserian stanza 169, 172
Spots of time 135, 136
Stoics 76
Sublime 5, 51, 136, 138, 139, 175, 199, 206
Synthesis 19, 46, 88, 94, 112, 162, 165
Tabula rasa 147
Terza rima 172
The Enquirer 78
Theology 4, 16, 24, 65, 68, 86, 149
Thou-shalt-not 35, 41, 49, 54
Titans 52, 56
Trimurti 174
Trinity 19, 86, 174

Tuberculosis 184, 189
Übermensch 55
Unmediated 72, 93, 117, 138, 148, 178
Unpremeditated 91, 117, 178-180, 186
Urizen 35-45, 48, 50, 53-56, 60
Utopia 2, 3, 13
Vishnu 174
Wagnerian leitmotifs 14
Western 50, 53, 54, 88, 174, 198
Willing Suspension of Disbelief 66, 69, 96, 98, 192
Wise Passiveness 80, 91, 114, 155
Wolfman 126
Word
Wye Valley 135, 137, 156
Xanadu 118, 124
Zen riddles 198
Zeus 52, 56, 126-129, 177

Other Titles of Interest

C. S. Lewis

C. S. Lewis: Views From Wake Forest - Essays on C. S. Lewis
Michael Travers, editor

Contains sixteen scholarly presentations from the international C. S. Lewis convention in Wake Forest, NC. Walter Hooper shares his important essay "Editing C. S. Lewis," a chronicle of publishing decisions after Lewis' death in 1963.

"Scholars from a variety of disciplines address a wide range of issues. The happy result is a fresh and expansive view of an author who well deserves this kind of thoughtful attention."
 Diana Pavlac Glyer, author of *The Company They Keep*

The Hidden Story of Narnia:
A Book-By-Book Guide to Lewis' Spiritual Themes
Will Vaus

A book of insightful commentary equally suited for teens or adults – Will Vaus points out connections between the *Narnia* books and spiritual/biblical themes, as well as between ideas in the *Narnia* books and C. S. Lewis' other books. Learn what Lewis himself said about the overarching and unifying thematic structure of the Narnia books. That is what this book explores; what C. S. Lewis called "the hidden story" of Narnia. Each chapter includes questions for individual use or small group discussion.

Why I Believe in Narnia:
33 Reviews and Essays on the Life and Work of C.S. Lewis
James Como

Chapters range from reviews of critical books, documentaries and movies to evaluations of Lewis' books to biographical analysis.
"A valuable, wide-ranging collection of essays by one of the best informed and most acute commentators on Lewis' work and ideas."
Peter Schakel, author of *Imagination & the Arts in C.S. Lewis*

C. S. Lewis: His Literary Achievement
Colin Manlove

"This is a positively brilliant book, written with splendor, elegance, profundity and evidencing an enormous amount of learning. This is probably not a book to give a first-time reader of Lewis. But for those who are more broadly read in the Lewis corpus this book is an absolute gold mine of information. The author gives us a magnificent overview of Lewis' many writings, tracing for us thoughts and ideas which recur throughout, and at the same time telling us how each book differs from the others. I think it is not extravagant to call *C. S. Lewis: His Literary Achievement* a *tour de force*."
 Robert Merchant, *St. Austin Review*, Book Review Editor

C. S. Lewis & Philosophy as a Way of Life: His Philosophical Thoughts
Adam Barkman

C. S. Lewis is rarely thought of as a "philosopher" per se despite having both studied and taught philosophy for several years at Oxford. Lewis's long journey to Christianity was essentially philosophical – passing through seven different stages. This 624 page book is an invaluable reference for C. S. Lewis scholars and fans alike.

Speaking of Jack: A C. S. Lewis Discussion Guide
Will Vaus

C. S. Lewis Societies have been forming around the world since the first one started in New York City in 1969. Will Vaus has started and led three groups himself. *Speaking of Jack* is the result of Vaus' experience in leading those Lewis Societies. Included here are introductions to most of Lewis' books as well as questions designed to stimulate discussion about Lewis' life and work. These materials have been "road-tested" with real groups made up of young and old, some very familiar with Lewis and some newcomers. *Speaking of Jack* may be used in an existing book discussion group, Sunday school class or small group, to start a C. S. Lewis Society, or as a guide to your own exploration of Lewis' books.

Mythopoeic Narnia: Memory, Metaphore, and Metamorphosis in C. S. Lewis's The Chronicles of Narnia
Salwa Khoddam

Dr. Khoddam, the founder of the C. S. Lewis and Inklings Society (2004), has been teaching university courses using Lewis' books for over 25 years. Her book offers a fresh approach to the *Narnia* books based on an inquiry into Lewis' readings and use of classical and Christian symbols. She explores the literary and intellectual contexts of these stories, the traditional myths and motifs, and places them in the company of the greatest Christian mythopoeic works of Western Literature. In Lewis' imagination, memory and metaphor interact to advance his purpose – a Christian metamorphosis. *Mythopoeic Narnia* helps to open the door for readers into the magical world of the Western imagination.

C. S. Lewis Goes to Heaven: A Reader's Guide to The Great Divorce (pub 2011)
David G. Clark

This is the first book devoted solely to this often neglected book and the first to reveal several important secrets Lewis concealed within the story. Lewis felt his imaginary trip to Hell and Heaven was far better than his book *The Screwtape Letters*, which has become a classic. Clark is an ordained minister who has taught courses on Lewis for more than 30 years and is a New Testament and Greek scholar with a Doctor of Philosophy degree in Biblical Studies from the University of Notre Dame. Readers will discover the many literary and biblical influences Lewis utilized in writing his brilliant novel.

George MacDonald

Diary of an Old Soul & The White Page Poems
George MacDonald and Betty Aberlin

The first edition of George MacDonald's book of daily poems included a blank page opposite each page of poems. Readers were invited to write their own reflections on the "white page." MacDonald wrote: "Let your white page be ground, my print be seed, growing to golden ears, that faith and hope may feed." Betty Aberlin responded to MacDonald's invitation with daily poems of her own.

Betty Aberlin's close readings of George MacDonald's verses and her thoughtful responses to them speak clearly of her poetic gifts and spiritual intelligence. Luci Shaw, poet

George MacDonald: Literary Heritage and Heirs
Roderick McGillis, editor

This latest collection of 14 essays sets a new standard that will influence MacDonald studies for many more years. George MacDonald experts are increasingly evaluating his entire corpus within the nineteenth century context.

This comprehensive collection represents the best of contemporary scholarship on George MacDonald. Rolland Hein, author of *George MacDonald: Victorian Mythmaker.*

In the Near Loss of Everything: George MacDonald's Son in America
Dale Wayne Slusser

In the summer of 1887, George MacDonald's son Ronald, newly engaged to artist Louise Blandy, sailed from England to America to teach school. The next summer he returned to England to marry Louise and bring her back to America. On August 27, 1890, Louise died leaving him with an infant daughter. Ronald once described losing a beloved spouse as "the near loss of everything". Dale Wayne Slusser unfolds this poignant story with unpublished letters and photos that give readers a glimpse into the close-knit MacDonald family. Also included is Ronald's essay about his father, *George MacDonald: A Personal Note*, plus a selection from Ronald's 1922 fable, *The Laughing Elf,* about the necessity of both sorrow and joy in life.

A Novel Pulpit: Sermons From George MacDonald's Fiction
David L. Neuhouser

"In MacDonald's novels, the Christian teaching emerges out of the characters and story line, the narrator's comments, and inclusion of sermons given by the fictional preachers. The sermons in the novels are shorter than the ones in collections of MacDonald's sermons and so are perhaps more accessible for some. In any case, they are both stimulating and thought-provoking. This collection of sermons from ten novels serve to bring out the 'freshness and brilliance' of MacDonald's message."

from the author's introduction

Behind the Back of the North Wind:
Critical Essays on George MacDonald's Classic Children's Book (pub 2011)
Editors, John Pennington and Roderick McGillis

This collection of 16 essays by various scholars is the first compendium on a particular MacDonald book – *At the Back of the North Wind*. This novel makes a good representative study because it bridges the world of the "realistic" and the fanciful, including a fairy tale and some nonsense poetry. Plus it deals with a central MacDonald theme - death. Essays run the gamut from exploring MacDonald's Christian worldview, to examining the tension between fantasy and reality, to grappling with *North Wind* as children's literature. In every case, the essays illuminate a complex book. This book is also an excellent companion to the critical and scholarly edition of *At The Back of the North Wind* by Pennington and McGillis published by Broadview Press.

Other Titles

To Love Another Person: A Spiritual Journey Through Les Miserables
John Morrison

The powerful story of Jean Valjean's redemption is beloved by readers and theater goers everywhere. In this companion and guide to Victor Hugo's masterpiece, author John Morrison unfolds the spiritual depth and breadth of this classic novel and broadway musical.

Through Common Things: Philosophical Reflections on Popular Culture
Adam Barkman

"Barkman presents us with an amazingly wide-ranging collection of philosophical reflections grounded in the everyday things of popular culture – past and present, eastern and western, factual and fictional. Throughout his encounters with often surprising subject-matter (the value of darkness?), he writes clearly and concisely, moving seamlessly between Aristotle and anime, Lord Buddha and Lord Voldemort. . . . This is an informative and entertaining book to read!"
    Doug Blomberg, Professor of Philosophy, Institute for Christian Studies

Remembering Roy Campbell: The Memoirs of his Daughters, Anna and Tess
Introduction by Judith Lütge Coullie, Editor
Preface by Joseph Pearce

Anna and Teresa Campbell were the daughters of the handsome young South African poet and writer, Roy Campbell (1901-1957), and his beautiful English wife, Mary Garman. In their frank and moving memoirs, Anna and Tess recall the extraordinary, and often very difficult, lives they shared with their exceptional parents. Over 50 photos, 344 footnotes, timeline of Campbell's life, and complete index.

CPSIA information can be obtained at www.ICGtesting.com
Printed in the USA
BVOW04s2213310714

361003BV00003B/536/P